A Reference Grammar of Northern Embera Languages

Studies in the Languages of Colombia 7

SIL International and
The University of Texas at Arlington
Publications in Linguistics

Publication 134

Publications in Linguistics is a series published jointly by SIL International and the University of Texas at Arlington. The series is a venue for works covering a broad range of topics in linguistics, especially the analytical treatment of minority languages from all parts of the world. While most volumes are authored by members of the Institute, suitable works by others will also form part of the series.

Series Editor

Donald A. Burquest, University of Texas at Arlington

Volume Editor

Rhonda Hartell

Production Staff

Bonnie Brown, Managing Editor
Laurie Nelson, Production Manager
Karoline Fisher, Compositor
Hazel Shorey, Graphic Artist

A Reference Grammar of Northern Embera Languages

Studies in the Languages of Colombia 7

Charles Arthur Mortensen

A Publication of
SIL International
and
The University of Texas at Arlington

© 1999 by SIL International
Library of Congress Catalog No: 99-64575
ISBN: 1-55671-081-x
ISSN: 1040-0850

Printed in the United States of America

All Rights Reserved

07 06 05 04 03 02 01 00   10 9 8 7 6 5 4 3 2 1

No part of this publication may be reproduced, stored in a retrieval system, or transmitted in any form or by any means—electronic, mechanical, photocopy, recording, or otherwise—without the express permission of SIL International, with the exception of brief excerpts in journal articles or reviews.

Copies of this and other publications of SIL International may be obtained from

International Academic Bookstore
SIL International
7500 W. Camp Wisdom Road
Dallas TX 75236-5699

Voice: 972-708-7404
Fax: 972-708-7433
Email: academic_books@sil.org
Internet: http://www.sil.org

Contents

Acknowledgements xi

Abbreviations xiii

1 Introduction 1
   1.1   Language affiliation 1
   1.2   Culture 2
   1.3   Note regarding transcription 4

1.4–1.7 Phonological sketch

   1.4   Phonological segments and variants 5
   1.5   Syllable and word structure 6
   1.6   Nasalization 7
   1.7   Contractions 8

1.8–1.19 Typological summary

   1.8   Case marking 8
   1.9   Constituent order 9
   1.10 Suffixes 10
   1.11 Head nouns and their modifiers 10
   1.12 Noun clauses and relative clauses 11
   1.13 Adposition order 11
   1.14 Negation 11
   1.15 Inflected auxiliary 12
   1.16 Comparatives 12
   1.17 Conditional clauses 12
   1.18 Purpose clauses 13

	1.19	Questions.	13
2	Word Classes.		15

2.1–2.7 Open classes

	2.1	Nouns.	15

2.2–2.4 Verbs

	2.2	Intransitive verbs.	16
	2.3	Transitive verbs.	17
	2.4	Bitransitive verbs.	17
	2.5	Descriptive adjectives.	17

2.6–2.8 Adverbs

	2.6	Time adverbs.	18
	2.7	Manner adverbs.	18

2.8–2.18 Closed classes

	2.8	Adverbs of location and direction.	19
	2.9	Pronouns and other pro-forms.	20

2.10–2.11 Noun adjuncts

	2.10	Postpositional suffixes.	20
	2.11	Quantifiers.	21

2.12–2.13 Statives

	2.12	Simple and descriptive statives	22
	2.13	Possessive and positional stems.	23
	2.14	Equative verb.	25
	2.15	Existential verb.	25
	2.16	Clitics.	26
	2.17	Vocatives.	27
	2.18	Interjections.	27
3	Derivational Morphology		29
	3.1	Denominalized adjectives.	29
	3.2	Deverbal predicate adjectives	29
	3.3	Derived nouns	30

3.4–3.7 Grammatically related phonological processes

	3.4	Intensification of adjectives	31
	3.5	Mitigation of adjectives	32
	3.6	Intensification of verbs	32
	3.7	Mitigation of verbs	32

Contents

4 Noun Phrase 33
   4.1   Simple nouns 33
   4.2   Compound nouns 33

4.3–4.7 Prenominal modifiers

   4.3   Possessive adjectives 34
   4.4   Demonstrative adjectives and pronouns 34
   4.5   Indexing adjectives 37
   4.6   Referential adjective 37
   4.7   Nouns modifying nouns 38

4.8–4.10 Post-nominal modifiers

   4.8   Descriptive adjectives 39
   4.9   Numerals 39
   4.10 Nominal quantifiers 40
   4.11 Compound noun phrases 40
   4.12 Plurality 41

4.13–4.15 Pronouns

   4.13 Personal pronouns 42
   4.14 Possessive pronouns 45
   4.15 Indefinite pronouns 45

5 Case 47
   5.1   Ablative 47
   5.2   Absolutive 49
   5.3   Indirect object 50
   5.4   Benefactive 50
   5.5   Possession 51
   5.6   Accompaniment 51
   5.7   Location 52
   5.8   Goal 53
   5.9   Movement down 55
   5.10 Movement from 55
   5.11 Origin 56
   5.12 Similarity 57
   5.13 Comparison 57

6 Verb 59
   6.1   Simple verb heads 59
   6.2   Serial verbs in the verb phrase 59
   6.3   Object-incorporated verbs 60

6.4–6.10 Derivational verb suffixes

6.4	Causative	62
6.5	Instrument	63
6.6	Volition	63
6.7	Affected object	64
6.8	Repetitive action	67
6.9	Verbs that indicate movement and direction	68
6.10	Other derivational morphemes	69

6.11–6.13 Tense

6.11	Past tense	73
6.12	Present tense	74
6.13	Future tense	75
6.14	Number in verbs	76

6.15–6.20 Aspect

6.15	Perfect aspect	77
6.16	Imperfective aspect	78
6.17	Completive	79
6.18	Habitual	80
6.19	Progressive	82
6.20	Durative	82

6.21–6.30 Mood and evidentiality

6.21	Declarative	83
6.22	Information interrogative	83
6.23	Polar interrogative	83
6.24	Uncertain interrogative	84
6.25	Hortatory	84
6.26	Imperative	85
6.27	Verification	85
6.28	Emphatic	85
6.29	Irrealis	85
6.30	Evidentials	86

7	Clause		89
	7.1	Order of clause constituents	89

7.2–7.7 Question formation

7.2	Polar questions	93
7.3	Information questions	93
7.4	Alternative tag questions	94
7.5	Leading questions	94

Contents

7.6	Uncertain questions	94
7.7	Questions used rhetorically	95

7.8–7.11 Imperatives

7.8	Direct imperatives	95
7.9	Polite imperatives	96
7.10	Hortatory imperatives	97
7.11	Imperatives in quotations	97

7.12–7.17 Negation

7.12	Standard negation	98
7.13	Negation of equatives	100
7.14	Habitual negation	100
7.15	Negative imperatives	100
7.16	Irregular negative verbs	101
7.17	Inherent negatives	101

8 Sentence ... 103

8.1	Sentence formation	103

8.2–8.6 Sentence introducers

8.2	Temporal relators	105
8.3	Extended time relators	108
8.4	Additive relators	108
8.5	Logical relators	108
8.6	Comparative relators	110
8.7	Conditional relators	110
8.8	*mãwã* as a pro-verb	110

9 Subordinate Clause ... 113

9.1–9.8 Adverbial clause

9.1	Overlapping event clause	113
9.2	Sequential event clause	116
9.3	Antecedence clause	119
9.4	Purpose clause	120
9.5	Conditional clause	122
9.6	Reason clause	124
9.7	Concessive clause	125
9.8	Repeated subordinate clause	126

9.9–9.10 Relative clause

9.9	Noun head	128
9.10	Headless relative clause	129

9.11–9.12 Complementation

- 9.11 Standard complementation 130
- 9.12 Reported quotations 131

10 Discourse and Pragmatic Considerations. 135
- 10.1 Demonstratives in discourse. 135
- 10.2 Introduction of participants. 137
- 10.3 Participant tracking 138
- 10.4 The referential adjective *či* in discourse 141
- 10.5 Pronouns in discourse 142

10.6–10.10 Highlighting

- 10.6 Absolutive focus and pivot 143
- 10.7 Important new information 145
- 10.8 Focus on given information 145
- 10.9 Certainty 146
- 10.10 Contrastive certainty. 146
- 10.11 Event line and background information. 146

Appendix A 155
Northern Embera Proper text 155

Appendix B 167
Embera-Katío text 167

References 193

Acknowledgements

Data for this study were collected by the author during five years of fieldwork in Northern Embera languages, two in Embera-Katío (1991–1993) and three in Northern Embera Proper (1995–1998). The fieldwork was carried out under the direction of the Summer Institute of Linguistics working in cooperation with the Colombian Ministry of the Interior. This reference grammar was adapted for Northern Embera Proper from *Epena Pedee Syntax: Studies in the Languages of Colombia 4* by Phillip Lee Harms, compared with other grammars of the Northern Embera languages and augmented to include more comparative data with Embera-Katío in cooperation with Mareike Schöttelndreyer, whose data collection began in 1965. The volume was revised in consultation with Dr. Stephen H. Levinsohn during the Grammar Writing Workshop for Chocó Languages, held in Pereira, Colombia, in August 1998.

The intention of the author is to present one reference grammar for the two Northern Embera languages, Embera-Katío and Northern Embera Proper, and point out differences as they arise.

Unless otherwise indicated, the illustrative examples are taken from Northern Embera Proper and represent the morphology and syntax of both languages but do not necessarily represent Embera-Katío speaking style.

I would like to express my sincere gratitude to the government and people of Colombia for the privilege of working and living in their country and to the Northern Embera people for patiently teaching me their language. I would also like to thank my friends and colleagues who work in other Embera languages, each of whom has been a source of help and a sounding board for my ideas: Phillip and Judy Harms, David and Penelope Pickens, Ron and Mary Jane Michael, Alan and Holly Wymore, James Lee Enemark, Douglas Schermerhon, Sharon Tibberts, Viviana Barrera, Edel Rasmussen, Sara Watkins, and especially Mareike Schöttelndreyer.

This grammar would not have been possible without the invaluable assessment of Stephen Levinsohn and the commitment of my wife and co-worker Helga Mortensen.

Abbreviations

ABL	ablative	ET	Embera-Tadó
ABS	absolutive	excl	exclusive pronoun
ACCOM	accompaniment	EXST	existential
ADV	adverb	FEM	feminine
ALT	alternate pronoun stem	FOC	focus
BEN	benefactive	FUT	future
C	complement	GEN	generalizer
CAUS	causative	GI	given information
CMPL	completive	HAB	habitual
COMP	comparative	HRSY	hearsay
COND	conditional	HYP	hypothetical
COREF	coreferent	IMM	immediate (future or past)
DECL	declarative	IMPF	imperfective
DESC	descriptive	IMPV	imperative
dev.	development	incl	inclusive pronoun
DIR	direction	indiv	individual
DO	direct object	INST	instrument
DS	different subject	INTENS	intensifier
DUR	durative	IO	indirect object
ECh	Embera-Chamí	IRR	irrealis
EMPH	emphatic	LIM	limiter
EK	Embera-Katío	LOC	locative
EQ	equative	NE	Northern Embera group
ERG	ergative	NEG	negative
ES	Epena-Saija	NEP	Northern Embera Proper

nondev.	nondevelopment	SIM	marker of similarity
O	object	SG	singular
OBL	oblique	Sp.	Spanish
ORIG	origin	sp.	species
PERF	perfect	SUBD	subordinate
PL	plural	SUM	summary action
POLAR	polar interrogative	T	time
POS	positional auxiliary verb stem	V	verb
		VER	verification
PPRT	past participle (relative past)	v.i.	intransitive verb
		VOL	volitional
PRES	present	VP	verb phrase
PURP	purpose	v.t.	transitive verb
Q	interrogative	1s	first-person singular
QUOT	quotation	1p	first-person plural
REF	referential adjective	2s	second-person singular
REPT	repetition	2p	second-person plural
RPRT	reportative	3s	third-person singular
S	subject	3p	third-person plural
SE	Southern Embera group	Ø	no suffix
		α	asyndeton

PANAMA
VENEZUELA
Area
of
enlargement
Bogotá
Pacific
Ocean
COLOMBIA
ECUADOR
BRAZIL
PERU

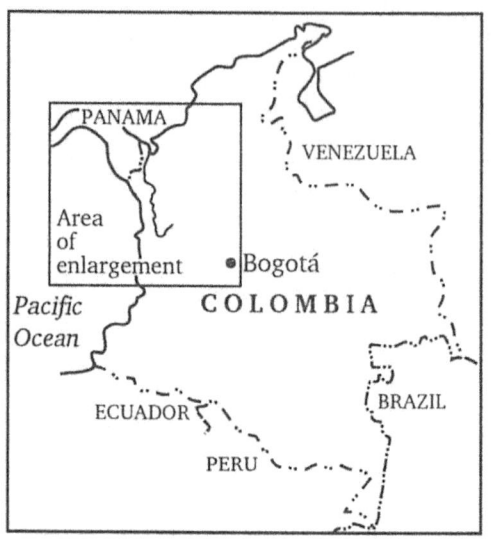

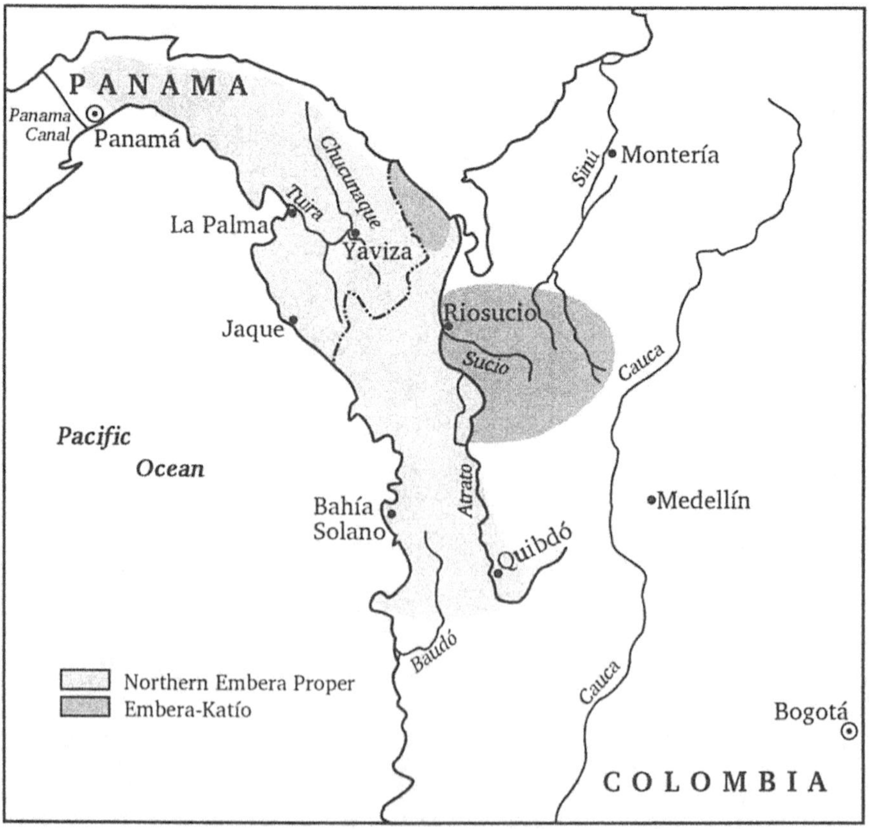
PANAMA
Panama
Canal
Panamá
Chucunaque
Tuira
La Palma
Yaviza
Sinú
Montería
Riosucio
Sucio
Jaque
Cauca
Pacific
Ocean
Atrato
Medellín
Bahía
Solano
Quibdó
Baudó
Northern Embera Proper
Embera-Katío
Cauca
Bogotá
COLOMBIA

1
Introduction

1.1 Language affiliation. Northern Embera (NE) is a member of the Chocó language family which is today thought to be alternatively Chibchan or Chibchan-Paezan (Greenberg 1987:106–22), Carib (Loewen 1963:244), or independent (Constenla-Umaña and Margery-Peña 1991:139–40, Pardo-Rojas and Aguirre-Licht 1993:270–92).

The Chocó family itself is grouped first into Waunana[1] and the six Embera languages. The Embera are divided into Southern and Northern groups. Four languages make up the Southern group: Chamí, Tadó, Saija,[2] and Baudó. Epena-Saija will be referred to by the initials ES. The two Northern languages are Embera-Katío (EK) and Northern Embera Proper (NEP). The language names are often preceded by the word Embera or a variant thereof in order to point out the common ethnicity of the speakers. Often NEP and the southern Baudó are combined under the term 'Embera' and clarified by 'Embera Embera'.

The Embera peoples call themselves *ēpērā* 'person' to distinguish themselves from Latins, but to distinguish the different Embera languages they use other names. Both the Katíos and Chamíes are referred to as *eyapida* 'mountain dwellers' and the Baudó and Saija groups call themselves *siapida* 'people of the wild cane'. The NEP are called *topida* 'river dwellers'.

---

[1]This group is also referred to as *Wounaan* 'people' and *Woun Meu* 'people's language'.
[2]In Harms (1994) the Saija language is referred to as 'Epena Pedee'. However, since all Embera languages have names very similar to that, in this volume each variety will be referred to by its regional name.

The Northern Embera Proper live in Panama, especially in the Chucunaque and Tuira basins in Darién province, and in Colombia in the northern half of the Department of Chocó, on tributaries of the Atrato River and along rivers which flow directly into the Pacific Ocean. Roughly 10,000 live in Panama and 15,000 in Colombia. The traditional EK homelands are the headwaters of the Sinú River basin in southern Córdoba department and the Sucio River basin in northwestern Antioquia department. A few more recently established communities are found in the far north of the Chocó and across the border in Panama. The total population of the Embera-Katíos is estimated to be as high as 20,000.

1.2 Culture. The status of the NE people cannot be understood properly without considering the different rates of development in Panama and Colombia. Although explorers entered the Atrato Basin of Colombia very early in the colonial period, most of the settlers of the region were emancipated slaves. Even today, the Colombian Department of Chocó is still sparsely populated and for the most part the indigenous people have not had to live alongside Spanish speakers. Consequently, the Emberas, especially the NEP, do not speak Spanish well and still practice traditional swidden agriculture. Crops include corn, rice, and plantain. The Emberas also hunt animals occasionally and catch fish almost daily. Many fruits are available as well.

In Panama the government has required that the Emberas organize themselves into communities in order to receive aid. While this has had a positive effect on the general well-being of the people, the great amount of contact with Spanish speakers and the availability of education in Spanish has led to the loss of the native language in some places, especially those closer to Panama City. Sadly, a number of Emberas have been forced to leave their native areas in the Darién by illegally armed groups. This results in settlements near the city and eventually the loss of the language in those places.

Organization into communities is a newer concept in Colombia. Traditionally, Emberas have preferred living in small family groups of a few houses each. Nevertheless, organization into communities is being done, mainly for political purposes. This outwardly imposed form of government has done away with the system of chiefs of rivers and has meant that those communities that understand the new government receive much more aid than those who do not.

Embera dress for men and boys is a pair of shorts and optional t-shirt. Shoes, long pants, and long-sleeved shirts are worn when they go to Latin towns. They also wear bead necklaces and bracelets made from brass chain. Little boys are allowed to go naked until they feel embarrassed about it. Girls' genitals are covered from birth either with old towels, shorts made from rags, or store-bought panties. Girls begin to wear traditional wrap-around skirts by the time they reach school age. Older girls and women may wear t-shirts or large pieces of cloth over their breasts unless they are nursing. They commonly wear ropes of colored beads around their necks. EK women wear special blouses of bright colors for festive occasions, when they go to town and when they are exposed to the sun, working in the fields. Both men and women paint themselves with black *jagua* (Sp.) or else red *achiote* (Sp.). This is for both cosmetic and health purposes. They may paint designs on their faces, arms, legs, or chests but also paint themselves entirely in order to retard sunburn and skin rashes caused by the extreme heat and humidity of the jungle.

Extended family dwellings are platform houses with thatched roofs. The platform is nearly two meters (5–6 feet) off the ground because of the dampness brought on from the heavy rainfall, about 400 inches (10,000 mm) per year. Walls are not usually built because of the need for air flow. Privacy for nuclear families is secured by the use of mosquito nets. The male youth of a community may live in one house together. Newly married couples usually live with the husband's family, although some EK couples live with the wife's family if land is more easily obtainable that way. When the wife becomes pregnant, the husband will begin building their own house.

The heavy rainfall retards the building of roads and encourages the use of dugout canoes for transportation. Makeshift rafts are also used if no canoe is available or for taking large shipments of produce to market. For longer trips outboard motors are highly prized even though gasoline and maintenance are expensive.

Some crops, fish, and hunted and domestic animals are sold in Latin towns for the purpose of getting cash to travel or buy clothes. The women weave baskets for their own use, although selling woven sleeping mats has become more popular recently.

Individuals own their property which is distributed among offspring at death. Land use privilege is passed on to all children. The spouse has no right to the land other than to help the household.

The traditional Embera religion accepts the existence of one God as the creator of the world and everything found in it. He is also all-powerful but not necessarily morally upright. Consequently, obedience to God is not an aspect of the culture. Shamanism is very strong, and its practitioners are usually blamed for unexplainable deaths. Revenge killings often involve the families of shamans. Whole communities are known to have dispersed because of this. The Embera-Waunana organization has urged that shamans not become involved in disputes and encourages practicing shamans to concentrate on healing the sick. Nontraditional religions include influences from the Pentecostal church and evangelical Christianity. Association with the Roman Catholic church is limited to infant baptism for the purpose of getting the child a *cédula,* the official identity card in Colombia.

Education is available in the NE language in some communities although at times there are no available teachers. In that case, some youths study in Spanish in Latin towns. Some educational literature is available in the language but has not been widely distributed.

1.3 Note regarding transcription. The phonological sketch is written using the symbols of the International Phonetic Alphabet (IPA). The affricates čʰ and č are resegmentations of /tʃʰ/ and /tʃʼ/. Nasalized vowels are indicated by a tilde (~) over the vowel. A limited number of verbs differ from one another only by stress pattern and this difference is shown when necessary. In the grammar portion of the book, phonemes are represented with IPA symbols with the following exceptions: all nasalized vowels are marked as such, the nasal variants of the voiced stops are marked as nasals (keeping in mind there are nasal consonant phonemes as well), the constricted stops are written as voiced unaspirated stops, and the vibrants /ɾ/ and /r/ are written as *r* and *rr,* respectively.

1.4–1.7 Phonological sketch

This section is an updating of my 1994 work on NE phonology. The major differences in this sketch are that nasalized vowels are not phonemes (see §1.6) and that NEP /j/ is the voiced alveopalatal affricate /ʤ/ in EK (Mortensen 1994:16–17).

Salient differences between NE phonologies and that of Epena-Saija (ES) are first the number of sibilants: while both NE languages have four, all SE languages like Epena-Saija have just two. Secondly, I include nasal consonant phonemes while Harms (1994:5–8) considers them to be variants of voiced stops.[3] Thirdly, NE languages do not have a voiced velar stop while ES does. A fourth difference is that in ES is the only Embera language to have seven vowels; all the others have six. This seventh vowel, written as *ë,* sometimes corresponds to /ɯ/ and even to /u/ in NE. Harms' inclusion of the glottal stop in is debatable; this is also the case for the NE languages. Motivation for including it would be its use as an infix in intensified adjectives (§3.4). A reason for leaving it out of the phonemic inventory is that it is not contrastive with other consonants.

---

[3]Aguirre-Licht (1995:11) posits nasal phonemes for Embera-Chamí.

Introduction

In addition to the phoneme correspondences mentioned above, the other phonemes also correspond except in the following cases: where Epena-Saija has /g/, the NE languages have /k'/. In all Embera varieties, post-stress /k'/ is often deleted; this is especially evident in SE languages like Epena-Saija. Finally, SE /s/ corresponds to NE /čʰ/ before high vowels and /sʰ/ in other environments. Likewise, SE /č/ corresponds to NE /č'/ before high vowels and /s'/ in other environments.

Stress systems are very different from NE to SE. Whereas in SE languages stress is predictably penultimate, NE stress tends to be ultimate on words in isolation but penultimate on suffixed words. This is an area for further study in the NE languages.

1.4 Phonological segments and variants.

(1) Consonants

	Bilabial	Alveolar	Alveopalatal	Back
Aspirated stops	pʰ	tʰ	čʰ	kʰ
Constricted stops	p'	t'	č'	k'
Voiced stops	b	d		
Aspirated fricative		sʰ		
Constricted fricative		s'		
Nasals	m	n		
Trill		r		
Sonorants	w	ɾ	j	h

(2) Vowels

	−back	+back/−round	+back/+round
+high	i	ɯ	u
−high	e	a	o

The p^h has an occasional affricated variant [pɸ] as well as a fricative variant [ɸ]. The constricted obstruents often sound voiced between vowels and when prenasalized.

(3)   *pʰɯɾukʼa wāsʰia*   [ɸɯɾɯgá wãⁿsía]   'walked in circles'
        hẽtʼa tʼiasʰia   [hẽⁿda tiasía]   'gave it back'

The voiced stops become nasals when in nasal morphemes, and all sonorants can be nasalized except for r, which does not occur in nasal environments.

(4) pʰuɾu + de   [pʰuɾúde]   'village-in' (NEP)
     mea + de   [mẽã́nẽ]   'jungle-in'
     hãwa   [hãw̃ã́]   'like that'
     ãyoɾe   [ãɲõɲẽ́]   'sister-in-law'

The w becomes the fricative [β] between high vowels.

(5) ewaɾi   [ewaɾí]   'day'
     pʰɯwɯɾɯ   [pɯβɯɾɯ́]   'bone'

Low back unrounded vowel a is raised preceding high back vowels. Nasalized /ɯ/ obtains a consonantal off-glide utterance-finally.

(6) tʼau   [təu]   'eye' (NEP)
     naɯ   [nə̃ɯ̃ŋ]   'this'

A feature of EK is that extended voicing onset time after velar stops causes allophonic variation. In other words, vowels following the aspirated stop /kʰ/ become temporarily voiceless, and the constricted stop /kʼ/ becomes affricated. This is most evident between low back vowels.

(7) sʼokʰo   [sʼokʰo̥ó] ~ [zokʰo̥ó]   'water jar'
     pʰoakʼa   [pʰoakxá] ~ [pʰoagγá]   'year'

1.5 Syllable and word structure. A word is typically composed of from one to four syllables. All syllables are open and the following patterns are attested: V, CV, CɾV, and CɾVⱽ.

(8) e   [ʔe]   'skin'
     ãikʼu   [ʔãĩŋkú]   'daughter-in-law'
     tʰɾɯ̃   [tʰɾɯ̃]   'name'
     tʰɾɯ̃apʼi   [tʰɾɯ̃ã́ᵐpi]   'song'

There are also numerous cases of vowel deletion in words with three or more syllables in unstressed syllables beginning with ɾ.

Introduction 7

(9)   *buɾuʃʰida*   [buɾsidá]   'happy' (NEP)
      buʃʰuɾida   [bus:ridá]   'happy' (EK)

Stress in NE languages tends to fall on the final syllable of words in isolation. In words that carry suffixes, stress falls on the penultimate syllable. The exception to these tendencies is in words with four or more syllables. In these cases NEP usually has antepenultimate stress and EK has penultimate stress, whether the words have suffixes or not.

(10)   *hãp'á*   'canoe'
      hãp'á + de   'canoe-in'
      hãp'a + dé + p'a   'canoe-in-from' (motion from within the canoe)
      p'ẽrówãrã   'spotted cavy' (NEP)
      p'ẽrõk'óɾã   'spotted cavy' (EK)

Some minimal pairs of verbs contrast with each other only by stress placement, the difference being most notable in the past tense forms.

(11)   *úʃʰia*   'planted'   *uʃʰía*   'swatted'
      kʰáʃʰia   'bit'   *kʰaʃʰía*   'wove'
      awáʃʰia   'carried it on his back'   *awaʃʰía*   'was given to doing that'

1.6 Nasalization. Nasalization in NE is progressive, spreading from the first voiced segment in a nasal morpheme through voiced stops and all sonorants to the end of the grammatical word.

(12)   *hũwuɾua*   [hũw̃ũɾ̃ũã]   'hot'
      mea + de   [mẽãnẽ]   'in the jungle'

When nasality encounters a voiceless obstruent, a transitional nasal is formed between the nasal vowel and the obstruent at the obstruent's place of articulation.

(13)   *hãp'a*   [hã^{m}pa]   'canoe'
      wẽʃa   [wẽ^{n}sa]   'dextrous'
      minič̃ʰia   [mĩnĩ^{n}č̃ʰia]   'ugly'
      õkʰo   [õŋkʰo]   'heron'

Morphemes are either oral or nasal. If a nasal morpheme precedes an oral one as in (14a), the nasality spreads to the oral morpheme in accordance with the rules above. In the speech of some people, phonetic nasality may spread backward to oral morphemes as in (14b).

(14) a. wẽra + a → [wẽɲãã] 'woman (IO)'
     b. usʰa + rã→ [[usaɲã] ~ [usãɲã] 'dog (PL)'

1.7 Contractions. There are few contractions in the NE languages. One mentioned in Rex (1975:4–5) for EK is that of identical vowel reduction. In (15) Rex's orthographic symbols have been replaced by actual phonemic characters.

(15) tʼe 'house' + eda 'GOAL' > tʼedá 'toward home' or > tʼéda 'at home'

Related to the above is the NEP tida, which has the same meaning as (15) with respect to the variations in stress but exhibits a vowel change as well.

(16) tʼe 'house' + eda 'into' > tʼidá 'toward home' or > tʼída 'at home'

This vowel change is related to an older, frozen form tʼikʼidá 'toward home', which is disappearing in NEP. In both languages mãwãmĩna, 'however' can be reduced to mãũmĩna, mãmĩna, or even mãmĩ.

1.8–1.19 Typological summary

The NE languages are fairly typical SOV languages. They are members of Greenberg's class 24 (1966:109) in that they exhibit possessives before the head noun, but postpositions, adjectives, and numerals that follow the noun. They are also fairly agglutinative in that morphemes are readily distinguishable and phonologically distinct. The verb has overt categories of number, tense, aspect, and mood.

1.8 Case marking. Languages whose verbs predominantly follow both the subject and the object almost always have a case system (Greenberg 1966:113). The NE group is no exception; it exhibits ergative-absolutive morphology on the major clause constituents. The subject of the transitive clause is marked by the ergative (ablative) suffix -pa. The ergative case will be glossed in this volume as ABL (ablative), since the suffix *-pa* does much more than mark transitive subject, as will become clear in §5.1. The alternate form of the ablative suffix, *-a*, is used on all pronouns except the first-person plural exclusive *tai* and the second-person plural *pārā*, which use *-pa*.

(17) mũ čapa-**pa**   beki-ta   pea-s^{h}i-a[4]
     1S brother-ABL deer-ABS^FOC kill-PAST-DECL
     My brother killed a deer.

(18) mũ-**a**   p^{h}ata   ú-s^{h}i-a
     1S-ABL   plantain   plant-PAST-DECL
     I planted plantain.

The object of a transitive clause and the subject of an intransitive clause are marked in the same way. See §5.2 for the conditions under which the absolute suffix is Ø, *-ra*, *-ta*, or *-tɨ*.

(19) mũ-**ra** Carlo-a
     1S-ABS   Carlos-DECL
     I am Carlos.

(20) iči-a   mũ-ra   ũnũ-s^{h}i-a
     3S-ABL 1S-ABS see-PAST-DECL
     He saw me.

1.9 Constituent order. Even though the Embera languages have ergative-accusative case marking, Harms (1994:10) points out that subject is still a relevant category since the verb is marked plural whenever the subject is plural. Normal clause constituent order is subject–object–verb (SOV). In the absence of an object, the order is SV. Oblique phrases and complements usually occur immediately after the subject (see further in §7.1).

(21) p^{h}ata-ra   warrá   b-ɨ-a
     plantain-ABS   tasty   be-PRES-DECL
     Plantain is delicious.

(22) ēpērā-rā-ra   wārāka   wã-s^{h}i-da-a
     person-PL-ABS up^river go-PAST-PL-DECL
     The people went up river.

---

[4]Hyphens are placed before suffixes but not before clitics.

(23) mũ kʰima-pa wárra-a pʰata-ra tia-sʰi-a
1S spouse-ABL offspring-IO plantain-ABS give-PAST-DECL
My wife gave my son a plantain.

1.10 Suffixes. All affixes in NE are suffixes; there are no prefixes although there are proclitics.

Nouns can be suffixed for case, number, and limit. Postpositions are also considered suffixes.

(24) aba-pe pa-sʰi-a
one-LIM EQ-PAST-DECL
There was only one.

(25) pʰuru-da hēta wã-sʰi-a
village-GOAL back go-PAST-DECL
He went back to the village.

Verbs can have suffixes of tense, number, mood, and condition. Overt aspect is shown only on auxiliary verbs.

(26) tama-pa kʰá-pʉrʉ akʰʉpari b-ʉ-ma wã-i-ta
snake-ABL bite-COND doctor be-PRES-LOC go-IRR-ABS^FOC

b-ʉ-a
be-PRES-DECL
If you are bitten by a snake, you have to go to the doctor.

(27) ĩyãpa tʰa-b-ʉ-a
breathe lie-be-PRES-DECL
He is lying down breathing.

Adverbs may have only suffixes which indicate origin.

(28) mãma-ʉ-pa wã-sʰi-da-a ya^barrea
there-LOC-ABL go-PAST-PL-DECL down^river
From there we went on down river.

1.11 Head nouns and their modifiers. Articles, demonstrative adjectives, possessives, and modifying noun phrases precede the head noun whereas numerals, quantifiers, and descriptive adjectives follow the head. This is in agreement with Greenberg's Universal 19 (1966:87): if the descriptive adjective follows the noun head, a minority of adjectives may precede it.

(29) či čapa-ta ūpea pʰan-a-sʰi-da-a
 REF brother-ABS^FOC three be^few-IMPF-PAST-PL-DECL
 They were three brothers.

(30) či bi waipʉa-ta
 REF belly big-ABS^FOC
 its big belly

1.12 Noun clauses and relative clauses. The relative clause has normal constituent order and is internally headed. The best evidence of this is that case markers applied to the modified noun are suffixed onto the end of the relative clause.

(31) mū ūmē wárra sʼe-da-ra
 1S with offspring come-PPRT-ABS
 the boy who came with me

(32) oro-sʰi-a nē^jõ pʰureka nū-m-ʉ-ra
 knock^down-PAST-DECL fruit ripe stand-be-PRES-ABS
 (he) knocked down fruit that was ripe

1.13 Adposition order. As is typical of SOV languages, NE adpositions follow the noun phrase.

(33) wā-na mōkara-ūrū beta wa-de
 go-PL rock-on fish carry-in
 Let's go up on that rock to fish.

(34) to sʼakʰe-de
 river small-in
 in a creek

1.14 Negation. There are three negative morphemes all with distinct uses. The standard negative is ẽ, a verbal enclitic which can receive the declarative and interrogative verb suffixes. Other verb suffixes are attached to the head verb or the auxiliary.

(35) mãwã   ẽ-a
     like^this NEG-DECL
     Not like that. *or* No.

(36) kʰawa ẽ   pa-sʰi-a
     know NEG EQ-PAST-DECL
     I didn't know.

(37) kʰawa-da ẽ-a
     know-PL   NEG-DECL
     We don't know.

The habitual negative is indicated by the suffix -kʰá.

(38) ẽpẽrã-rã-pa   tama kʰo-da-kʰá
     person-PL-ABL snake eat-PL-NEG^HAB
     Emberas never eat snake(s).

A negative command is marked by the suffix -rã.

(39) mãwã   o-rã-tua
     like^this do-NEG^IRR-IMPV
     Don't do it like that!

1.15 Inflected auxiliary. The inflected auxiliary verb follows the head verb as in most SOV languages.

(40) Ariel-ta   huersʲa ipʰida b-a-sʰi-a
     Ariel-ABS^FOC force   laugh be-IMPF-PAST-DECL
     Ariel was laughing so hard.

1.16 Comparatives. The order for comparatives is Entity–Standard–Marker–Adjective of Comparison.

(41) kʰare-ta   kʰekʰerre kʰãyãpara waibʉa-ra b-ʉ-a
     parrot-ABS^FOC parakeet than   big-COMP be-PRES-DECL
     The parrot is bigger than the parakeet.

1.17 Conditional clauses. Conditional clauses usually precede their accompanying result clauses.

(42) sʰukʰura-ta   to-di-pɨrɨ   pāči huware-pa   hue
     cane^juice-ABS^FOC drink-FUT^PL-COND 2p   right^hand-ABL scoop

   to-da-tua
   drink-PL-IMPV
   If you're going to drink some cane juice, scoop it out with your right hand and drink it!

(43) ačʰe hosʰo   pɨ-a mū-ta kʰĩrã čupuria-ra mū-a
     friend anteater 2S-ABL 1S-ABS face mercy-COND 1S-ABL

   kʰimi hõ-ta   ūnū iru-b-ɨ-a
   bee   fruit-ABS^FOC see have-be-PRES-DECL
   Anteater, my friend, if you do me a favor, I'll show you where some honey[5] is.

1.18 Purpose clauses. Subordinated purpose clauses follow the main clause.

(44) wã-na mōkara-ūrū beta wa-de
     go-PL rock-on   fish carry-in
     Let's go up on that rock to fish.

1.19 Questions. Polar interrogatives end with the suffix *-kʰa* and rising intonation.

(45) pia b-ɨ-**kʰa**
     good be-PRES-POLAR
     Are you well?

Information questions begin with a question word. Questions may be preceded by a nominal orientation phrase, as in (46).

(46) pɨ s'es'a sʰãma b-ɨ
     2S father where be-PRES
     Where is your father?

---

[5]Not all NEP speakers agree that *kʰimi hõ* means 'honey'.

2
Word Classes

The inventory of parts of speech in the NE languages includes open classes (nouns, verbs, adjectives, and certain adverbs) and closed classes (other adverbs, pronouns and other pro-forms, auxiliary verbs, clitics, vocatives, and interjections).

2.1–2.7 Open classes

2.1 Nouns. Nouns typically refer to concrete objects or things (animate beings or inanimate entities), are either common or proper, and function as the heads of arguments.[6]

Nouns may occur with or without suffixes. The four possible noun suffix categories are number, case, limit, and postposition. In (47) *kʰuriwa* 'guatín'[7] is suffixed for ergative (ablative) case and *kʰimi^hõ* 'bee fruit' is suffixed for focus in the absolutive case.

(47) ara mãũ-ta **kʰuriwa**-pa **kʰimi hõ**-ta haratia-sʰi-a
 same this-SUBD guatín-ABL bee fruit-ABS^FOC teach-PAST-DECL
 Then the *guatín* showed [the anteater] where the honey was.

Stress on nouns seems to be ultimate when the word occurs unsuffixed or in isolation. Stress becomes predictably penultimate when nouns are

---

[6]Harms (1994:19) has not found any abstract nouns in ES.
[7]The *guatín* (Sp.) is a gray rodent the size of a rabbit with small ears and no tail. It is the subject of many Embera folktales.

suffixed. Nouns with four or more syllables, whether suffixes are included in the count or not, have antepenultimate stress in NEP and penultimate stress in EK. For examples of this refer to §1.5.

2.2–2.4 Verbs

Verbs function as the heads of verb phrases. They are either active (§§2.2–2.4) or nonactive (closed classes; see §§2.12–15). Verbs may occur with only a subject argument, with both subject and direct object, or with subject, direct object, and indirect object. They may be inflected for or reflect in their meanings number, aspect, tense, and mood.

Verbs are stressed on the penultimate syllable unless, in NEP, there are four or more syllables in the word, including the suffixes, in which case stress is usually antepenultimate (see further below).

(48) s'e-s^{h}i-a   [s'es^{h}í.a]
come-PAST-DECL
came

(49) s'e-s'e-s^{h}i-da-a   [s'es'és^{h}ida]   (NEP)
come-come-PAST-PL-DECL
came one by one

Some clarification is in order since some verb forms seem to have ultimate stress. This is because two morphemes of identical vowel quality are juxtaposed: in (50) note that the plural suffix -da is followed by the declarative suffix -a. This shifts the stress to the ultimate phonetic syllable since the second-to-last vowel nucleus is carrying the stress: -dáa. This is akin to stress in ES (Harms 1994:8). This phenomenon, however, does not trigger the NEP four-syllable stress shift.

(50) wã-s^{h}i-**da-a**   [wã^{n}sidá]   *[wã^{n}sída.a]
go-PAST-PL-DECL
(plural) left

2.2 Intransitive verbs. Intransitive verbs have only one nominal constituent, which is marked by an absolutive suffix.

Word Classes

(51) iči-**ra** kʰãĩ-sʰi-a
    3S-ABS sleep-PAST-DECL
    He slept.

(52) tai-**ra** mẽã wã-sʰi-da-a
    1pl-ABS jungle go-PAST-PL-DECL
    We went into the jungle (to hunt).

2.3 Transitive verbs. Transitive verbs have two arguments: the subject and the direct object. The subject is marked with an ergative (ablative) suffix, and the direct object receives an absolutive suffix.

(53) hãũ ẽpẽrã-**pa** mṹ sʼesʼa-**ra** pea-sʰi-a
    that person-ABL 1S father-ABS kill-PAST-DECL
    That man killed my father.

One or both arguments in a transitive sentence may be omitted.

(54) mũ kʰima-pa ũnũ-sʰi-a
    1S spouse-ABL see-PAST-DECL
    My wife saw (him/her/it).

(55) beki-ra batʰa pea-sʰi-a
    deer-ABS shoot kill-PAST-DECL
    shot and killed a deer

(56) sʼruka-sʰi-da-a
    steal-PAST-PL-DECL
    (plural subject) stole (DO known from context)

2.4 Bitransitive verbs. These have three arguments; the subject and direct object as described above, and the indirect object which is marked by the suffix -a. In EK this suffix receives stress.

(57) mũ-**a** pari tia-sʰi-a
    1S-IO free give-PAST-DECL
    He gave it to me free.

2.5 Descriptive adjectives. Adjectives follow nouns within the noun phrase or appear as pre-verbal complements in the sentence.

(58) hãpa waibᵾa-ta o-sʰi-a
canoe large-ABS^FOC make-PAST-DECL
He made a big canoe!

(59) pio waibᵾa b-ᵾ-a
very large be-PRES-DECL
It's very big.

The only suffix attached exclusively to adjectives is the *-ra* denoting comparison (§5.13). Adjectives also carry the case suffixes if they are the last constituent in a noun phrase, as in (58).

2.6–2.8 Adverbs

Adverbs include a broad range of words. They can be defined as modifiers of those constituents that are not nouns. In this section three classes of adverbs are considered: time and manner (which are open classes) and location direction (closed classes). Most adverbs occur at the beginning of the verb phrase.

2.6 Time adverbs. The default position for adverbs of time is before the main clause constituents (see further §7.1).

(60) ***idi tiapʰeda*** mẽã wã-sʰi-a
today morning jungle go-PAST-DECL
He left early this morning to go hunting.

2.7 Manner adverbs. The deictics *nãwã* 'like this', *hãwã (kʰãwã* in EK) 'like that', and *mãwã* 'like the previous' are commonly used to express manner. Manner can also be indicated by other adverbs.

(61) Ariel-ta ***huers'a ipʰida*** b-a-sʰi-a
Ariel-ABS^FOC force laugh be-IMPF-PAST-DECL
Ariel was laughing so hard.

mãwã is also used to introduce reported speech, especially in EK; see §9.12.

Word Classes

2.8–2.18 Closed classes

The remaining parts of speech to be discussed are closed classes, that is, those classes that have limited numbers of members.

2.8 Adverbs of location and direction. Deictics consisting of a demonstrative root plus the locative suffix -*ma* (§4.4 and §5.7) are commonly used to indicate location.

(62) nãma   hãma   mãma
     here   there   location previously mentioned

In EK, the directional suffix -*idu* 'into' can be added to the demonstrative roots.

(63) nã-ĩnũ   hã-ĩnũ   mã-ĩnu
     in-here   in-there in-previously^mentioned^place

(64) mã-ĩnu   hũẽ-puru-para   (EK)
     there-into arrive-PRES-time
     when I got into there

Location can be indicated by locative words.

(65) bas^{h}i   warĩ
     place down river   place up river

Direction can be indicated by adverbs.

(66) barrea   barek^{h}are   wãrãka   wãrã   wãtek^{h}are
     down river   down river   up river   up river   up river
     (far)   (near)   (far)   (general)   (near)

     trua   truarik^{h}a   mẽã   na   hẽta
     inland   inland   into the   ahead   back
                   (near)   jungle

(67) barrea   wã-s^{h}i-da-a
     down^river   go-PAST-PL-DECL
     They went downstream.

Some adverbs can also function as postpositional suffixes (§2.10).

2.9 Pronouns and other pro-forms. Pronouns and other pro-forms substitute for nouns, noun phrases, clauses, or larger units. The referent of a pro-form is usually identifiable from its context. In NE there are pronoun stems to which are added case endings, possessives which usually look like the pronoun stems without endings, and alternative pronoun stems, which can be used as possessives as well. These are listed in §§4.13–4.14. There is no pronominal marking in verbs.

Pro-sentences are single words which take the place of complete sentences. Answers to polar questions are often pro-sentences, like the answer to the question in (68).

(68)   pia   hũẽ-s^{h}i-k^{h}a
       good arrive-PAST-POLAR
       Did you arrive well?

          mãẽ
          Yes.

Pronouns by themselves occur in the same position in the sentence as the noun they replace.

(69)   ***iči-ra*** huers'a ip^{h}ida b-a-s^{h}i-a
       3S-ABS force laugh be-IMPF-PAST-DECL
       S/he was laughing so hard.

2.10–2.11 Noun adjuncts

Elements in NE that occur with nouns to form noun phrases are postpositions and quantifiers.

2.10 Postpositional suffixes. Postpositional suffixes in NE are attached to the noun phrase. That they are not enclitics is shown by the fact that nasal base words spread their nasality to oral postpositions.

(70)   p^{h}uru-***de***
       village-in
       in the village

Word Classes

    *to-hã-**ne***
    river-expanse-in
    in the water of the river, at the bottom of the river

Some postpositions act as adverbs when they are not affixed to nouns.

(71) a. *to-**eda**   bae-s^hi-a*
       river-into descend-PAST-DECL
       He went down to the river.

   b. *eda   wã-s^hi-a*
       into go-PAST-DECL
       He went inside (or down).

2.11 Quantifiers. Numbers and other quantifiers usually follow the head noun.

(72) *tači s'rõã-ena-pema ẽpẽrã-ta   s^hida **k^hĩmãrẽ***
     1p old-into-ORIG person-ABS^FOC also^ABS four
     A long time ago there were four men.

(73) *mũ-a hãẽpʉrʉ imama-ra **hũma** k^hẽnã-ya-a*
     1S-ABL now   jaguar-ABS all   slaughter-FUT-DECL
     Now I am going to kill all of the jaguars.

(74) *hãũ-kʉ   mõkara-de **eda** pio^para ẽpẽrã-ta   b-ʉ-ra*
     that-very rock-in   into lots^of person-ABS^FOC be-PRES-ABS
     [I tell you that] inside that very rock is a whole bunch of people.

2.12–2.13 Statives

    A small set of stative verb roots is used in adjectival and locative constructions as well as in auxiliaries. Their root reflects the number of the subject, and they are obligatorily inflected for aspect. Two of these roots are optionally preceded by the possessive root *eru-* 'have, own' and/or by one of a set of positional roots.
    The internal structure of these stative verbs is, therefore, as follows: ± possessive root ± positional root + stative root + aspect + tense + mood.
    Tense and mood suffixes are discussed in §§6.11–13 and §§6.21–30; the mood suffix is replaced by nominal suffixes in subordinate clauses.

2.12 Simple and descriptive statives. Simple statives are roots that indicate the number of the subject. These are obligatorily marked for aspect. The roots are singular *b-*, plural (few) *pʰan-*, and plural (many/all) *tuan-*. Often the plural indicator *-da* found on regular verbs appears with the stative roots in NEP. In EK, the different statives suffice to indicate number.

The tense-aspect vowel that follows the stative root is obligatory. The present tense, which by default has imperfective aspect, is marked by *-ʉ*. Nonpresent imperfective aspect is marked by *-a*. Perfect aspect is signaled by *-e*. If the present imperfective *-ʉ* is used, no other tense marking is necessary. The nonpresent imperfective *-a* and the perfect *-e* require further tense marking. These are exemplified in (75) with the singular stative root *b-*.

(75) a. *b-ʉ-a*
 be-PRES-DECL
 am/are/is

 b. *b-a-sʰi-a*
 be-IMPF-PAST-DECL
 was/were

 c. *b-e-sʰi-a*
 be-PERF-PAST-DECL
 stayed

One additional stative root is *bea*, which is a plural form used to refer to all the individuals of a group. It cannot accept the three tense-aspect suffixes mentioned above, although it can accept other aspectuals, tense markers, and mood suffixes (§§6.11–13, 6.15–6.30).

(76) *ũkʰʉrʉ ũrũ-pema nẽ^ẽã čʰu-**bea**-sʰi-a carro-ra* (EK)
 some upon-ORIG without sit-be^indiv-PAST-DECL car-PIVOT
 Some of the cars were without tops.

Descriptive sentences use the simple stative *b-* or the special auxiliary *kʰir-*.[8] The present tense-aspect vowel for this verb is *-u*, not *-ʉ*. The past tense is also an irregular form, *kʰer-* + *-a*. In EK *kʰir-* describes female subjects; male subjects are described with *čir-*. The latter form is no longer used by most speakers of NEP.

---

[8]This also has diminutive and affective connotations.

Word Classes

(77) ẽpẽrã-ra   porekea   b-ʉ-a
      person-ABS fat   be-PRES-DECL
      The man is fat.

(78) ẽpẽrã-ra   porekea   kʰir-u-a
      person-ABS fat   DESC-PRES-DECL
      I would describe the guy as fat.

2.13 Possessive and positional stems. A small set of positional roots, which cannot occur in simple past tense form, is obligatorily followed by the singular root *b-* or the plural *pʰan-* to form the following positional verb stems:

(79)   singular   plural
                                                              (few)

sitting⁹   čʰũ-m- (NEP);   čʰũ-pʰan-
                                        čʰu-b- (EK)

standing and progressive   nũ-m-   nũ-pʰan-
positional/short durative¹⁰   kʰo-b-   kʰo-pʰan-
lying down   tʰa-b-   —

The stems in (79) are intransitive, and the resulting verbs can be used independently. In (80) the root *čʰũ-* 'sitting, leaning' has combined with the singular stative root *b-* to become the positional verb stem *čʰũm-* 'sit'. The exact meaning of the combined verb is determined by the tense-aspect vowel. *-e* indicates inceptive (perfect) aspect, and *-a* marks imperfective aspect.

(80) a. čʰũ-m-**e**-sʰi-a
          sit-be-PERF-PAST-DECL
          sat down

      b. čʰũ-m-**a**-sʰi-a
          sit-IMPF-PAST-DECL
          was sitting

---

⁹In EK the 'sitting' positional stem *čʰu-b-* is also a descriptive auxiliary and is used similarly to the way *kʰir-* (§2.12) is used in NEP. Another 'sitting' positional is *akʰʉ-*, which also means 'look'; the positional use is commonplace in SE but rare in NE.

¹⁰The short durative is as in 'the dog wagged its tail a few times' (David Pickens personal communication).

c. *čʰũ-m-ʉ-a*
   sit-be-PRES-DECL
   is sitting

All of the positional verbs can also act as auxiliaries.[11] The positional roots *nũ-* and *kʰo-* have also taken on aspectual functions, the progressive and short durative, respectively (see §§6.19–6.20).

(81) nẽ   kʰo čʰũ-m-a-sʰi-a
     GEN eat sit-be-IMPF-PAST-DECL
     was sitting and eating

(82) nẽ   kʰo **nũ**-m-a-sʰi-a
     GEN eat stand-be-IMPF-PAST-DECL
     was standing eating (positional) or was eating (progressive)

(83) akʉ   **kʰo**-b-e-sʰi-a
     look POS-be-PERF-PAST-DECL
     looked for a minute

The possessive root *eru-* 'have, own' (also *iru-* and *ero-* in NEP) behaves like a positional in that it must occur in combination with another verb and does so most commonly with a stative root. It can also combine with some positional roots. In any case it forms a transitive verb.

(84) mũ   pʰapʰa   čora-pa   wárra-rã   hueshoma **eru**-b-a-sʰi-a
     1S   mother old-ABL offspring-PL five   have-be-IMPF-PAST-DECL
     My grandmother had five children.

   *Mũ pʰapʰa čora-pa warra-rã hueshoma eru-sʰi-a.

(85) poro-de-pema-trʉ   **eru**-kʰo-b-e-sʰi-a
     head-in-ORIG^FOC^GI^ABS   have-POS-be-PERF-PAST-DECL
     He held it in place on his *head*.

The positionals can also combine with the independent verb *bʉya* 'put, place, write' to form compound verbs that mean placing an object in a certain position (see §6.10).

---

[11]The motion verbs *wã* 'go' and *sʼe* 'come' can act as auxiliaries in purpose clauses (see §6.9).

Word Classes

The root *hira* 'hang, lift, be up high' is unusual in that it can function with a stative root as a positional auxiliary and as a member of a serial verb stem (§6.2).

(86) či   katisolo ūtʰʉ **hira**-b-e-sʰi-a
      REF coatí   up   hang-be-PERF-PAST-DECL
      The coatí stayed up there.

(87) imama-ra   ēkʰarra-de **hira** eta-sʰi-a
      jaguar-ABS back-on   hang   take-PAST-DECL
      He picked up and carried the jaguar on his back.

2.14 Equative verb. Equative clauses do not use a separate verb or copula in the present tense. A declarative mood suffix on the nominal complement is sufficient. In the past tense the equative root *pa-* is used but never with a plural suffix. *pa-* is also the auxiliary used in past negatives (§7.12).

(88) Reinaldo-ra   Roberto   sʹesʹa-a
      Reinaldo-ABS Roberto   father-DECL
      Reinaldo is Roberto's father.

(89) hāʉ̄ ēpērā-ta   iči poro **pa**-sʰi-a
      that person-ABS^FOC   3S   head EQ-PAST-DECL
      That man was his boss.

Equative *pa-* is also used with temporal nouns in stative clauses even though there is no equivalent complement of the time expression.

(90) kʰewara   **pa**-pʉrʉ-de sʹe-sʰi-a   tida
      afternoon EQ-PRES-in   come-PAST-DECL   home
      When it was afternoon he came home.

2.15 Existential verb. The verb stem *para*, which is related to the equative *pa-*, is used for the existential as in (91). *para* can also mean 'have' if the possession is not viewed as temporary and if a stative auxiliary verb is used in the present tense as in (92). For temporary possession, the possessive root *eru-* is used (§2.13).

(91) wadi   čikʰo **para**-a
      still food   EXST-DECL
      There is still food.

(92) pakʰuru-pa kʰitua **para** b-ʉ-a
 tree-ABL leaf EXST be-PRES-DECL
 The tree has (lots of) leaves.

pa- and para are related in that the past tense existential verb uses pa- as its root rather than para.¹² If para occurs in the past tense, it must mean 'have (nontemporary)'. Interestingly enough, having a wife is not considered temporary; see (94).

(93) mãũ nãpua b-ʉ-mae   mõkara waibʉa-ta   **pa-sʰi-a**
 this deep be-PRES-LOC rock   large-ABS^FOC EQ-PAST-DECL
 At this deep place, there was a large rock.

(94) kʰima   **para-sʰi-a**
 spouse EXST-PAST-DECL
 He took a wife (got married).

2.16 Clitics. Clitics are metrically bound to words they precede or follow but are not in the same realm of nasalization as suffixes. Whereas suffixes in NE are always nasalized if nasality spreads to the end of a word, clitics in NEP are not obligatorily subject to nasalization rules. In EK the nasalization is not passed to or from clitics at all.

A common enclitic is bari, a derivational verb morpheme discussed in §6.10. It is optionally nasalized after nasal verb stems.

(95) /wã baɾi/ → [wãᵐbaɾi] ~ [wãmãɲĩ]   'go' + 'upward' = 'fly'

The common generalizing proclitic nẽ is not a prefix since its nasality is spread optionally instead of obligatorily.

(96) /nẽ ba/ → [nẽᵐba] ~ [nẽmã]   GEN + 'liquid' = 'soup'

nẽ often makes the referent of a noun generic.¹³ For example, whereas etʰerre 'chicken' and the referential adjective či (§4.6) identify the procedence of ũmũ 'egg', nẽ makes its meaning general.

(97) etʰerre ũmũ   'chicken egg'
 či ũmũ   'its egg, the egg'
 nẽ ũmũ   'an egg, any kind of egg'

---

¹²To avoid confusion, pa- is always glossed as equative and para- as existential.
¹³Harms (1994:41) discusses nẽ in §3.9.

Word Classes

The other common use of *nẽ* is to make the object of a verb generic. The object is then incorporated (see §6.3).

(98)   o   nu-m-ʉ-a
       make   stand-be-PRES-DECL
       He is making it.

(99)   nẽ   o   nũ-m-ʉ-a
       GEN make stand-be-PRES-DECL
       He is making something/doing something/working.

2.17 Vocatives. Many nouns can be used as vocatives, including *čapa* 'brother', *čapawẽrã* 'sister', *kʰima* 'spouse', other kinship terms, and *kʰurra* 'neighbor'. *ačʰe* 'friend', however, is only used in the vocative.

2.18 Interjections. NE has interjections to express emotion. They have no lexical meaning.

(100) **ai**   ačʰe   mũ   huwa!
       ow   friend   1s   hand
       Ow, man, my hand!

3
Derivational Morphology

This chapter limits itself to derivational processes which change the part of speech (§§3.1–3.3) and to phonological processes which intensify or mitigate the meaning of a word (§§3.4–3.7). Derivational suffixes that are added to a verb stem but do not change the part of speech are discussed in §§6.4–6.10.

3.1 Denominalized adjectives. The suffix *-ida* is added to nouns in order to form an adjective 'full of X' or 'given to X'.

(101) *hãũ ẽpẽrã-ra s^hewa-**ida** b-ʉ-a*
 that person-ABS lie-full^of be-PRES-DECL
 That guy is full of lies.

3.2 Deverbal predicate adjectives. Whereas ES uses the suffix *-ya* meaning 'someone who does X a lot' to form predicate adjectives from verbs, this suffix in NEP means 'likely or bound to do X'. It is identical to the future tense suffix but in order to convey this particular meaning, a stative verb is needed in addition. In the EK form, *-ya* is shortened to *-i*.

(102) *nãũ tiamas^hi itua to-**ya** b-ʉ-a*   (NEP)
 this night liquor drink-FUT be-PRES-DECL
 Tonight he is bound to drink liquor (get drunk).

To convey 'someone who does/likes to do X a lot', the irrealis suffix *-i* is used as in (103) and (104).

(103) *itua   to-i   pia   b-ɨ-a*
      liquor drink-IRR good be-PRES-DECL
      He likes to drink/often drinks liquor.

(104) *itua   to-i   awa   b-ɨ-a*
      liquor drink-IRR be^given^to be-PRES-DECL
      He likes to drink/often drinks liquor.

3.3 Derived nouns. Habitual suffixes on verbs or verb phrases may function as agentive nominalizations or headless relative clauses. The phonetically identical sentences below can be interpreted as active or as equative. In the equative sentence (106), the noun *čõpari* 'soldier' is derived from the active verb form *čõ-pa-ri-a* 'habitually fights' from (105). The derived noun is in turn suffixed with the declarative -a to form an equative sentence.

(105) *iči-ra   čõ-pa-ri-a*
      3S-ABS   fight-HAB-SG-DECL
      He always fights.

(106) *iči-ra   čõpari-a*
      3S-ABS   soldier-DECL
      He is a soldier.

The difference between the active and equative sentences in (107) and (108) is seen first in the case marking on the subject. In (107) the speaker is saying that Miguel takes care of their teeth. Therefore, the subject receives ergative (ablative) case marking. In (108) the phrase *tači kʰida wakapari* 'caretaker of our (= human) teeth' has been derived from the predicate *tači kʰida waka-pa-ri-a* 'habitually takes care of our teeth'. The subject *Miguel* receives absolutive case marking and the derived noun is suffixed with the declarative -a to form an equative sentence.

(107) *Miguel-**pa**   tači   kʰida   waka-pa-ri-**a***
      Miguel-ABL 1p   tooth care^for-HAB-SG-DECL
      Miguel habitually takes care of our teeth.

(108) *Miguel-ra   tači   kʰida   wakapari-a.*
      Miguel-ABS 1p   tooth   caretaker-DECL
      Miguel is a dentist.

Derivational Morphology

3.4–3.7 Grammatically related phonological processes

Lengthening of syllables, insertion of glottal stops, reduplication of syllables and whole roots, and extra heavy stress all have a grammatical function in NE.

3.4 Intensification of adjectives. One intensified form of an adjective in NEP involves the lengthening of and heavier stress on the stressed syllable, which cause resyllabification of the intensified word as shown in (110). In EK the intensified adjective uses a glottal stop, as shown in (111).

(109) *pia   b-ʉ-a*
      good be-PRES-DECL
      I'm fine.

(110) ***piya***   *b-ʉ-a*   (NEP)
      very^good be-PRES-DECL
      I'm very well.

(111) ***pi?ia***   *b-ʉ-a*   (EK)
      very^good be-PRES-DECL
      I'm very well.

Harms (1994:39) says that the occurrence of the two types of intensifiers is predictable: one-syllable words are lengthened, and multisyllabic words receive -ka. This is not always true in NE, although both of these types of intensification exist. In (112) the adjective *kʰuara* 'yellow' is intensified by the addition of -ka.

(112 *mããpʉrʉ   waya   we-kʰua   nũ-m-e-sʰi-a*
      [new^dev.]   again   vomit-REPT stand-be-PERF-PAST-DECL

      *kʰuara-**ka***
      yellow-INTENS
      Then I started throwing up again; it was *yellow*.

In still another type of intensification, a glottal stop is inserted between partially reduplicated forms.

(113) a. *pʰãwãrã*
         blue

b. *pʰã?pʰãrã*
   bright blue

3.5 Mitigation of adjectives. To tone down the quality of a given adjective, up to the first two syllables of the root are reduplicated.

(114) a. *pʰãwãrã*
         blue
      b. *pʰãwãpʰãwãrã*
         greenish-blue

(115) a. *kʰačirua*
         bad, sinful, adulterous
      b. *kʰačikʰačirua*
         marginally acceptable

3.6 Intensification of verbs. The suffix *-ka* that intensifies adjectives also intensifies verbs.

(116) *pʰurrua-sʰi-a*
      go^circle-PAST-DECL
      went in a circle

(117) *pʰurru-ka-sʰi-a*
      go^circle-INTENS-PAST-DECL
      went around in circles

3.7 Mitigation of verbs. Verbs are mitigated in the same way adjectives are: by reduplication.

(118) *ipʰida-sʰi-a*
      laugh-PAST-DECL
      laughed

(119) *ipʰida-ipʰida-sʰi-a*
      laugh-laugh-PAST-DECL
      smiled

4
Noun Phrase

The noun phrase is composed of a noun head, which may be singular or plural and simple or compound. The noun may be preceded by a possessive adjective, demonstrative adjective, indexing adjective, referential adjective or another noun. It may be followed by a descriptive adjective, numeral, or quantifier. It is not usually preceded or followed by more than one element. For more complex constructions, relative clauses are used (§§9.9–9.10).

4.1 Simple nouns. Many noun phrases are simple nouns.

(120) *usʰa-ra houhou-sʰi-a*
dog-ABS bark-PAST-DECL
The dog barked.

(121) ***María*-*pa*** *pʰata o-sʰi-a*
María-ABL plantain make-PAST-DECL
María cooked plantains.

4.2 Compound nouns. Compound nouns are formed from a noun plus another noun, from a descriptive adjective acting in a derivational role, or from a verb. Also, the generalizing proclitic *nẽ* may proceed the noun in order to form a different noun (§2.16). In practice, nouns are considered compound if the sum of the semantic parts does not equal the meaning of the whole. For example, the word for 'thumb' is formed from the nouns *huwa* 'hand' and *pʰapʰa* 'mother'. Since hands do not have mothers, the roots are joined for 'thumb', as in (122).

(122) mū **huwapʰapʰa** pʰúa-sʰi-a
 1s thumb   hurt-PAST-DECL
 I hurt my thumb.

The NEP word *toi* 'paddle' is formed from the noun *to* 'river' and the verb stem *wi* 'stir'. The EK equivalent is *towiki*. The NEP word is written with its parts joined in (123) not only for the semantic criterion stated above but because the two monosyllabic words have become one: *toi*, not *towi*.

(123) mā̃ṹ hăpa-de **toi**   ũmẽ pʰan-ʉ-a
 this canoe-in paddle two be^few-PRES-DECL
 In this canoe are two paddles.

4.3–4.7 Prenominal modifiers

Prenominal modifiers may be possessive adjectives, demonstrative adjectives, indexing adjectives, the referential proclitic, or nouns.

4.3 Possessive adjectives. Possessive adjectives are personal pronouns (§4.13) used to show a possessive relationship. They always precede the head noun.

(124) **mū** sʼesʼa
 my father

4.4 Demonstrative adjectives and pronouns. The table in (125) indicates the spatial and discourse functions of the demonstratives, which can occur preceding nouns or by themselves in similar roles.

(125)   *nā̃ṹ* 'this'   *hā̃ṹ* 'that'   *mā̃ṹ* 'this, the'

Spatial:	close	physically or psychologically distant	—
Discourse:	cataphoric	anaphoric	always anaphoric; main theme in the context

References to objects physically proximate to the speaker are usually assigned *nā̃ṹ* 'this', although they need not be physical objects. In (126)

Noun Phrase

the demonstrative denotes a temporal proximity. In (127) it denotes a physical proximity.

(126) **nãũ** kʰewara nẽ   asʰea-ta   to-di-a   mũ tida
      this afternoon GEN bitter-ABS^FOC drink-FUT^PL-DECL 1s home
      This afternoon we will drink chicha at my house.

(127) **nãũ** hiwa-ta   bari-di-a
      this bend-ABS^FOC   fish-FUT^PL-DECL
      Let's fish this riverbend.

Objects physically, temporally, or psychologically distant from the speaker are assigned the demonstrative *hãũ* (*kʰãũ* in EK). Example (128) is of a physical distance. The distance in (129) is psychological, since the *guatín* is angry at the vulture. In (130), which is from EK, the locative *kʰã-má* is used to signal emotional distance even though the speaker means 'here', where he is.

(128) ačʰe   **hãũ** kʰuriwa beya   tʰrũ-ni-a   tači pʰera-pue-da
      friend that   guatín whistle call-FUT-DECL   1p   fear-VOL-PPRT

      pera   (NEP)
      because
      Hey, let's call that *guatín* (rodent) out by whistling, because he's scared of us.

(129) kʰuriwa-pa kʰrĩčʰa hᵾrᵾ   b-e-sʰi-a   mũ-ã   **hãũ**
      guatín-ABL think   search be-PERF-PAST-DECL 1s-ABL that

      ãkosʰo-ra   pea-ya-a   (NEP)
      vulture-ABS KILL-FUT-DECL
      The guatín's only thought became, "I will kill that vulture."

(130) mũ kʰãrẽã   sⁱokʰa-sʰi-tʰa **kʰãmá** plata nẽ^ẽã-ra   kʰãrẽ-ma
      1s REASON send-PAST-FOC   there   money without-PIVOT what-LOC

      sⁱe-sʰi-tʰa   (EK)
      come-PAST-FOC
      Why did you send me to this place with no money?! What have I come for?!

When objects are in sight, *s'a* 'here' and *hari* 'there' are joined with present tense forms of stative verbs (§§2.12–2.13) to form demonstratives. These combinations can be translated as 'this here' and 'that there', respectively. These are deictics in the pure sense. They have no discourse function other than to point out participants as they introduce them. One way in which they are unique is that they can occur before and after the nouns they modify. (131) uses *s'a* 'here' with *b-ʉ* 'be-PRES' and (132) employs *hari* 'there' with *nū-m-ʉ* 'stand-be-PRES'.

(131) māwã   b-ʉ-de   s'e-sʰi-a   ūmākʰīrã   **s'a**   **b-ʉ**-ta
      like^this be-PRES-in come-PAST-DECL man   here   be-PRES-ABS^FOC
      While this was happening, there came a man who looked like him.

(132) čapa   **hari** **nū-m-ʉ**   s'āmo-ta   māwã   bia
      brother   there   stand-be-PRES   curassow-ABS^FOC like^this yell

      b-ʉ-a
      be-PRES-DECL
      [We said,] "Brother, that there *curassow* (large jungle turkey) calls like this."

The thematic demonstrative *mãũ*, which is best translated as 'this' or 'the', is often assigned to nouns once they have been mentioned in a given context (see §10.1).

(133) hãpa-de-pa   hũē-sʰi-da-a   nãpua b-ʉ-mae   **mãũ** nãpua
      canoe-in-ABL arrive-PAST-PL-DECL deep   be-PRES-LOC this   deep

      b-ʉ-mae
      be-PRES-LOC
      We came by canoe to a deep place. At this deep place

Addition of the suffix *-kʉ* to the demonstrative adjectives gives them an emphatic sense.

(134) hãũ-**kʉ**   mōkara-de   eda   pio^para   ēpērã-ta   b-ʉ-ra
      that-very   rock-in   into   lots^of   person-ABS^FOC be-PRES-ABS
      [I tell you that] inside that very rock is a whole bunch of people.

(135) mã̄ũ-**ku** pʰāka-pa   tai hāpa   barru-pue-sʰi-a
       this-very speedboat-ABL 1p canoe turn^over-VOL-PAST-DECL
       This *very* speedboat capsized our canoe.

Demonstratives can occur without nouns but carry the proper case marking, making them true demonstrative pronouns.

(136) ãči-a   kʰrīčʰa-sʰi-da-a   **hã̄ũ-pa**   sʰāwã-ẽrã   warrá
       3p-ABL think-PAST-PL-DECL that-ABL how-because tasty

       o-pa-ri
       make-HAB-SG
       They thought, "How does that guy make it taste so good?"

4.5 Indexing adjectives. The indexing adjective *ara* 'same, right' placed before demonstratives and sentence introducers (§8.2) indicates that the referent is both specific and the same as before.

(137) **ara**   mãma-pe nẽpᵻrᵻ pa-sʰi-a
       same there-LIM story   EQ-PAST-DECL
       The story ends right here.

A word with a similar function, *abari* 'same', is used to indicate that something else is in the same class as the previously mentioned object. See also §5.12.

(138) **abari** pedea b-ᵻ-a
       same word be-PRES-DECL
       It means the same thing.

4.6 Referential adjective. The referential proclitic *či* precedes the noun phrase head and indicates that the noun is something already overtly mentioned, related to something already mentioned, or obviously understood by the context. For this reason, some linguists have called *či* a definite article; see (139) and (140). More often, however, the referent is the possessor of the head noun, as shown (141). When the referential proclitic precedes a verb, the action concerned is reciprocal; see §6.3. The discourse function of *či* is discussed in §10.4.

(139) batʰa ẽ   pa-sʰi-a   či   kʰatʰisʰolo ũtʰʉ hira-b-e-sʰi-a
     shoot NEG EQ-PAST-DECL REF coatí   up   hang-be-PERF-PAST-DECL
     [Since I had no rifle] I didn't shoot it. The *coatí* (racoon-like animal) stayed up there.

(140) beko-ta   nũ-m-a-sʰi-a   či   beko-ra   s'au
     avocado-ABS^FOC stand-be-IMPF-PAST-DECL REF avocado-ABS produce

     nũ-m-a-sʰi-a
     stand-be-IMPF-PAST-DECL
     There was an avocado tree. The avocado tree was producing fruit.

(141) mãũ-ne   čipari-ta   wã-sʰi-a   to   sʰu-de   či   kʰima
     this-in owner-ABS^FOC go-PAST-DECL river spear-in REF spouse

     ũmẽ
     two
     Then the owner [of the above tree] went to spear fish with his wife.

4.7 Nouns modifying nouns. Heads of noun phrases can also be modified by proper or common nouns or noun phrases. If the relationship between the nouns is possessive, the possessor precedes the possessed noun.

(142) **pʰema poro-ra** tʰu   hita-sʰi-a
     fish^sp. head-ABS chop grab-PAST-DECL
     cut the pema fish's head off

(143) ẽpẽrã   pʰuru
     person village
     Embera village

(144) či   s'es'a   te
     REF father house
     his/her father's house

In descriptive relationships the modifier follows the head noun.

(145) pʰata   kʰũmũ
     plantain bunch
     plantains in bunch form

Noun Phrase

(146) et^{h}erre wẽrã
  chicken female
  hen

4.8-4.10 Post-nominal modifiers

Nouns may be followed by descriptive adjectives, numerals, or quantifiers.

4.8 Descriptive adjectives. Adjectives follow the nouns they modify.

(147) wárra s'ak^{h}e
  offspring small
  baby

(148) mãũ nãpua b-ʉ-mae mōkara **waibua-ta** pa-s^{h}i-a
  this deep be-PRES-LOC rock large-ABS^FOC EQ-PAST-DECL
  At this deep place there was a large rock.

4.9 Numerals. There are five common numerals in NE. The term hues^{h}oma 'five' is derived from huwa hōma 'whole hand'. These numbers were once combined with the words for 'hand', 'body', and 'foot' to form larger numbers (see Harms 1994:53). For example, 'one hand plus three' equaled eight. These days, however, the great majority of Northern Emberas use Spanish words for the numbers over five and sometimes for the numbers five and under.

(149) aba ūmẽ[14] ũpea k^{h}ĩmārẽ hues^{h}oma
  'one' 'two' 'three' 'four' 'five'

Numbers follow the nouns they quantify; the appropriate case marking is suffixed onto the head noun.

(150) ẽpẽrã-ta ūmẽ mẽã wã-s^{h}i-da-a
  person-ABS^FOC two jungle go-PAST-PL-DECL
  Two men went into the jungle (= went hunting).

Numbers can be suffixed with the limiter -pe 'only'. The EK form is -pai.

---

[14]The same morpheme is used as an enclitic to indicate accompaniment (§5.6).

(151) **aba-pe** nẽ ẽ-a   (NEP)
one-LIM GEN NEG-DECL
There's not even one.

Numbers can also act as the head of a noun phrase when the head is understood from the context.

(152) **ūpea** wã-sʰi-da-a   traha-de
three go-PAST-PL-DECL work-in
Three of them went to work.

(153) mãũ sʰukʰura-ra   ãči **ūpea-pema-pa** warrá to-sʰi-da-a
this cane^juice-ABS 3p three-ORIG-ABL tasty drink-PAST-PL-DECL
The other three of them heartily drank this cane juice.

4.10 Nominal quantifiers. Quantifiers also follow the head noun (154) and, like numbers, do not take case marking (155).

(154) ãči-de-ra **hūma** kʰotʰa-pa-či-da-a
3pl-in-ABS all gobble-HAB-PAST-PL-DECL
They gobbled up all of their own, just as they had before.

(155) **mãũ-ku** ẽpẽrã-rã nũrẽma-s'a   traha-pa-či-da-a
this-very person-PL next^day-every work-HAB-PAST-PL-DECL
These same men worked every day.

4.11 Compound noun phrases. In compound noun phrases the various nominals are often separated by the additive *tewara* 'others, the rest, also'. *ičaba* 'and, also' separates clauses (see §8.4).

(156) s'e-sʰi-da-a   Reinaldo-ta   **tewara** Kolako-ta   **tewara**
come-PAST-PL-DECL Reinaldo-ABS^FOC also Kolako-ABS^FOC also

   Terecino-ta
   Terecino-ABS^FOC
Those who came along were Reinaldo, Kolako, and Terecino.

Neither of the above additives, however, is obligatory. It is sufficient to mark each of the constituents of a compound noun phrase with absolutive focus as in (157), if that constitutes appropriate case marking for the phrase. Otherwise, the final noun in the phrase is followed by one of the following

Noun Phrase

enclitics: *sʰida* in absolutive phrases (158) or *pida* in nonabsolutive cases. The first noun in such situations need not be overt (159).

(157) tači sʰrōā-ēnā to^kʰēpɨ-da wã-sʰi-da-a ūmākʰīrã-ta
1p old-into headwaters-GOAL go-PAST-PL-DECL man-ABS^FOC

 wẽrã-ta
 woman-ABS^FOC
 A long time ago a man and a woman went to the headwaters.

(158) Anancio-pa pʰata tia-sʰi-a nẽ ba sʰida
Anancio-ABL plantain give-PAST-DECL GEN liquid also^ABS

 tia-sʰi-a
 give-PAST-DECL
 Anancio gave them plantains and also soup.

(159) mū-a **pida** warrá o-ya-a hāēpɨrɨ
1S-ABL also tasty make-FUT-DECL now
Now I, too, will make it tasty.

(160) māmī pʰua-pa kʰāī b-e ẽ pa-sʰi-a ewari-de
however pain-ABL sleep be-PERF NEG EQ-PAST-DECL day-in

 miã **tiamasʰe** pida
 GEN night also
 However, because of the pain I couldn't sleep day or night.

4.12 Plurality. Plurality, which is obligatory in the verb phrase, is marked optionally in the subject noun phrase as in (161). The subject noun carries no plural marker except for the number *ūmē* 'two'. The verb has the plural suffix *-da*.

(161) ēpẽrã-ta ūmē mẽã wã-sʰi-**da**-a
person-ABS^FOC two jungle go-PAST-PL-DECL
Two men went into the jungle (= went hunting).

Plural marking on the noun phrase only becomes obligatory if large numbers are being talked about.

(162) pʰaraskua-**rã**-pa   tai-ra toya   tʰrŭ-sʰi-da-a
      armed^men-PL-ABL 1p-ABS riverside call-PAST-PL-DECL
      Some armed men called us to shore.

When talking about the habits of animals, the singular is used. When talking about people's customs, the plural is used.

(163) hue^hõpʉ-pa   bʉčʰa-ta   kʰo-pa-**ri**-a
      harpy^eagle-ABL sloth-ABS^FOC eat-HAB-SG-DECL
      The harpy eagle eats sloth.

   *hue^hõpʉ-rã-pa bʉčʰa-rã-ta kʰo-pa-ta-a

(164) ãtia-ta   hũ-pa-či-**da**-a
      g^string-ABS^FOC tie-HAB-PL-DECL
      We used to wear g-strings.

4.13–4.15 Pronouns

The NE languages have personal, possessive, and indefinite pronouns.

4.13 Personal pronouns. Pronouns and other pro-forms substitute for nouns, noun phrases, clauses, or larger units. The referent of a pro-form is usually identifiable from its context. In NE there are pronoun stems to which are added case endings, possessive adjectives which are the stems without endings (§4.3), and coreferent pronoun stems, which are possessives as well.[15] There is no pronominal marking on verbs. Note in chart (165) the alternate ergative case marking taken by some regular stems.

(165)

person and number[16]	regular stem	ergative (ablative)	absolutive	indirect object	coreferent stems
1s	mũ	mũ-a	mũ-ra	mũ-a	mũči
2s	pʉ	pʉ-a	pʉ-ra	pʉ-a	pʉči
3s	iči	iči-a	iči-ra	iči-a	iči
1p excl	tai	tai-pa	tai-ra	tai-a	
1p incl	tači	tači-a	tači-ra	tači-a	tači

---

[15]Harms (1994:58) calls the coreferent pronoun stems 'marked pronouns', which he analyzes as the simple root plus a morpheme -či.
[16]The plural stems take on the plural noun suffix -rã when their referent is a large number of people.

person and number	regular stem	ergative (ablative)	absolutive	indirect object	coreferent stems
2p	pārā[17]	pārā-pa	pārā-ra	pārā-a	pāči
3p	āči	āči-a	āči-ra	āči-a	āči

Two additional third-person stems are also found: *iru* (SG) and *ārā* (PL); see below. Pronouns by themselves occur where the noun they replace would normally be.

(166) *iči-ra huers'a ipʰida b-a-sʰi-a*
 3S-ABS force laugh be-IMPF-PAST-DECL
 S/he was laughing so hard.

The coreferent forms of the first- and second-person pronouns are most often used in NE as possessive adjectives when the referent is the subject of the sentence.[18] In the oblique phrases in (167) and (168), first- and second-person coreferent posessives, respectively, are used because the subjects of the sentences are the same referents as those indicated by the possessives. In (169) the second-person coreferent possessive is used because *pʉ-a* 'you-ABL' is the subject of the complement clause.

(167) *mʉ-a **mʉči** hĩrũ-ne hũẽ nũ-m-ʉ-ya-a   pʉ-a*
 1S-ABL 1S^COREF leg-in hook stand-be-place-FUT-DECL 2S-ABL

  errebari mārẽā
  pull   PURP
 I will hook it on my leg so you can pull me out.

(168) *yarre pʉ-ra **pʉči** kʰʉwʉrʉ s'area-pa kʰore-pa*
 monkey 2S-ABS 2S^COREF ear   hard-ABL crocodile-ABL

  kʰo-ya-a
  eat-FUT-DECL
 Monkey, because you won't listen (lit., because of your hard ear) you will be eaten by a crocodile!

---

[17]In EK this form is *mārā*.

[18]When the coreferent forms are used as subjects, Enemark and Schermerhorn (n.d.) comment, "The second person [SG] *pʉči* and [PL] *pāči* seem to indicate a derogative, scolding attitude, i.e., 'Get **your** kid!' or '**Your** grades are lousy!' The first person *mūči* is used in the sense of a superior, proud, uplifted attitude." In ES, in contrast, the alternate forms of the first- and second-person pronouns are used to emphasize whose will is dominant (Harms 1994:59).

(169) mũ-a   ara   mãũ-ne   kʰawa-ya-a   pʉ-a   **pʉči**   pedea hara
      1S-ABL same this-in know-FUT-DECL   2S-ABL 2S^COREF   word say

       wã-i-tʰa   kʰrĩña   b-ʉ-tʰa
       go-IRR-FOC want   be-PRES-FOC
then I will know that you want me to go and preach your word

The regular third-person pronouns *iči* and *ãči* may also be used as possessive adjectives when the referent is the subject of the sentence. See §10.5 for the reason for selecting *iči* rather than the referential adjective *či*.

(170) ara   mãũ-ta   werã   iči wárra   sʼakʰe ẽkʰarra-de atʰau
      same this-SUBD woman 3S   offspring small   back-in   carry

       eta-sʰi-a
       bring-PAST-DECL
Then the woman took her son along tied on her back.

The NEP examples (171) and (172) suggest that the alternate third-person pronoun stems are used to set off the party marked by them as the adversary of the main character.[19] In (171) the main character, who is speaking, has to kill the evil beings indicated by *ãrã,* who want to control or kill him as well as his family.

(171) ãrã-ra   peu   kʰãĩke-da   kʰarea   mũ-a   hũma
      3S^ALT-ABS drunk fall^asleep-PPRT DS   1S-ABL all

       kʰẽna-ya-a
       slaughter-FUT-DECL
After they are drunk and have fallen asleep, I will kill them all.

In (172) the alternate third-person singular *iru* also marks an adversary.

(172) **iru**-a   mũ-ra   pʰoya-sʰi-a   mãwã-mĩna   iči poro-ra
      3S^ALT-ABL 1S-ABS conquer-PAST-DECL like^this-though 3S   head-ABS

---

[19]Rasmussen and Mesúa (1985:126) say the third-person singular is used to indicate affection, pity, or scorn. However, available examples are limited to those in this section.

Noun Phrase 45

    urua   b-e-s^{h}i-a
    shine be-PERF-PAST-DECL
    He beat me, but his head became bald!

Almost completely opposite of this is the EK use of *iru* and *ā̃rā̃*. These are used to defend someone who is being charged with a crime.

4.14 Possessive pronouns. Possessive pronouns for the first and second singulars are formed by adding *-re* to the regular stem. For the other pronouns this is done with the suffixation of *-de*. Due to this fact, *-de* is occasionally seen suffixed to the first- and second-person singulars.

(173) *pu-**re**-a*
     2S-POSS-DECL
     It's yours.

(174) *iči-**de**-a*
     3S-in-DECL
     It is his.

4.15 Indefinite pronouns. As in ES, there are three indefinite pronouns in NE, two of which use the generalizing proclitic *nẽ* (§2.16). *nẽ t^{h}at^{h}a* means 'things' and *nẽ hūma* means 'everything'. A form which includes *nẽ* in ES (Harms 1994:61) leaves it off in NE: *ina* means 'what-cha-ma-call-it, what's-his-name, etc.'.

(175) *tači Āk^{h}õrẽ-pa **nẽ^hūma** o-s^{h}i-a*
     1p God-ABL   everything make-PAST-DECL
     God made everything.

(176) *p^{h}uru-da wã-puru-de mũ-a ũnũ-s^{h}i-a   hãũ ẽpẽrã*
     town-GOAL go-PRES-in 1S-ABL see-PAST-DECL that person

     ina
     what's-his-name
     When I was going to town I saw that guy—what's his name—you know...

Another indefinite pronoun in NEP uses *hūma* 'all' and the post-positional suffix *-eda* in its nasal form, *-ēnā*, to make *hūmaēnā* 'everyone'.[20]

(177) **hūma-ēnā**   hʉrʉ-sʰi-da-a   māwā-mīna   tai-ra nē nē
       all-into   search-PAST-PL-DECL   like^this-though   1p-ABS GEN GEN

       ẽ   pʰan-a-sʰi-da-a
       NEG   be^few-IMPF-PAST-PL-DECL

They searched everyone. Even though [they did] this, we didn't have any [weapons] at all.

---

[20]*hūmaēnā* is probably a frozen form. For more discussion of the uses of *-eda/-ēnā*, see §§5.8–5.11.

5

Case

The NE case system is ergative-absolutive, that is, the subject of the intransitive clause and the object of the transitive clause receive identical suffixation. Marking of the transitive subject is distinct. The case marking is a suffix on the last member of the phrase in question. Similar case systems are found in all Embera languages as well as in Waunana, the only other Chocó language (Rex 1975:38–40, Rasmussen and Mesúa 1985:115–17, Pardo-Rojas and Aguirre-Licht 1993:308–9, Harms 1994:65–78).

In this chapter the basic uses of the case markers will be illustrated along with the use of the ergative (ablative) suffix in combination with other morphemes.

5.1 Ablative. The suffix -*pa* marks the transitive subject or ergative case within the main clause. By itself, however, it also marks instrument and reason. Together these uses share the sense of cause or origin. All of these notions are subsumed under the term "ablative." Example (178) shows the normal use of -*pa* as the ergative.

(178) *tai-**pa** hita-s^{h}i-da-a*
 1p-ABL grab-PAST-PL-DECL
 We took it.

(179) and (180) are examples of the instrumental use of -*pa*. As is usual, the suffix is placed on the last member of the phrase.

(179) tʰu-da-pʰeda   nekʰo   sʲakʰe-**pa**   či   kʰĩpu-are   tʰoa-kʰua-pa-ta-a
       chop-PL-after knife small-ABL REF nose-area split-REPT-HAB-PL-DECL
       After we chop it, we split the ends with a small knife.

(180) hãpa-de-**pa**   hũẽ-sʰi-da-a   nãpua   b-ʉ-mae
       canoe-in-ABL arrive-PAST-PL-DECL deep   be-PRES-LOC
       We arrived by canoe at a deep place.

When a pronoun in the ergative case is being emphasized, a second suffix -*pʉrʉ* is added to the ergative suffix -*a*. For all other emphasized ergative nominals, -*pʉrʉ* replaces the normal -*pa*; it is not added to it.

(181) mũ-**a-pʉrʉ**   sʰãwã-ẽrã   hãwã   o-pʉrʉ
       1S-ABL-FOC^GI how-because like^that make-PRES
       How am *I* going to make it like that?

(182) hãũ-**pʉrʉ**   sʰãwã-ẽrã   warrá   o-pa-ri
       that-ABL^FOC how-because tasty   make-HAB-SG
       How does *he* make it tasty?

Examples (183) and (184) from the same story show how -*pa* and -*pʉrʉ* give NE speakers a choice of where to put any emphasis. In (183) the woman finally comes to the conclusion that she has been taken away by a demon; that is why *animarã* 'demon' is suffixed with -*pʉrʉ*. In (184) the husband does not really know how his wife has disappeared. Most Emberas would assume, though, that any unexplainable phenomenon had to do with the spirit world. Therefore, to say that a demon has taken his wife away is not surprising. That is why the normal -*pa* has been used instead of -*pʉrʉ*. See also §10.8.

(183) mãũ-ne-*pʉrʉ*   wẽrã-pa   kʰawa-sʰi-a   mũ-ra   animarã-**pʉrʉ**
       this-in-FOC^GI woman-ABL know-PAST-DECL 1S-ABS demon-FOC^GI

       hãwã   ete   wã-pʉrʉ-kʰa
       like^that take go-PRES-POLAR
       That's when the woman realized, "Am I being taken away by a demon?"

(184) mãũ-ne   ũmãkʰĩrã-pa kʰawa-sʰi-a   mũ   kʰima-ra   animarã-**pa**
       this-in man-ABL   know-PAST-DECL 1S spouse-ABS demon-ABL

ete   wã-pɨrɨ-ta
   take go-PRES-ABS^FOC
About that time the man realized, "My wife has been taken by a demon."

5.2 Absolutive. Nouns in the absolutive case can be marked in four ways: Ø (nonactivated), -ra (nonfocal), -ta (introductory focus), or -trɨ (focus on given information). Stephen Levinsohn (personal communication) suggests that zero marking is associated with nouns that have not yet been activated or brought into focus in a text or have temporarily been inactivated or put out of focus. In (185) the husband is inactivated because he leaves the stage for a while.[21]

(185) nũrẽma   ũmãkʰĩrã-Ø   mẽã   wã-sʰi-a
      next^day   man-ABS   jungle go-PAST-DECL
      The next morning the man [husband] went into the jungle.

Example (186), which precedes (185) in the same story, is of the nonfocal absolutive suffix -ra marking the intransitive subject werã 'woman', who is remaining on stage.

(186) mãẽpɨrɨ   werã-ra   kʰãĩ   b-e-sʰi-a
      [new^dev]   woman-ABS   sleep be-PERF-PAST-DECL
      Then the woman fell asleep.

Example (187) shows the same suffix -ra marking the transitive direct object.

(187) wibari-da-pʰeda tai kʰɨda-ra   hũma trua wa-sʰi-da-a
      land-PL-after   1p baggage-ABS all land carry-PAST-PL-DECL
      After we landed the boat, we took all of our baggage onto shore.

The absolutive focus suffix (ABS^FOC) is used the first time an object or participant is mentioned in a text or recalled from the background (see also §10.6, 10.8). In (188) and (189) are intransitive and transitive uses, respectively.

(188) nũrẽma   ewari-de aba hũã-sʰi-da-a   čapa   Roberto-ta
      next^day   day-in   one wait-PAST-PL-DECL   brother Roberto-ABS^FOC
      All day the next day we waited for brother Roberto.

---

[21]For a fuller discussion of the discourse function of the absolutive suffixes, see §§10.6–10.8.

(189) wã-pʉ-ta-ta   mãũ-ne tai-pa yerrehe-ta   ũnũ-sʰi-da-a
      go-PRES-PL-SUBD this-in 1p-ABL chimpanzee-ABS^FOC see-PAST-PL-DECL

   ũmẽ
   two

Going along we then saw chimpanzees, two of them.

The focus on given information suffix -tʉ can also be substituted. See §10.8.

5.3 Indirect object. The indirect object in bitransitive clauses is indicated by the suffix -a (-á in EK) at the end of the respective phrase. This is quite different from ES, which uses one suffix -ma to mark the indirect object and others for several other types of "inherent goal" (see §5.7 and Harms 1994:67 for a discussion of -má).

(190) mãũ-ne wárra   sʲakʰe-a nẽ pʰōno-ta   bʉa
      this-in offspring small-IO GEN blossom-ABS^FOC break

   tia-sʰi-a
   give-PAST-DECL

Then he picked a flower and gave it to the little boy.

The notion of indirect object also includes the addressee in a conversation.

(191) mãẽpʉrʉ   wẽrã-a   a-sʰi-a   kʰima
      [new^dev]   woman-IO say-PAST-DECL   spouse

Then he said to the woman, "Wife,..."

5.4 Benefactive. While in ES the suffix -itʰee marks both future tense and benefactive, the cognate NEP enclitic itʰea or itʰá (suffix -itʰa in EK) is only one of two ways to indicate benefactive. The subordinating conjunction kʰãrẽã/kʰarea (also kʰãrī in EK) also marks recipients of a benefactive action.

(192) sʲa b-ʉ   libro pʉ itʰea b-ʉ-a
      here be-PRES book 2S BEN be-PRES-DECL

This book is for you.

(193) s'a   b-ʉ   libro pʉ kʰãrẽã b-ʉ-a
      here be-PRES book 2S REASON be-PRES-DECL
      This book is for you.

In (192) *pʉ itʰea* can be contracted to *pʉ-tʰá* 'for you'.

5.5 Possession. The locative postposition *-de* 'in, at, on, while, within the limits of' (see §5.7 and §9.1) may be attached to a pronoun (§4.14) or noun (phrase) to denote possession.

(194) ãči-*de*-ra hũma kʰotʰa-pa-či-da-a
      3p-in-ABS   all   gobble-HAB-PAST-PL-DECL
      They gobbled up all their own, just as they had before.

5.6 Accompaniment. Accompaniment is most often indicated by the enclitic *ũmẽ* 'two'.

(195) mãũ-ne čipari-ta   wã-sʰi-a   to   sʰu-de   či   kʰima
      this-in owner-ABS^FOC go-PAST-DECL river spear-in REF spouse

      ũmẽ
      two
      Then the owner [of a certain tree] went spear-fishing with his wife.

Another form used for accompaniment is *pawara*. This is now used only by older speakers of NEP. In EK this indicates a family group as in 'these people lived together'.

(196) pʰoaka aba tači **pawara** b-a-sʰi-a
      year   one 1p   ACCOM   be-IMPF-PAST-DECL
      He lived with us for one year.

Another accompaniment construction unique to EK is *kʰaidu wãsʰia* 'went along'; in NEP the same sentence means 'followed'.

Verbs preceding accompaniment phrases may occur with a singular subject or with a plural subject which includes the participant in the accompaniment phrase. Harms (1994:121) says this inconsistency has to do with (lack of) coordination of the participants. In (197) the NE verb morphology is plural yet the implied subject seems to be singular, as 'he' goes with his wife.

(197) nūrēma   nẽ   kʰo-da-pʰeda wã-sʰi-da-a   pʰata   tʰu-de či
next^day GEN eat-PL-after go-PAST-PL-DECL plantain cut-in REF

     kʰima   ūme   hãpa   waibʉa-de
     spouse two   canoe   big-in
The next day after eating, he and his wife went in a big canoe to cut plantain.

5.7 Location. Stationary location is indicated by a number of adverbs, deictics (§2.8), and postpositions. Two of the more common locative postpositions are *-de* and *-ma*.

The difference between *-de* and *-ma* is that *-ma* defines more precise points while *-de* marks more loosely defined points; it allows the sense of 'within'. *-de* usually indicates a stationary or temporal location and can be suffixed to nouns and subordinated verbs.[22] It only indicates the goal of movement if the verb *hũẽ* 'arrive' is used, as in (200).

(198) wã-pʉrʉ-ta   mãũ-ne hūkʰara-pa hĩrũ pʰepʰena-de hũẽ
go-PRES-SUBD this-in vine-ABL foot fan-in   hook

     toko-sʰi-a
     go-PAST-DECL
Going along, he then tripped when the top of his foot caught on a vine.

(199) tai-ra   pʰan-a-shi-da-a   ewari ūpea   Vigía-de
1p-ABS be^few-IMPF-PAST-PL-DECL day   three Vigía-in
We were in Vigía for three days.

(200) kʰewara   hũẽ-sʰi-da-a   Loma-de kʰãpʰūrĩã pʰuru
afternoon arrive-PAST-PL-DECL Loma-in Latin   village
In the afternoon we arrived at Loma, a Latin village.

Stationary location can also be marked with *-ma* if the location is expressed with a demonstrative adverb (§2.8), in a relative clause, a noun (phrase), or a pronoun. The location need not be literal, as seen in (203).

---

[22]For the use of *-de* with motion verb auxiliaries, see §6.9. The use of *-de* with overlapping event clauses is discussed in §9.1. The use of *-de* with immediate purpose clauses is presented in §9.4.

Case 53

(201) *pɨ paito to-pa-ri-**ma*** *kʰore waibɨa-ta b-ɨ-a*
2s water drink-HAB-SG-LOC crocodile big-ABS^FOC be-PRES-DECL
Where you always drink water there is a big crocodile.

(202) *udu hĩtrɨ toko-de mãɨ̃-ne ẽpẽrã-pa hĩrũ-**ma***
down jump go-in this-in person-ABL leg-LOC

    tʰu-pue-sʰi-a
    chop-VOL-PAST-DECL
Jumping out of the way, the man chopped her on the leg.

(203) *tai wárra-**ma** kʰrĩčʰa ẽ-kʰa*
1p offspring-LOC think NEG-POLAR
Don't you think about our son?

The locative suffix *-ma* is also used commonly for the goal of movement (§5.8). Less specific location is indicated by *-are*.

(204) *tʰu-da-pʰeda nekʰo sʲakʰe-pa či kʰĩpu-**are** tʰoa-kʰua-pa-ta-a*
chop-PL-after knife small-ABL REF nose-area split-REPT-HAB-PL-DECL
After we chop it, we split the ends with a small knife.

5.8 Goal. The notion of goal is commonly marked with *-da*. In EK the corresponding suffix is *-eda*.[23]

(205) *martes ewari-de sʲe-sʰi-da-a Peñitʰa-**da***
Tuesday day-in come-PAST-PL-DECL Peñita-GOAL
On Tuesday we came to Peñita.

(206) *ete wã-pɨrɨ-ta ete wã-pɨrɨ-ta ĩpɨ-**da** pʰoa*
take go-PRES-SUBD take go-PRES-SUBD sand-GOAL dry

    nũ-m-e-sʰi-a
    stand-be-PERF-PAST-DECL
Being taken a long ways [through the water], he made it onto dry sand.

---

[23]While the EK and NEP forms look related, it is possible that NEP *-da* is actually a contraction of *-de* plus *-a* 'indirect object'. This is possible since some NEP material written in Panama represents *-da* as *-daa* and because Colombian speakers from the southern edge of the language area pronounce *-da* as *-de-a*. If this analysis of *-da* is accepted it could imply that *-a* is actually a goal marker, as in the SE languages. However, this cannot be widely substantiated. For discussion of the nasal postposition *-ẽnã* 'into', see §5.11.

Goal is also indicated by postpositions. The postposition in (207) can also be used as an adverb (§2.8 and §2.10).

(207) to-**eda**   wã-s^{h}i-a
river-into   go-PAST-DECL
He went down to the river.

The suffix -*ma* can also be put on goals of movement with respect to the restrictions in §5.7. This suffix also appears lengthened as -*maa* and -*mae*. It appears that -*mae* coincides with *hũẽ* 'arrive', which is also the only motion verb to use the stationary locative -*de*. One 25-year-old speaker of NEP said the forms of -*ma* were interchangeable.

(208) mãẽpɨrɨ   či   p^{h}ãka   tai-**ma**   s'e-s^{h}i-a
[new^dev] REF speedboat 1p-LOC   come-PAST-DECL
Then the speedboat came to us.

(209) ara   mãũ-ta   tai-ra   s'e-s^{h}i-da-a   či   carro
same   this-SUBD 1p-ABS   come-PAST-PL-DECL REF car

nũ-m-ɨ-**ma**
stand-be-PRES-LOC
Right then we came to where the car was parked.

(210) wã-pɨ-ta-ta   hũẽ-s^{h}i-da-a   k^{h}ãp^{h}ũrĩã   hãpa
go-PRES-PL-SUBD   arrive-PAST-PL-DECL Latino   canoe

ũ-m-ɨ-**mae**
float-be-PRES-LOC
We went along and arrived at the place where the Latino's canoe was floating.

In (211) both -*ma* and -*mae* occur in the same context. Notice the juxtaposition of the latter form with *hũẽ* 'arrive'.

(211) ete-tua   či   eya ɨra   hira-b-ɨ-**ma**   či   eya ɨra
take-IMPV REF hill cave^in   hang-be-PRES-LOC REF hill cave^in

    *hira-b-ʉ-**mae**   hũẽ-pʰeda*
    hang-be-PRES-LOC   arrive-after
    Take him to where the cave-in has left an overhang in the mountain! After you arrive at the place where the cave-in has left an overhang…

5.9 Movement down. The notion of movement down can be expressed by postpositions. The two postpositions used for 'down' are *-eda* and *-idu*. The former, in (212), is general and can be used to mean both 'into' and 'inside' as well as 'down'. The latter, in (213), when used for downward motion, always implies entrance into a place, such as a river.

(212) *to-**eda**   bae-sʰi-a*
    river-into descend-PAST-DECL
    went down to the river

(213) *to-**idu**   bae-sʰi-a*
    river-down descend-PAST-DECL
    fell into the river

Related to the postpositional suffix *-idu* is the adverb *udu* 'down', which has no other meaning except motion to the ground. Its counterpart is *uda*, which indicates motion toward the ground but not necessarily reaching it, as in (214).

(214) *mãũpe tai-ra **uda** sʲe-pʉ-ta-de   mũ abari-kʰa udu*
    then   1p-ABS down come-PRES-PL-in 1s same-SIM down

    wã-sʰi-a
    go-PAST-DECL
    Then as we were climbing down the tree, my twin brother fell to the ground.

5.10 Movement from. The notion of movement from a place is usually expressed by combining two already familiar suffixes. The first is *-de* and the second is the ablative suffix *-pa,* showing in this case the idea of origin (see also §5.1 and 5.11). As in §5.7, *-de* indicates general locations.

(215) *ara   mãũ-ta   tai-ra eya-**de-pa** eda sʲe-sʰi-da-a*
    same this-SUBD 1p-ABS hill-in-ABL into come-PAST-PL-DECL
    Then we came down from the mountain.

(216) čʰirua-**de-pa** uča akʰʉ-pʉ-ta-de tida nẽ ẽ pa-sʰi-a
brush-in-ABL come^out look-PRES-PL-in home GEN NEG EQ-PAST-DECL
As we came out of the brush looking, there was no one home.

When movement is from a specific location indicated by -ma (§5.7) rather than -de, -ma is lengthened to -*maʉ* and followed by -pa.

(217) nūrẽma tai-ra sʲe-sʰi-da-a Lomita-*maʉ-pa* ya^barrea
next^day 1p-ABS come-PAST-PL-DECL Lomita-LOC-ABL down^river
The next day we came down river from Lomita.

5.11 Origin. While the suffixes -de-pa and *ma-ʉ-pa* (§5.10) indicate movement from a location, -pema indicates the native origin of the referent. It can also make general reference to the word to which it is suffixed, as in the title of a story. -pema can be attached to nouns and nominalized verbs, as well as to adverbs. It often occurs in EK following -*ʉrʉ̃* 'about, upon' and rarely appears in NEP apart from the locative suffix -de (§5.8), which precedes it.

(218) wãrãta kʰuriwa-pa pea-sʰi-a tači-rã-**ne-pema**-ra
truly guatín-ABL kill-PAST-DECL 1p-PL-LOC-ORIG-ABS
Truly the guatín has killed one from among us.

(219) Roberto-ra Čikʰue-**de-pema** b-ʉ-a
Roberto-ABS Chicué-in-ORIG be-PRES-DECL
Roberto is from the Chicué River.

(220) beta či ẽkʰarra-**de-pema** ʉrʉ ʉrʉa-pa huwa-ra
fish REF back-in-ORIG spine spine-ABL hand-ABS

kʰõãrẽ-sʰi-a
scratch-PAST-DECL
The spines on the fish's back scratched his hand

In NEP, the one word -pema is not preceded by -de but by -ẽnã, the nasal form of the postposition -eda (§5.9). sʲrõã-ẽnã-pema is a frozen form which is used in the first and last sentences in most stories, whether ancient or recent.

(221) ara mãma-pe tači **sʲrõã-ẽnã-pema** nẽpʉrʉ
same here-LIM 1p old-into-ORIG story
The story from our old times ends right here.

Case 57

5.12 Similarity. All manners of expressing similarity use a combination of the words *abari* 'same' (§4.5), *kʰīrã* 'face', and the suffix *-kʰa*: *kʰīrã* 'face' + *-kʰa* = 'like'; *abari* 'same' + *-kʰa* = 'exactly the same'; *abari kʰīrã sʲa pʰanʉa* 'same face appearing' = 'looking exactly the same'.

(222) *mẽrã ūnū ẽ   pa-sʰi-a   yerrehe-ta   tʰũ   pea*
        nice see NEG EQ-PAST-DECL chimpanzee-ABS^FOC lice kill

        čʰū-m-ʉ-ta   ẽpẽrã   kʰīrã-kʰa
        sit-be-PRES-ABS^FOC person face-SIM
        I didn't like seeing a chimpanzee sitting there killing lice like a human does.

(223) *mãũpe tai-ra uda   sʲe-pʉ-ta-de   mũ   **abari-kʰa** udu*
        then   1P-ABS down come-PRES-PL-in 1S same-SIM down

        wã-sʰi-a
        go-PAST-DECL
        Then as we were climbing down the tree, my twin brother fell to the ground.

5.13 Comparison. The comparative relationship in NE is expressed by marking the object of comparison with the enclitic *kʰãyãpara* and the quality or quantity in question with the suffix *-ra*. The subject exhibits normal case marking.

(224) *kʰare-ta   kʰekʰerre **kʰãyãpara** waibʉa-ra b-ʉ-a*
        parrot-ABS^FOC parakeet than   large-COMP be-PRES-DECL
        The parrot is bigger than the parakeet.

6
Verb

In this chapter the various constituents of the verb phrase are presented except for adverbs, which are discussed in §§2.7–2.9. The verb phrase has the following order:

± adverb(s) ± incorporated object + verb stem ± auxiliary + tense ± mood

The positions of the negatives are discussed in §§7.12–7.17.

6.1 Simple verb heads. Verb phrases may consist of a single verb root (a simple stem) with minimal suffixation.

(225) wã-s^hi-da-a
 go-PAST-PL-DECL
 They left/went.

(226) mũ-a k^hrĩč^ha-s^hi-a mĩpu-ta
 1S-ABL think-PAST-DECL fish^sp.-ABS^FOC
 I thought it was a *mĩbu* fish.

6.2 Serial verbs in the verb phrase. Some verbs may be strung together to form a serial verb stem. Each of the verb roots in (227) and (228) can also appear as an independent verb. A plus sign (+) is put between the two parts of the serial verb for clarification. Their meaning is italicized in the free translation.

(227) mũ-ra animarã-puru hãwã   ete+wã-puru-kʰa
     1s-ABS demon-FOC^GI like^that take+go-PRES-POLAR
     Am I being *taken away* by a demon?

(228) Pilaku-pa pʰõwã-pa batʰa+pea-sʰi-a
     Pilaku-ABL rifle-ABL shoot+kill-PAST-DECL
     Pilaku *shot and killed* it with his rifle.

6.3 Object-incorporated verbs. Some transitive verbs may incorporate their object, giving the object nonspecific reference. In these cases the object occurs before the verb as it normally would but it carries no absolutive case marking. The subject is marked as the absolutive because the clause has become intransitive.

(229) mãũ-ne čipari-ta   wã-sʰi-a   to   sʰu-de   či   kʰima
     this-in owner-ABS^FOC go-PAST-DECL river spear-in REF spouse

     ũmẽ
     two
     Then the owner went *spear-fishing* with his wife.

(230) Silisio-ra hĩka wã-pʰeda **beta wa** nũ-m-e-sʰi-a
     Silisio-ABS not^far go-after *fish carry* stand-be-PERF-PAST-DECL
     After Silisio went a little ways off he started *to fish*.

In (231) the subject has absolutive case marking. Therefore, the word *pʰata* 'plantain' refers to food or a meal and is considered incorporated. If the subject had normal ergative case marking, the meaning of the sentence would specifically reflect the object.

(231) ara   mãũ-ta   Anancio-ra pʰata   o-sʰi-a
     same this-SUBD Anancio-ABS plantain make-PAST-DECL
     Right then Anancio made dinner.

     *Right then Anancio prepared plantain.

Another way that NE incorporates objects without mentioning them is by the use of the generalizing proclitic *nẽ* (§2.16). In (232) the subject is in the absolutive case, showing that the object has been incorporated.

(232) tai-∅ nẽ kʰo pan-ʉ-ne   tai-ra be-si-a   carro-pa
      1p-ABS GEN eat be^few-PRES-in 1p-ABS stay-PAST-DECL bus-ABL
      While we were eating [lunch], the bus left us behind.

Another proclitic, mīã, also incorporates objects by giving the respective verb a more specific meaning; this makes mention of the object superfluous.

(233) ara   mãũ kʰewara   mīã huru-de wã-sʰi-da-a   mũ čapa
      same this afternoon GEN seek-in go-PAST-PL-DECL 1S brother

      ūmẽ
      two
      That same afternoon my brother and I went to seduce [a certain young woman].

When the referential proclitic či (§4.6) precedes a verb, the action concerned is reciprocal.

(234) ewari aba pokʰorro-ta   beki ūmẽ či ūnū-sʰi-da-a
      day one toad-ABS^FOC deer two REF see-PAST-PL-DECL
      One day a toad and a deer saw each other.

6.4–6.10 Derivational verb suffixes

The suffixes between the verb stem and the aspect and tense markers are derivational. The use of these suffixes gives the speaker flexibility in adding color to his speaking, putting focus on certain items or removing it from others, or giving additional description to the action of the verb itself.

Derivational suffixes differ from serial verb stems in that each member of a serial stem can occur by itself whereas the derivational suffixes do not. Harms (1994:87–88) does not strictly distinguish the two types of element. He asserts that in ES they are inextricably related in that the derivational suffixes developed from verb roots. Harms does distinguish between the two types, however: if the verb root changes phonological form in the derivational affix position it is a derivational suffix. If the verb root maintains its form it is part of a serial verb.

The point on which Harms bases phonological change is loss of vowel length. The ES verb kʰaa 'bite' becomes -kʰa, a derivational verb suffix meaning 'do something with one's teeth'. Obviously, these two forms are related. In NE, however, the vowel length distinction quite evident in ES and other SE languages has been lost or displaced. Therefore, loss of vowel length cannot be a test for morphological identity. Instead, I use fidelity to the basic meaning of the verb as a test, along with the first point, that serial verb morphemes must be able to appear on their own.

A sample of the richness of NE verb derivation is given in (235), using the simple verb stem *poka* 'grind'. The suffix *-ya* is the future tense marker and is used as the citation form.

(235) *pokaya* 'grind something in a cup'
 poka bariya 'bleed, menstruate'
 pokačhiraya 'scrub, roll back and forth between hands'
 pokakhuaya 'grind repeatedly, grind up several objects'
 pokapeya 'remove by hitting (e.g., corn from cob, dust from pants)'
 pokapiya 'have something ground, make to grind'
 pokapueya 'grind up one object'
 pokatrᵾya 'bubble up from the ground (water), move in ocean waves'
 pokathᵾya 'push down into something, make a ball of something'
 pokawiya 'grind to powder'
 pokas'oaya 'fall and break to pieces'

I now discuss the most productive derivational verb suffixes.

6.4 Causative. The suffix *-pi* indicates causative or obligative. In NE, this morpheme is uncommon compared to the SE languages (Harms 1994:89). In SE the causee is marked as an indirect object if the verb root is transitive.

(236) *hãũ čapa-ra   wã-pi-shi-da-a*
 that brother-ABS go-CAUS-PAST-PL-DECL
 They made that guy leave. *or* They obligated that guy to leave.

(237) *mũ-a silla thōtrᵾ-pᵾrᵾ-pa udu bae-pi-shi-a*
 1S-ABL chair bump-PRES-ABL down fall-CAUS-PAST-DECL
 By bumping into the chair I made it fall down.

(238) *Atilio-ra wã-shi-a beta wa-de či wárra-rã kho-pi-i*
 Atilio-ABS go-PAST-DECL fish carry-in REF offspring-PL eat-CAUS-IRR

kʰãrẽã
REASON
Atilio went fishing in order to feed his children.

If there is more than one causee, the causative morpheme is *-pika*.

(239) *usʰa waibᵻa-pa wárra   s'akʰe-rã hĩã-**pika**-sʰi-a*
  dog big-ABL   offspring small-PL cry-CAUS^PL-PAST-DECL
  The big dog made the little children cry.

6.5 Instrument. As in ES (Harms 1994:90), the use of the derivational verb suffix *-pʰe* indicates an instrument is being used to perform an action but does not specify the instrument. In NE this suffix is often followed by another derivational morpheme *-tʰa* (§6.7). In ET and Embera-Chamí (ECh) the two are always together (Pickens pers. comm.).

This derivational suffix does not seem to have any relation to the independent verb stems *pʰe* 'collect' and *pʰetʰa* 'blow away'. There are verbs (*tʰiapʰetʰaya* 'cut underbrush, weeds') that have the derivational suffix but no attested simple form. In the list in (240) the simple verbs are followed by their forms with *-pʰe/-pʰetʰa*. The meaning of the derived form is 'do X with an instrument' unless otherwise indicated in the column on the right. If there is no listing in the left column, there is no attested simple form of the verb.

(240) *berraya* 'smash, destroy'   *berrapʰetʰaya*
  ẽrãya 'free, loosen, untie'   *ẽrãpʰetʰaya*   'free an animal from a pen'
  mẽrãya 'hide something'   *mẽrãpʰetʰaya*   'pound in so peg is hidden'
  nĩãkaya 'kiss'   *nĩãpʰetʰaya*   'caress'
  okaya 'come unglued'   *okapʰetʰaya*   'strip off bark'
    poropʰetʰaya   'mistreat, throw to ground'
    tʰiapʰetʰaya   'cut underbrush, weeds'
  tʰoaya 'split'   *tʰoapʰetʰaya*

6.6 Volition. The volitional suffix apparent in ES (Harms 1994:90) is cognate with NE *-pue*, which when suffixed to verb roots often adds the meaning of 'send'. Since sending is inherently volitional, it stands to reason that *-pue* can be used to add the volitional element.

(241)

		pueya[24]	'send, let go'
auya	'find, discover'	aupueya	'set free, place, put, toss, leave in order to pick up later'
bariya	'grab, snatch (v.t.); arrive (v.i.)'	baripueya	'toss, beat against (waves against a boat)'
itu	'back' as in 'he put it back'	itu pueya	'give permission'
nẽtoya	'buy'	nẽtopueya	'sell'
pʰeaya	'spill, splatter'	pʰeapueya	'throw to a dog'
tiaya	'give'	tiapueya	'send something'

A pragmatic use of -*pue* is to highlight singular direct objects. For example, *kʰoshia* means 'ate it', whereas *kʰopueshia* means 'ate it whole' or 'ate it all up'. The use of -*pue* in (243) may put focus on the one direct object, perhaps to take it off the speaker.

(242) Anancio-pa   kʰo-i   b-a-da   pʰata-ra   ǎči-a   hũma
     Anancio-ABL eat-IRR   be-IMPF-PPRT   plantain-ABS 3S-ABL all

   kʰo-**pue**-sʰi-da-a
   eat-VOL-PAST-PL-DECL
   They ate all of what Anancio was going to eat.

(243) tiamasʰi mĩčʰi-pa mũ ũmẽ sʲe-da   wárra-ra pia
     night   cat-ABL   1S two come-PPRT   boy-ABS   good

   pʰera-**pue**-sʰi-a
   scare-VOL-PAST-DECL
   [That] night a cat really scared the boy who had come along with me [but it didn't scare me].

6.7 Affected object. Harms (1994) mentions *-tʰaa* as an ES morpheme which most commonly indicates action away from the speaker or participant. It also can indicate a specific singular object and a specific understood object which is not overtly stated (1994:91).

In NE the cognate derivational suffix *-tʰa* communicates that the action is punctiliar or summary and that the object is totally affected.[25] Both of these notions increase the transitivity of the verb (Hopper and Thompson

---

[24]The verb *pueya* 'send' discussed here is not often used independently and is unrelated to *puéya* 'pile up, load'.

1980:252). The effect is best illustrated with *pea* 'kill'. *peasʰia* means 'killed' but *peatʰasia* indicates that the action on the object was summary ('struck or shot and killed'). The difference is illustrated also in *beroya* 'put into' (e.g., put a shoestring into a small hole in shoe) versus *berotʰaya* 'put into' (put some object into a pocket, basket, box, mouth, etc.). Carrying out the action of *beroya* requires careful attention over a period of time. On the other hand, the action of *berotʰaya* involves a single, punctiliar insertion. *beroya* is a contraction of the more common *berahuya*.

A list of simple verbs and their meanings with *-tʰa* is given in (244).

(244)

		tʰaya	[no meaning]
ānāya	'cover, fill in'	ānātʰaya	'cover up, fill in hole, erase'
batʰaya	'shoot, throw'	batʰatʰaya	'throw away'
beoya	'break'	beotʰaya	'break by bending in two'
beroya	'put in a small hole'	berotʰaya	'put in a pocket, basket, box, can'
čʰāya	'push steadily'	čʰātʰaya	'shove'
ẽũya	'pull up'	ẽũtʰaya	'extract a tooth, remove from skin or eye'
haya	'cut off' (one meaning)	hatʰaya	'castrate'
hīzoaya	'splash, carom'	hīzoatʰaya	'pick off flower petals'
hʉreya	'scare away, throw out'	hʉretʰaya	'expel, throw out'
kʰoya	'eat'	kʰotʰaya	'gobble up'
kʰōrāya	'break (off)'	kʰōrātʰaya	'twist off, break by twisting'
okaya	'come unglued, open eyes'	okatʰaya	'come unglued'
okoroya	'swell up'	okorotʰaya	'punch'
piraya	'fill'	pirutʰaya	'fill up but not overflow'

---

[25]Stephen Levinsohn (personal communication) points out that even in those derived *-tʰa* verbs for which the meaning is intransitive, the absolutive is still totally affected as in *okatʰaya* 'become unglued all at once or completely unglued'.

pʉraya	'roll'	pʉratʰaya	'wrap, roll'
		pʉratʰatʰaya	'turn a screw'
sʰusʰuaya	'rest, then sleep'	sʰusʰuatʰaya	'sleep on one's back with one's knees up'
sʰuya	'point, poke, lance'	sʰutʰaya	'lance'
trʉya	'shoot an arrow'	trʉtʰaya	'hit (with an arrow)'
tʰoaya	'cut lengthwise'	tʰoatʰaya	'split, cut in two'
tʰuya	'chop'	tʰutʰaya	'cut in two, vertically'
tʰʉkaya	'step'	tʰʉkatʰaya	'kick'
ʉre hiraya	'swing'	ʉre hiratʰaya	'get a sudden chill'
ʉraya	'slide, touch'	ʉratʰaya	'touch lightly, massage'
wẽãya	'take off clothes'	wẽãtʰaya	'throw off, down'

The EK prefix *ma-* indicates that the object is completely affected. Rex (1975:27, 29) calls this the superlative number occurring in totality position. It probably comes from the word *hōma* 'all' (Schöttelndreyer, personal communication).

(245) **ma**-kʰo-sʰi-a   (EK)
all-eat-PAST-DECL
He ate all of it.

The derivational suffix *-sʼoa* always adds a 'to pieces' shade to the main verb. All of the attested verbs which have *-sʼoa* are intransitive and do not necessarily come from verbs.

(246)			
		bʉkʉsʼoaya	'become rotten or withered and at the point of breaking'
čʰĩya	'wither'	čʰĩsʼoaya	'become infected (where a thorn entered the skin)'

		ēhĩs'oaya	'run away together (animals)'
		ẽs'oaya	'winnow'
hãrãtruya	'separate from'	hãrãs'oaya	'disperse (v.i.)'
hedea	'wide, spacious'	hedes'oaya	'extend branches'
hĩ bariya	'have a runny nose'	hĩs'oaya	'sprinkle, splash, or fly off like pieces of rock when they hit another rock'
hurruya	'fall out (loose tooth)'	hurrus'oaya	'fall, disintegrate'
kʰōrōya	'break (v.i.)'	kʰōrōkos'oaya	'fall and break to pieces'
pokaya	'grind'	pokas'oaya	'fall and break to pieces'
		pʰučʰis'oaya	'give off sparks [lit., pieces of fire]'
tʰodos'oa	'cave-in'	tʰodos'oaya	'break to pieces, cave in'

6.8 Repetitive action. What Harms (1994:92) describes as a suffix indicating intensity is the morpheme -*kʰua*, which in NE and ECh indicates repetitive action associated with the absolutive case. Whereas *wesʰia* means that the subject vomited, *wekʰuasʰia* means that s/he vomited over and over.

(247) mũ-ra we-**kʰua**-sʰi-a   čikʰo kʰo-da hũma we-sʰi-a
       1S-ABS vomit-REPT-PAST-DECL food eat-PPRT all   vomit-PAST-DECL
       I threw up over and over the food I had eaten. I threw up all of it.

The repetitive action is also applied to absolutives in transitive object roles.[26] In these cases, -*kʰua* indicates repeated action in the sense that similar actions are done to a number of direct objects. While *kʰosʰia* means 'ate it', *kʰokʰuasʰia* communicates that the subject ate many pieces of the object.

(248) oro-sʰi-a   nẽ^hõ pʰureka nũ-m-ʉ-ra
       knock^down-PAST-DECL fruit   ripe   stand-be-PRES-ABS

---

[26]Comrie (1978:337ff) points out that ergative-absolutive systems refer not only to case marking but also to verb agreement and syntax.

*oro-**k^h^ua*** *nũ-m-e-s^h^i-a*
knock^down-REPT stand-be-PERF-PAST-DECL
He knocked down the fruit that was ripe. He started knocking down a lot [of the fruit]. *or* He started knocking it down and did so for quite some time.

6.9 Verbs that indicate movement and direction. While ES indicates movement and direction in the verb by means of suffixes (Harms 1994:93ff.), NE employs the common verbs *s'e* 'come' and *wã* 'go'. These verbs indicate motion to or from a point of reference, which is often the speaker's house or village or the place at which the speaker is located at the time of the utterance. *s'e* 'come' always refers to motion toward the point of reference. This is in contrast with *wã* 'go'. In (249) a woman is being taken away from her home by a demon appearing as her husband, who has been away hunting. The demon gets her to leave her house in order to help him carry home a large animal.

(249) *mʉ̃-a pʉ eta-de **s'e**-s^h^i-a ara mãʉ̃-ta wẽrã ete*
1S-ABL 2S get-in come-PAST-DECL same this-SUBD woman take

wã-s^h^i-a
go-PAST-DECL
"I came [home] to get you." So he took the woman along (away from home).

In (249) it is important to note that the subject *mʉ̃-a* '1S-ABL' has case agreement with the transitive verb *eta* 'get' in the purpose clause, not with the intransitive verb in the main clause. In this way, the motion verbs *wã* 'go' and *s'e* 'come' act as auxiliary verbs.

In (250) the morphology of the verb phrase *ũnũ-ne wã-s^h^i-a* allows for two meanings. The first possibility interprets the suffix *-ne* (nasal form of *-de*) as an immediate purpose marker (§9.4) and the verb *wãs^h^ia* 'went' as the main verb. The second possibility interprets *wãs^h^ia* 'went' as the auxiliary of *ũnũ* 'see', adding the sense of 'see while walking'. The presence of the absolutive focus (§5.2) marker *-ta* on the end of the noun phrase *eya ʉra hirabʉ* 'mountain that caved in left an overhang' renders the first possibility ungrammatical. *wãs^h^ia,* then, is the auxiliary of *ũnũ* 'see'.

(250) *wã-pʉrʉ-ta wã-pʉrʉ-ta eya ʉra hira-b-ʉ-**ta***
go-PRES-SUBD go-PRES-SUBD hill cave^in hang-be-PRES-ABS^FOC

ũnũ-ne wã-sʰi-a
see-in go-PAST-DECL

Going a long way, he saw while walking along that a cave-in had left an overhang in the mountain.

*Going a long way, a cave-in that had left an overhang in the mountain went to see it.

6.10 Other derivational morphemes. The derivational enclitic *bari* presents a special case. Although written as a word separate from the verb root, *bari* is not usually a typical serial verb (§6.2). Its function is derivational and its effect is not always clear. In some cases, however, it derives an intransitive or reflexive meaning or a sense of imminence from the root verb. It is not readily apparent that this effect is carried over from the meanings of the independent verb *bariya*.

(251)   bariya   'appear, arrive, become (v.i.); grasp (v.t.)'[27]

ãnãya	'cover, fill in'	ãnẽ bariya	'cover oneself up'
čʰãya	'push'	čʰã bariya	'push'
erreya	'pull'	erre bariya	'pull along, drag'
hidiya	'pull, tug'	hidi bariya	'for kids to fight over a toy'
hupʰiya	'hiccup'	hupʰi bariya	'have the hiccups'
hũrẽã	'curved, twisted'	hũrẽ bariya	'go around a curve'
norra		norra bariya	'become weak, melt'
okaya	'pull apart'	oka bariya	'open one's eyes, pay attention'
peuya	'die, be drunk'	peu bariya	'be at the point of death'
pʉraya	'roll'	pʉra bariya	'turn around or over'
pʰiraya	'run'	pʰira bariya	'stand up, get up'
pʰʉrrʉa	'in a circle'	pʰʉrre bariya	'turn away from'
tau	'eye'	tau bariya	'divine'
trʉ(tʰa)ya	'shoot an arrow, hit'	trʉtʰa bariya	'hit with an arrow shaft'

---

[27]*bariya* is different from *hũẽya* 'arrive' in that it does not imply a starting point.

tʰeoya	'dive in'	tʰeo bariya	'disappear inside'
tʰuya	'cut'	tʰu bariya	'bury a corpse'
ũya	'float'	ũ bariya	'float, swim'
wã	'go'	wã bariya	'fly'
wiya	'stir, paddle'	wi bariya	'stop on a river trip'

Whereas *bari*, *-tʰa*, *-pue*, *-s'oa*, and *-kʰua* all form new verbs, the derivational suffix *-tru* can create verbs or nouns.

(252)

		truya	'shoot an arrow (v.t.); flow (v.i.)'
barruya	'capsize'	barrutruya	'duck down'
bukaya	'make noise'	bukatruya	'make a noise'
eraya	'sharpen'	eratruya	'stare' (three other meanings also)
erreya	'drag or pull'	erretruya	'coil up like a snake'
hãrãhãrã	'sediment'	hãrãtruya	'separate from'
hipʰiya	'hiccup'	hipʰitru	'hiccup(s)'
hiraweya	'be tossed by waves'	hiratru	'a current'
hũãya	'make someone wait'	hũãtruya	'make someone wait; guard, shield'
hũẽya	'catch on something'	hũẽtruya	'link, make a chain'
ira	'sipping, sucking'	iratruya	'bubble or foam up, get angry'
kʰũrã	'cool (breeze)'	kʰũrãtru	'shade'
okaya	'become unglued'	okatruya	'open one's mind, pay attention'
oraya	'blister'	oratruya	'blister'
pokaya	'grind'	pokatruya	'bubble up, move in waves'
puraya	'roll, wrap'	puratruya	'wrap around, wrap up'
pʰiraya	'run'	pʰiratruya	'stand up, be resurrected'

sʰo 'heart' bae 'falling'		sʰobaetrᵾya	'feel fear or sadness in one's heart'
tʰōya	'accidentally hit'	tʰōtrᵾya	'bump into something'
ᵾraya	'slide (land)'	ᵾratrᵾya	'slide away from, crawl'
ūnaya	'shine, clear up'	ūnatrᵾya	'dawn, wake up'

The nominalizer -mia forms nouns from verbs and verb phrases.

(253)	kᵾwaya	'have a fever'	kᵾwamia	'a fever'
	ᵾreya	'to shake'	te ᵾremia	'earthquake (lit., a house-shaking)'

The independent verb bᵾya 'put, place, write' can be prefixed with the positional roots (§2.13) to form transitive verbs meaning placement in a certain position. The verb bᵾya is distinguished from the present singular stative b-ᵾ by its ability to take the future and past tense suffixes -ya and -sʰi, respectively. Therefore, the vowel in the compound forms in the third column of (254) is from bᵾya, not the auxiliary.[28]

(254)			bᵾya	'put, place, write'
	čʰū-	'sitting'	čʰūmᵾya	'put a child on a seat'
	hira	'hanging, lifting, being high'	hirabᵾya	'place or hang in a high place'
	kʰo-	'positioning'	kʰobᵾya	'place something carefully'
	nū-	'standing'	nūmᵾya	'stand an object up'
	tʰa-	'lying down'	tʰabᵾya	'lay an object flat'

6.11–6.13 Tense

Past, present, and future tense forms are shown in (255):

---

[28]For further discussion of the positional auxiliaries, see §2.13 and §§6.15–6.20.

(255)   Past   Present   Future
        Standard   -s^hi -и (-ригн, -ри-ta)   -ya, -di[29]
        Habitual (following -pa)   -či   -ri, -ta   —
        Subordinate clause   -da   -и (-ригн, -ри-ta)   -i, -di

The two forms listed for present standard and habitual and for subordinate present and future are for singular and plural subjects, respectively.

Immediate past and future tenses in EK are expressed using -podo and -toko, respectively.[30]

(256) a. *wã-**podo**-a*
         go IMM^FUT-DECL
         He is about to leave.

      b. *wã-**toko**-a*
         go-IMM^PAST-DECL
         He just left.

Tense in subordinate clauses is relative, not actual. Subordinate clauses are often in the present tense even though they describe a past event or state. This is true of the SE languages as well. Harms (1994:97) says that the tense of the subordinate clause depends on its temporal relationship to the main clause. If the tense of the subordinate clause is present, the subordinate clause event occurred or the subordinate clause state existed in the same time frame as that of the main verb. In (257) the subordinate forms are in the present tense, so they indicate that the repeated 'going' is in the same tense as the main verb 'arrived'.

(257) *wã-pи-ta-ta*   *wã-pи-ta-ta*   *hũẽ-s^hi-da-a*   *iči te*
      go-PRES-PL-SUBD   go-PRES-PL-SUBD   arrive-PAST-PL-DECL   3S house

---

[29]NEP only; see §6.13.

[30]While NEP also has the immediate future -podo, the NEP cognate of EK -toko is tokoya, which can be used as an independent verb 'to go' or as an auxiliary which means 'do while going away'.
      ara mãũ-pa bиa   toko-s^hi-mana
      very this-ABL break go-PAST-HRSY
      The very same thing broke him as he was running away.
The counterpart of the auxiliary tokoya is tukeya 'to come' or 'do while coming toward'. See appendix B, sentence 118.

Verb

>   *to-eda*
>   river-into

Walking for a long time, they arrived at the river's edge below his house.

Similarly, if the tense of the subordinate clause is past, the subordinate clause event occurred or the subordinate clause state existed before that of the main verb. The relative past suffix *-na* (nasal form of *-da*; see §6.11) indicates that the arrival of the parents occurred before the soup was served.

(258) *čipari-rã   kʰewara   tida   hũẽ-na   kʰarea ara   mãũ-ta*
      parent-PL afternoon home arrive-PPRT DS   same this-SUBD

>   *kʰuriwa-pa nẽ   ba-ra   tʰue   tia-sʰi-a*
>   guatín-ABL GEN liquid-ABS scoop give-PAST-DECL

After the parents came home, the guatín served them the soup.

6.11 Past tense. The standard suffix *-sʰi* indicates past tense.

(259) *ara   mãũ-ta   kʰui-sʰi-da-a*
      same this-SUBD bathe-PAST-PL-DECL
      So they bathed.

Another morpheme, *-či*, indicates past tense in the habitual aspect, which can either refer to action habitually done in times gone by or to a single action which is similar to one done previously in a story.

(260) *kʰurruma kʰa-da-ta   āpura-ta*
      beads   weave-PPRT-ABS^FOC bead^belt-ABS^FOC

>   *hũ-pa-či-da-a*
>   wear-HAB-PAST-PL-DECL

We used to wear belts woven from beads.

(261) *mãũ-ne či   tʰusʰi-ra hei hei hei a   wãmãrĩ-pa-či-a*
      this-in REF guan-ABS hei hei hei say fly-HAB-PAST-DECL
      Then the guan flew away calling, "Hei, hei, hei," just as it did before.

Past tense forms in subordinate clauses are marked with *-da* and not *-sʰi*.

(262) tiamasʰi mĩčʰi-pa mũ ũmẽ s'e-**da** wárra-ra pia
night cat-ABL 1S two come-PPRT offspring-ABS good

    pʰera-pue-sʰi-a
    scare-VOL-PAST-DECL
[That] night a cat really scared the boy who had come along with me.

If the past tense subordinate clause describes an event that is no longer relevant, -pʰedada or -pʰenana can be used. However, this is rare in natural text material.

6.12 Present tense. Because present tense and aspect marking are so intertwined in NE, the discussion on present tense forms includes some discussion of aspect.

As in ES (Harms 1994:99), present tense is indicated by:
1. an aspectual stative auxiliary verb with the present tense suffix -ʉ (§2.12);
2. the use of -ri or -ta following the habitual -pa (see (255)); and
3. the use of -pʉrʉ or -pʉ-ta, provided the conditional is not in use and no other tense is marked.[31]

(263) kʰuriwa-pa pia b-**ʉ**-a a-sʰi-a
guatín-ABL good be-PRES-DECL say-PAST-DECL
'That's fine,' the guatín said.

(264) mãpe hũma bi-sʰi-ra ẽhũã-ne čʰũ-m-e-pʰeda
then all pull^apart-PAST-COND ground-in sit-be-PERF-after

    kʰa-pa-**ta**-a
    weave-HAB-PL-DECL
Then, once we have pulled it all apart, after we sit down we weave it.

(265) nẽ kʰo-pa-ta hora ara pa-**pʉrʉ**-a
GEN eat-HAB-PL hour same EQ-PRES-DECL
It's time to eat right now.

Negated verbs in the present tense have no tense suffix (see §§7.12–7.17).

---

[31]In active verbs, -pʉrʉ and -pʉta may be viewed as 'present progressives' (§6.19). There is also a conditional marker -pʉrʉ (§9.5).

Verb

6.13 Future tense. Unlike in ES, where the future tense is marked by -*it^{h}ee*, NE employs irrealis -*i* (possibility) or the future tense marker -*ya* (certainty).

(266) mũ-ã hãũ ãkos^{h}o-ra pea-**ya**-a
1S-ABL that vulture-ABS kill-FUT-DECL
I will kill that vulture.

(267) wã-**i**-ta mũ-ra
go-IRR-FOC 1S-ABS
I'd better get out of here.

The future plural is -*di*, or in a nasal verb, -*ni*. These are derived from the plural marker -*da* plus the irrealis -*i* or future -*ya*. In EK and older NEP data, the future plural marking is -*da-ya*. Although these are translated as actual futures they can also be rendered as hortatives, as in (269).

(268) nãũ hiwa-ta bari-**di**-a
this bend-ABS^FOC fish-FUT^PL-DECL
We will fish this bend of the river.

(269) čapa-rã wã-**ni**-a te-da
brother-PL go-FUT^PL-DECL house-GOAL
Brothers, we will go home. *or* Let's go home.

It can be argued that the future marker -*ya* is a resyllabified combination of irrealis -*i* and declarative -*a*. Following this argument, in EK the combination -*y-a* has become the future tense suffix -*ya* and the declarative -*a* is added to it, forming a phonetically long vowel which receives stress.

There is apparent contrast, however, between -*i* and -*ya* in (270). The contrast between *pea-ya* and *pea-i* is upheld by ECh data which demonstrate that the two futures contrast in identical environments.

(270) a. pea-**i**-ta b-ʉ-a
kill-IRR-FOC be-PRES-DECL
He is obligated to kill it.

  b. pea-**ya** b-ʉ-a
kill-FUT be-PRES-DECL
He is likely to kill it.

6.14 Number in verbs. The unmarked number in finite verbs which do not use auxiliaries is singular. The one case which does not fit this pattern is the present habitual construction, where the singular is *-pari*. Plural verb marking is with *-puta* in the present (progressive), *-pata* in the present habitual, and *-da* after the past tense suffix.[32] The future plural *-di* is suffixed directly to the verb stem.

(271) mãpe či kʰɨrɨ-ta ũpea-pe o-**pa-ta**-a
then REF loop-ABS^FOC three-LIM make-HAB-PL-DECL
Then we make loops, just three of them.

(272) sʲe-**pɨ-ta**-ta hũẽ-sʰi-**da**-a te to-eda
come-PRES-PL-SUBD arrive-PAST-PL-DECL house river-into
Coming along, we arrived at the river's edge below our house.

(273) nẽ kʰo-**di**-a
GEN eat-FUT^PL-DECL
(Pl.) will eat. *or* Let's eat!

The same markers of plural and, where relevant, singular are used in subordinate clauses (274) except that when the past participle suffix *-da/-na* occurs with *kʰarea* (§9.2) no plural marker is used in Colombian NEP. (275) reflects this.

(274) hũẽ-**na**-pʰeda te o-sʰi-da-a
arrive-PL-after house make-PAST-PL-DECL
After arriving they made a house.

(275) čipari-rã kʰewara tida hũẽ-**na** kʰarea ara mãũ-ta
parent-PL afternoon home arrive-PPRT DS same this-SUBD

---

[32]Just as there are various plural stative verbs (§2.12) for different sizes of groups, occasionally, there is additional plural marking in active verbs to indicate large groups. Rasmussen and Mesúa (1985:76) indicate that for *wã* 'go', the large group plural marking is *-pɨrɨ*.

māwã-**pɨrɨ**-de [imama tuan-a-rã]-ra hɨma-ēnã pʰira-kʰua
like^this-PRES-in [jaguar be^many-IMPF-PL]-ABS ALL-INTO RUN-REPT

wã-**pɨrɨ**-sʰi-da-a
go-PL^MANY-PAST-PL-DECL
When he said this, all of those who were big cats ran away.

Verb

    kʰuriwa-pa nẽ ba-ra   tʰue   tia-si-a
    guatín-ABL GEN liquid-ABS scoop give-PAST-DECL
    After the parents arrived home in the afternoon, the guatín served them the soup.

Number in relative present subordinate clauses is indicated the same way as in the present progressive. Whereas *-pʉrʉ* indicates singular, *-pʉta* indicates plural.

(276) kʰaidu wã-**pʉrʉ**-ta hũẽ-sʰi-a
      follow go-PRES-SUBD arrive-PAST-DECL
      Following along, he arrived.

(277) wã-**pʉ-ta**-ta   wã-pʉ-ta-ta   hũẽ-sʰi-da-a
      go-PRES-PL-SUBD go-PRES-PL-SUBD arrive-PAST-PL-DECL
      Going along for a long time, they arrived.

6.15–6.20 Aspect

Perfect and imperfective aspects are indicated by the use of the stative verb (§2.12) with the appropriate aspect suffix. Perfect aspect is marked with *-e* and the imperfective is shown by *-a*. The attachment of a certain positional root to the imperfective has a similar effect to progressive and durative aspect markers in other languages. Habitual aspect is indicated with verb suffixes. The perfective aspect is characterized by the absence of any aspectual marker.

6.15 Perfect aspect. The principal use of the perfect suffix *-e* is to portray an action as beginning (inceptive) and continuing.

(278) Anancio-pa pio akʰʉ nũ-m-e-sʰi-a
      Anancio-ABL very look stand-be-PERF-PAST-DECL
      Anancio started looking at it very carefully.

(279) tai-pa pedea pʰan-e-sʰi-da-a   kʰãrẽ-pa tʰʉpʉ
      1p-ABL talk be^few-PERF-PAST-PL-DECL what-ABL fire

      kʰoa-di-ta
      light-FUT^PL-ABS^FOC
      We began to talk about how we were going to light a fire.

Another common use of -e is for true perfects, which describe an event as having lasting effects or a change of state as lasting a long time.

(280) iči hāpa-ra   iči b-a-pa-ri-ma   trua urrahu b-e-s^hi-a
      3S canoe-ABS 3S be-IMPF-HAB-SG-LOC land drag   be-PERF-PAST-DECL
At the place where he lived, he dragged his canoe onto land for good [until it was finished].

(281) k^huriwa-ra harra-pa   vale^ẽã   b-e-s^hi-a
      guatín-ABS hunger-ABL worthless   be-PERF-PAST-DECL
The guatín became defenseless because of hunger.

A couple of the stative verb stems can be used in the perfect form without a main verb and in these cases have meanings appropriate to the perfect aspect. The simple stative b- plus the perfect suffix -e means 'stay'.[33]
In (283) the 'sitting' stem čhũm- plus -e means 'sit down'.

(282) k^huwa   nũ-m-a-era   b-e-s^hi-a   tida
      have^fever   stand-be-IMPF-because   be-PERF-PAST-DECL   home

      mũ-tuba b-e-s^hi-a
      1S-oneself
      be-PERF-PAST-DECL
Because I had a fever, I stayed home. I stayed by myself.

(283) baitia   čhũ-m-e-s^hi-a
      at^edge   sit-be-PERF-PAST-DECL
He sat down at the edge [of the platform house, ready to jump off].

6.16 Imperfective aspect. As in ES (Harms 1994:106), imperfective aspect is signaled in a number of ways. Any stative stem with the imperfective suffix -a or the present suffix -ʉ, as well as the present progressive and habitual suffixes, indicates the imperfective. In contrast with the combination of the 'sitting' stem čhũm- and the perfect -e, čhũm- plus the imperfective -a means 'was sitting'.

---

[33]The perfect aspect marker is appropriate here because, typically, some other action caused the absolutive to stay, e.g., others leaving or, as in the example, 'because I had a fever'. The sentence below is unusual in that the verb bes^hia 'stayed' is transitive; it agrees in number with 'bus', not 'we/us'.

   tai-Ø   nẽ   k^ho phan-ʉ-ne   tai-ra   be-s^hi-a   carro-pa
   1p-ABS GEN   eat be^few-PRES-in   1p-ABS   stay-PAST-DECL   BUS-ABL
While we were eating [lunch], the bus left us behind/we were left by the bus.

(284) idu   čʰū-m-**a**-sʰi-a
      inside sit-be-IMPF-PAST-DECL
      He was sitting inside [his hole].

(285) contains two means of indicating the imperfective in the same word, a stative with the suffix -a and the habitual suffix. This relative clause means 'the place where he lived', or literally, 'where he habitually was'.

(285) iči hãpa-ra   iči b-**a**-pa-ri-**ma**   trua urrahu b-e-sʰi-a
      3S canoe-ABS 3S be-IMPF-HAB-SG-LOC land drag   be-PERF-PAST-DECL
      At the place where he lived, he dragged his canoe onto land for good.

6.17 Completive. Harms (1994:107) says the completive -da has not been found in any Chocó language besides ES. However, both NEP and EK have this: the past participle suffix -da mentioned in §§6.13–6.14.[34] When suffixing nasal verbs it is realized as -na, as in (287) and (288).

(286) mũ ũmẽ wárra   sʲe-**da**-ra   (NEP)
      1S two offspring   come-PPRT-ABS
      the boy who had come with me

(287) mãũ wã-**na** b-a-sʰi-a   waa sʲe ẽ   pa-sʰi-a   (NEP)
      this go-PPRT be-IMPF-PAST-DECL   more come NEG EQ-PAST-DECL
      He was gone. He didn't come back.

(288) iči-ra wã-**na**-ta   sʲe-sʰi-a   wakʰusʰa   (EK)
      3S-ABS go-PPRT-FOC   come-PAST-DECL again
      He left and came back later.

In addition to -da, EK uniquely uses -ma to portray an action or change of state as having been completed.

(289) a. pʰata   ču-**ma**
         plantain cook-CMPL
         boiled plantain

      b. čʰičʰi pa-**ma**
         meat   grind-CMPL
         ground beef

---

[34]This same suffix is also attested in ET and ECh.

c. wã-**ma** ũpea
      go-CMPL three
      having gone three times

In fact, one example of the completive mentioned in Harms (1994:108) has an exact parallel in NE. The ES form *piu-da-čí* 'got dead' is obviously related to NE *peu-da* 'dead' or 'drunk' and can mean 'got drunk' in ES (Phill Harms, personal communication).

6.18 Habitual. The habitual aspect suffix *-pa* designates actions characteristic of a single person or people group. As shown in (255), the present habitual suffixes are singular *-pa-ri* and plural *-pa-ta*. The past habituals are singular *-pa-či* and plural *-pa-či-da*.

(290) *Iloriza-pa kʰisʰapʰa-ta kʰo-**pa-ri**-a*
      Iloriza-ABL sardine-ABS^FOC eat-HAB-SG-DECL
      Iloriza eats sardines regularly.

(291) *tewara kʰa-**pa-ta**-a ãkosʰo pʰepʰena-ta*
      also weave-HAB-PL-DECL vulture fan-ABS^FOC
      We [Embera women] also weave "vulture" fans.

(292) *Čʰori-ra mẽã wã-**pa-či**-a*
      Chorí-ABS jungle go-HAB-PAST-DECL
      Chorí used to go into the jungle [to hunt].

(293) *ãtia-ta hũ-**pa-či-da**-a*
      g^string-ABS^FOC tie-HAB-PAST-PL-DECL
      We [Embera men] used to wear g-strings.

As mentioned in §6.11, the habitual past can be used for a past tense event that is the same or similar to one that happened before.

(294) *ãči-a hara-**pa-či**-da-a Anancio pɨ-ra peu-tua*
      3p-ABL say-HAB-PAST-PL-DECL Anancio 2S-ABS die-IMPV
      They said, just like before, "Anancio, die!"

Negative habituals are expressed with the suffix *-kʰá*. The plural form inserts *-da* before *-kʰá*.

Verb

(295) ūnū-**kʰá**
see-NEG^HAB
I've never seen that.

(296) ēpērā-rā-pa   tama   kʰo-**da-kʰá**
Embera-PL-ABL snake eat-PL-NEG^HAB
Emberas never eat snakes.

The combination of the imperfective aspect and the future tense marker is tantamount to a future habitual, which is usually employed to communicate eternity.

(297) nẽ   kʰo-ya-a
GEN eat-FUT-DECL
will eat

(298) nẽ   kʰo **b-a-ya**-a
GEN eat be-IMPF-FUT-DECL
will always [have enough to] eat

Another verb used as a habitual is nĩpaya 'walk'. When used as a habitual it has the meaning 'carry on a lifestyle'. (For an example of nĩpaya, see (396).) This irregular verb is found in all Embera languages. In SE languages the stem nĩpa can only be used in the past and future tenses. While in NE languages nĩpa is most commonly used in the same way, it can also be used in the present tense in combination with a stative auxiliary or with -pʉrʉ in a subordinate clause.

Nevertheless, it is far more common in the present tense to use nĩ or nĩmi. The former is like a regular verb stem in that it can be accompanied by stative auxiliaries and tense and aspectual suffixes and can also be suffixed with future -ya. nĩmi, which is unique to the NE languages, can only be used in the present tense with a singular subject. Both nĩmi (obligatorily) and nĩ (optionally) are suffixed directly with declarative -a. Both can also be used in present subordinate clauses (§6.12) without -pʉrʉ: nĩmine, nĩne 'while walking.'

The present tense phenomena of the SE cognate nipa are as follows. Most like the NE languages is ES, in which the present tense form is ni, which acts very similar to its NE counterpart (Phillip Harms, personal communication). ECh ni is similar to this but is also used to describe things (Alan Wymore, personal communication). ET has no present tense form (David Pickens, personal communication).

6.19 Progressive. The equivalent of progressive aspect manifests itself in two different ways. One is through the stative stem *nũ-m-*. The other is with the present progressive forms used in subordinate clauses. (299) demonstrates the use of *nũ-m-* and (300) the present progressive.

(299) *ũrĩ-tua   tikʰo-ta   hĩkua   nũ-m-ʉ-a*
       hear-IMPV *diko*-ABS^FOC make^noise stand-be-PRES-DECL
       Listen! The Victrola is sounding.

(300) *pʉ mãwã   tida   pʰira s'e-pʉrʉ-de   iči-a   mãũ-ne   iwidi-ya-a*
       2S like^this home   run   come-PRES-in 3S-ABL this-in   ask-FUT-DECL
       When you come running home like that, he will ask you a question.

6.20 Durative. The NE cognates of the ES durative markers (Harms 1994:113) are not used as duratives in NE. As mentioned above, NE *nũ-m-* is used to portray progressive aspect. The probable NE cognate of the ES plural durative *hon-* is *hõ*, a verb root meaning 'end, run out'. The only durative use of the ES markers is in the derived EK form *nũmina*.

(301) *mũ-a   tai s'es'e-a   widi b-e-sʰi-a   kʰãrẽ-ne-pa   mũ kʰaya*
       1S-ABL 1p   father-IO   ask   be-PERF-PAST-DECL what-in-ABL   1S sick

   nũmina-tʰa (EK)
   DUR-FOC
   I began asking God what had been making me sick for so long.

A short durative in NEP is marked by the positional-stative stem *kʰo-b-*.[35]

(302) *usʰa-ta   beru b-ʉ-ta   ũrĩ-sʰi-a   ara   mãũ-ta*
       dog-ABS^FOC bark be-PRES-ABS^FOC hear-PAST-DECL same this-SUBD

   kʰuriwa-ra   akʰʉ   kʰo-b-e-sʰi-a
   guatín-ABS   look   POS-be-PERF-PAST-DECL
   He heard a dog barking. So the guatín looked around briefly.

---

[35] I am grateful to David Pickens for making this observation about the equivalent positional stative in Embera-Tadó.

6.21–6.30 Mood and evidentiality

The mood suffix is the final morpheme on the verb, except in the case of the information interrogative, which has no overt suffix. NE distinguishes five moods: declarative, information interrogative, polar interrogative, imperative, and verification moods. In contrast, ES distinguishes four additional moods: uncertain interrogative, hortatory, emphatic, and irrealis. Evidentials in NE are declarative, verificatory, reportative, and hearsay.

6.21 Declarative. The declarative mood suffix is a simple -*a*. This is in contrast to ES, where declaratives have no mood suffix unless found in a quotation. The NE declarative is illustrated in (303) (see further in §6.30).

(303) *māēpɨrɨ či pʰāka   tai-ma   s'e-sʰi-a*
      [new^dev.] REF speedboat 1p-LOC come-PAST-DECL
      Then the speedboat came to us.

6.22 Information interrogative. As mentioned above, the information interrogative has no mood suffix.

(304) *sʰāwā b-ɨ*
      how   be-PRES
      How are you?

(305) *ačʰe kʰuriwa pɨ-ra kʰārē kʰārēā s'e   b-ɨ*
      friend guatín 2S-ABS what REASON come be-PRES
      Well, guatín, my friend, why have you come? (lit., are you coming)

6.23 Polar interrogative. The polar interrogative is formed by adding the mood suffix -*kʰa*.

(306) *pārā nē kʰo-sʰi-da-kʰa*
      2p   GEN eat-PAST-PL-POLAR
      Did you eat?

It can also be used with a negative, with a rhetorical effect similar to that of English.

(307) *harra ē-kʰa*
      hunger NEG-POLAR
      Aren't you hungry?

6.24 Uncertain interrogative. Uncertain interrogatives take the polar interrogative suffix but have sentence intonation rather than rising intonation. They indicate that the speaker is unsure about the answer to his question. In (308) the woman wonders whether or not she is being taken by a demon. See also §6.30.

(308) mũ-ra animarã-puru   hãwã   ete   wã-puru-kʰa
       1S-ABS demon-ABL^FOC like^that take go-PRES-POLAR
       Am I being taken away by a demon?

This same marking can also be used to express surprise at discovering something one did not know previously.

(309) imama čara-ra   hãwã warrá b-u-ta   mũ-a   atua
       jaguar meat-ABS that tasty be-PRES-ABS^FOC 1S-ABL be^unaware

       b-a-sʰi-kʰa
       be-IMPF-PAST-POLAR
       I didn't know jaguar meat tasted this good!

6.25 Hortatory. NE does not have a special hortatory mood marker. Instead, a declarative or verification mood marker or an absolutive emphasis marker is used with an indicator of plurality.

(310) tači-ra kʰui-di-a   nãma
       1p-ABS   bathe-FUT^PL-DECL here
       Let's bathe here/now. *or* We will bathe here/now.

One less common form of the hortatory is identical to the ES form *-dama* (Harms 1994:115). This form is likely made up of the plural morpheme *-da* and the verification mood marker *-ma* (§6.27). More common is *-datru*, which is most likely formed from *-da* and the emphatic absolutive *-tru* (§6.28).

(311) nẽ   kʰo-da-ma
       GEN   eat-PL-VERI
       Let's eat!

(312) nẽ   kʰo-da-tru
       GEN   eat-PL-FOC^GI^ABS
       Let's eat!

Verb

6.26 Imperative. The direct imperatives are singular *-tua* and plural *-da-tua*. NE has no form like the ES imperative found in quotations (Harms 1994:116).

(313) pɨ-ra ɨbɨa s'e-**tua**
 2S-ABS srtong come-IMPV
 Hurry up!

(314) hŭmaẽnã ẽs'oa-**da-tua**
 everyone disperse-PL-IMPV
 Everyone get off the bus!

Negative imperatives carry the suffix *-rã* before the imperative mood marker. See §§7.8 and 7.15.

6.27 Verification. The mood suffix *-ma* is found in NEP but not in EK. It is a verificatory declarative, often used to repeat what someone else has said or even to repeat what one has said oneself. This is also used as an evidential (§6.30). (315) and (316) come from the same story.

(315) ačʰe tʰro mũ-ra pɨ-ma s'e b-ɨ-a
 friend armadillo 1S-ABS 2S-LOC come be-PRES-DECL
 Armadillo, my friend, I (have) come to you.

(316) mũ-ra s'e b-ɨ-**ma** pɨ-ma kʰĩrã čupuria iwidi-i kʰãrẽã
 1S-ABS come be-PRES-VER 2S-LOC face poor ask-IRR REASON
 I have come to you to ask a favor.

6.28 Emphatic. NE does not have the same emphatic mood suffix as in ES (Harms 1994:116–17). However, it does use *-tru* (§6.25) and *-i-ta* (§6.29).

6.29 Irrealis. NE does not have an irrealis mood. Instead the combination of the future markers *-i/-di* and the focus marker *-ta* are used to signal future conditionals, potential action, past intention, obligation, and contrary-to-fact conditions. In effect, *-i-ta/-di-ta* becomes the mood marker. (317) shows both a future conditional and potential action, which together make a contrary-to-fact statement.

(317) mũ-ta   ũtʰʉ wã-i-pʉrʉ   mũ pʉwʉrʉ-ra bʉa-i-ta
      1S-ABS^FOC up   go-IRR-COND 1S bone-ABS   break-IRR-FOC
      If I climb up there, my leg will break. *or* If I were to climb up there, my leg would break.

(318) Cabezón pʉ-ra wã-i-ta
      Cabezón 2S-ABS go-IRR-FOC
      Bighead, you should climb up.

(319) wã-i-ta   mũ-ra
      go-IRR-FOC 1S-ABS
      I'd better get out of here!

6.30 Evidentials. Information that the speaker believes or purports to be certain is marked with the declarative suffix *-a* (§6.21) or reiterated with *-ma* (§6.27).

(320) ačʰe tʰro   mũ-ra pʉ-ma s'e   b-ʉ-**a**
      friend armadillo 1S-ABS 2S-LOC come be-PRES-DECL
      Armadillo, my friend, I (have) come to you.

(321) mũ-ra s'e   b-ʉ-**ma**   pʉ-ma kʰĩrã čupuria iwidi-i kʰãrẽã
      1S-ABS come be-PRES-VER 2S-LOC face poor   ask-IRR REASON
      I have come to you to ask a favor.

Information that the speaker is reporting, purportedly saying exactly what the "horse's mouth" said to him, is marked with *-pida* (Rasmussen and Mesúa 1985:108).

(322) a. wãrã-kʰa   Abundio-pa te   čiwidi-ta   o-sʰi-ta
         true-POLAR Abundio-ABL HOUSE NEW-ABS^FOC make-PAST-ABS^FOC
         Is it true that Abundio built a new house?

      b. o-sʰi-**pida**
         make-PAST-RPRT
         [He told me that] he made one.

Commands repeated by someone who heard the command are also marked with the reportative *-pida*.[36] This gives more emphasis to the

---

[36]This morpheme may be cognate with the Epena-Saija *-pade*, which is used to mark reported commands (Harms 1994:116).

Verb   87

command, according to Rasmussen and Mesúa, from which the example is taken (1985:107–8).

(323) a. či s'es'a-pa   či wárra-a   hara b-ʉ-a   s'e-tua
         REF father-ABL REF offspring-IO say be-PRES-DECL come-IMPV
         The father says to his son, 'Come!'

   b. mã̃ʉpe či pʰapʰa-pa či wárra-a   hara b-ʉ-a
      then REF mother-ABL REF offspring-IO say be-PRES-DECL

      s'e-sʰi-**pida**
      come-PAST-RPRT
      Then the mother says to her son, "He told you to come!"

Information along the line of hearsay, often found in NEP legends, is marked with -*mana*. (324) comes from a legend about three brothers. The last brother died because he was so skinny that a little twig broke him.

(324) pakʰuru s'akʰe-pa čhōtʰa kʰir-u-pa   iči hīrū-ne sʰu-sʰi-ma
      stick   small-ABL skinny DESC-PRES-ABL   3S leg-in   poke-PAST-DECL

      ara   mã̃ʉ-pa bʉa   toko-sʰi-**mana**
      same this-ABL break go-PAST-HRSY
      He was poked in the leg by a skinny little stick. That very stick, they say, broke him apart while he was running away.

Mere conjecture is marked with -*kʰa* as in a polar question (§6.23) but has the intonation of a declarative sentence.

(325) mã̃ʉnē-pʉrʉ werã-pa   kʰawa-sʰi-a   mū-ra animarã-pʉrʉ
      then-FOC^GI woman-ABL know-PAST-DECL   1S-ABS demon-ABL^FOC

      hãwã   ete   wã-pʉrʉ-**kʰa**
      like^that bring go-PRES-POLAR
      That's when the woman realized: "Am I being taken away by a demon?"

7

Clause

In this chapter the elements of the clause are discussed. Section 7.1 provides a description of the normal order of clause constituents. Sections 7.2–7.7 consider the formation of interrogative clauses. Sections 7.8–7.11 give a description of imperative clauses, and §§7.12–7.17 discuss negation.

7.1 Order of clause constituents. Typically, following any preposed constituents, constituents such as the subject, direct and indirect object, and obliques precede the verb. Sentences (326)–(330) demonstrate normal constituent order.

(326) Existential (S/V)
mōkara /para b-a-s^{h}i-a/
rock   /EXST be-IMPF-PAST-DECL/
S   /   V   /
There was a bunch of rocks.

(327) Copular (S/C)
mũ-ra /ẽpẽrã   pia/   pẽrã   mũ-a   pɨ-a   hara-ya-a
1S-ABS /person good/   because 1S-ABL 2S-IO   say-FUT-DECL
S   /   /
Since I am a good person, I will tell you.

89

(328) Intransitive (S/V)
   mū-ra māũ to   s'akʰe wārā   /wā-pʉrʉ-a/
   1s-ABS this river small upstream   /go-PRES-DECL/
   S   Obl   /V/
   I am walking up this creek.

(329) Transitive (S/O/V)
   Anancio-pa /Tío   Cabeza-ra/ ēkʰarra-de hira eta-sʰi-a
   Anancio-ABL /Uncle Head-ABS/ back-in   hang get-PAST-DECL
   S   /O/   Obl   V
   Anancio picked up Uncle Head and carried him on his back.

(330) Bitransitive (S/IO/DO/V)
   māũ-ne wárra   s'akʰe-a /nẽ pʰōnō-ta/   bʉa
   this-in offspring small-IO /GEN blossom-ABS^FOC/ break
   IO   /DO/   V

   tia-sʰi-a
   give-PAST-DECL
   Then [he] picked a flower and gave it to the little boy.

(331) māũ-ne čapa   Carlo-pa   /tai-a/ hara-sʰi-a
   this-in brother Carlos-ABL /1p-IO/ say-PAST-DECL
   S   /IO/   V
   Then brother Carlos said to us...

Phrases indicating instrument usually occur pre-verbally, between the subject and the object, if present. This is contrary to the tendency in ES, where they end the clause they affect (Harms 1994:121).

(332) māũ-ne hĩrū-pa   /tambora-ta/   s'a nū-m-e-sʰi-a
   this-in foot-ABL   /drum-ABS^FOC/ play stand-be-PERF-PAST-DECL
   INST   /DO/   V
   Then he started playing a drum with his feet.

(333) ara māũ-ta   kʰāpʰūrīā s'rōā-pa /pʰōwā-pa/ batʰa-sʰi-a
   same this-SUBD   Latino   old-ABL /rifle-ABL/ shoot-PAST-DECL
   S   /INST/   V
   Then the old Latino shot it with his rifle.

Accompaniment phrases (§5.6) often follow the main verb. They are marked by the enclitic ūmẽ 'with, two'.

Oblique constituents usually precede or follow the core constituents, though at times they may occur between subject and object. Their placement, however, in a given sentence depends mostly on discourse and pragmatic considerations.

Time words and phrases usually begin the clause to which they relate because they set the scene for what follows.

(334) nũrēma ũmākʰīrã mẽã wã-sʰi-a
 next^day man jungle go-PAST-DECL
 T S V
 The next morning the man went into the jungle [to hunt].

In contrast, time words and phrases are placed after the verb to highlight them. In (335) the time word *tiamasʰi* 'night' is placed last to highlight it; Emberas, especially women, do not walk trails at night.

(335) mãẽpʉrʉ /wã-sʰi-a/ tiamasʰi
 [new^dev.] /go-PAST-DECL/ night
  /V/ T
 Then she left while it was still dark.

Other constituents are also postposed for highlighting. Notice also the adverb *mũ-tuba* following the verb. This occurs post-nucleus rather than as the first constituent in the verb phrase to highlight it, because going into the jungle by oneself can be dangerous. Incidentally, in (336), not only does a time phrase occur first in the clause, another one occurs post-subject.

(336) /ewari aba/ mũ /viernes ewari-de/ mẽã wã-sʰi-a /mũ-tuba/
 /day one/ 1s /Friday day-in/ jungle go-PAST-DECL /1s-alone/
 /T/ S /T/ V /Adv/
 One day, on a Friday, I went into the jungle by myself.

(337) has two pre-verbal constituents and three post-verbal ones. It is likely that 'in a big canoe' occurs last since it is the most salient constituent. In the story, the man and his wife cut a lot of plantains and needed a big canoe to ferry them all.

(337) nũrēma nẽ kʰo-da-pʰeda /wã-sʰi-da-a/ pʰata tʰu-de
 next^day GEN eat-PL-after /go-PAST-PL-DECL/ plantain cut-in
 T /V/ IMM PURP

/či kʰima ũme/ hãpa waibʉa-de
/REF spouse two/ canoe big-in
/ACCOM/ LOC
The next day after eating, he and his wife went *in a big canoe* to cut plantain.

Important new or discontinuous information, especially main clause constituents, is signaled by occurrence in post-verbal position. (338) is an example of a rhetorical device used to slow down the story prior to the significant information the woman is about to divulge, which is important to the resolution of the story.

(338) mãũ-ne tewara hara-sʰi-a wẽrã-pa kʰima ãči-ra nane
 this-in also say-PAST-DECL woman-ABL spouse 3p-ABS later

  kʰewara itua to-di-a
  afternoon liquor drink-FUT^PL-DECL
 Then the woman also said, "Husband, tonight they are going to drink chicha."

Postposing of major constituents can also be used merely for purposes of clarification. In the complex sentence in (339) the subjects of the two clauses are overtly mentioned for clarification, and the second subject is also postposed for the same purpose.

(339) wẽrã-pa eda akʰʉ-pʉrʉ-de mãũ-ne ũnũ b-e-sʰi-a
 woman-ABL into look-PRES-in this-in see be-PERF-PAST-DECL

  ũmãkʰĩrã-pa
  man-ABL
 While the woman was looking down [from the house], the man saw her. *or* She was seen by the man.

7.2–7.7 Question formation

NE has both polar and information questions. Polar questions take the polar interrogative mood marker -kʰa on the independent clause. Information questions use interrogative pro-forms and do not include a mood marker. Interrogatives may be straightforward (§§7.2–7.4), leading (§7.5), uncertain (§7.6), or rhetorical (§7.7).

7.2 Polar questions. Polar interrogatives have normal constituent order with the polar question suffix -k^ha in the mood position (clause final). They also have rising intonation, in contrast with the uncertain interrogative (§6.24).

(340) $ač^he$ $pʉ$-ta /$wadi$ $č^hiwa$ b-$ʉ$-k^ha/
       friend   2S-ABS^FOC /still   urinate   be-PRES-POLAR/
       S   /V/
       Hey, are you still urinating?

7.3 Information questions. Information questions begin with interrogative pronouns unless a nominal orientation phrase is mentioned first. A list of the interrogative pronouns is given in (341).

(341) k^hai who $s^hãma$ where
       $k^hãrẽ$ what; which $s^hãũ$ which
                           (in NEP)
       $k^hãrẽ$ $k^hãrẽã$ why $s^hãwã$ how
       $k^hãrẽa$ why (EK only) $s^hãpe$ ($s^hõpe$ in EK)   when
       k^has^ha what (NEP only) $hõmas^ha$ how much
                                                                                                                           (NEP only)

(342)   /$s^hãwã$/ b-$ʉ$
       /how/   be-PRES
       /Q/   V
       How are you?

In (343) the nominal orientation phrase occurs before the interrogative pronoun, i.e., the nominal is topicalized.

(343) $pʉ$-ra /$s^hãwã$/ s^le-s^hi
       2S-ABS   /how/   come-PAST
       S   /Q/   V
       How did you get here?

Harms (1994:122–3) says that in ES questions in which information is sought about a constituent other than the subject, the subject usually follows the rest of the clause unless it is topicalized. In (344), the first NE example, the overt point of reference, in headless relative clause form, is sentence-final. However, (345) and (346) exhibit topicalization of the subject.

(344) /sʰãma/   b-ʉ-ta   /mãwã   pedea b-ʉ-ta/
      /where/ be-PRES-QUOT /likeˆthis talk   be-PRES-ABSˆFOC/
      /Q/   V   /S/
      Where is the one who is talking like that?

(345) ačʰe   /pʉ-a/   sʰãwã-ẽrã   /warrá o-pa-ri/
      friend /2S-ABL/ how-because   /tasty make-HAB-SG/
              /S/   Q   /V/
      Friend, how do you make it so tasty?

(346) Anancio /pʉ-a/   kʰãrẽ-ta   /tida   ero-b-ʉ/
      Anancio /2S-ABL/ what-ABSˆFOC   /atˆhome   have-be-PRES/
               /S/   Q   /V/
      Anancio, what do you have in your house?

7.4 Alternative tag questions. Alternative tag questions begin with an interrogative pro-form and contain at least two alternatives; the pro-form and all of the alternatives are suffixed with the absolutive focus marker *-ta*.

(347) sʰãʉ̃-ta   kʰĩrĩã-i   sʲa   b-ʉ-ta   wa hari b-ʉ-ta
      which-ABSˆFOC want-IRR here be-PRES-ABSˆFOC or there be-ABSˆFOC
      Which do you want? This one or that one?

7.5 Leading questions. Leading questions are common in all Embera languages, including EK and NEP. This question type seeks a specific kind of response. Usually, a negative question elicits a positive response. (348) is about a *guatín* (rodent) who was tricking a mother jaguar into allowing the guatín to care for her cubs.

(348) tia-i   ẽ   b-ʉ-kʰa
      give-IRR NEG be-PRES-POLAR
      Won't you give [me some work]?

7.6 Uncertain questions. According to Harms, these differ from rhetorical and other questions because, in uncertain questions, the speaker is not sure if he knows the answer or not. In the other types of questions he either knows the answer or is completely in the dark (1994:125). As for their form, uncertain questions look like polar interrogatives in NE, either in the affirmative or negative. (349) is about a man who was trying to shoot a magic guan pheasant.

Clause 95

(349) mũ-a   wãrãta hãũ   tʰusʰi-ra   pʰoya pea ẽ-kʰa
      1s-ABL truly   that guan-ABS   can   kill NEG-POLAR
      Can I really not kill that guan pheasant?

7.7 Questions used rhetorically. Rhetorical questions take the same form as the above question types with the distinction that they do not require a response nor is one necessarily desired. The rhetorical question in (350) was posed to a man by his wife, who missed their young son after being away from home for a month. The point of the woman was to rebuke her husband rather than to elicit a verbal response from him.

(350) tai wárra-ma   kʰrĩčʰa ẽ-kʰa
      1p offspring-LOC   think   NEG-POLAR
      Don't you think about our son?

7.8–7.11 Imperatives

In this section the imperative constructions are presented—the direct imperative in singular and plural forms and the indirect imperative found in quotations and indirect speech.

7.8 Direct imperatives. Direct imperatives use the suffix -tua in place of the tense and mood suffixes. This morpheme is always final in an imperative.

(351) pɨ-ra   ɨbɨa   sʲe-**tua**
      2S-ABS   strong   come-IMPV
      (You) hurry up! *or* literally, Come more quickly!

(352) Anancio pɨ-a   mũ-ra   ete-**tua**
      Anancio 2S-ABL 1S-ABS take-IMPV
      Anancio, take me along!

Imperatives can be formed from stative verbs as well as with stative verbs. NE has several forms in which the 'be' verb and other statives can be used as commands in the imperfective and other aspects. They are used with regular verbs also, in order to add color or scope to the command. In example (353) the simple stative *b-* is augmented by the perfect aspect suffix *-e* to form the stem for 'stay'. In (354) the plural auxiliary *pʰan-* is colored by the imperfective suffix -a to indicate that the command is to be carried out over a period of time.

(353) mãẽtʰara pɨ-ta   ya   b-e-**tua**   tida
      if^so   2S-ABS^FOC now be-PERF-IMPV home
      Well, then, *you* stay home now!

(354) pãrã-pa wãrãka   akʰɨ   pʰan-a-**tua**
      2P-ABL up^river look   be^few-IMPF-IMPV
      You guys keep looking up river!

The regular plural imperative is formed by adding the suffix -*da* before the imperative suffix.

(355) sʰukʰura-ta   to-di-pɨrɨ   pãči huware-pa   hue
      cane^juice-ABS^FOC drink-FUT^PL-COND   2p   right^hand-ABL scoop

   to-**da**-**tua**
   drink-PL-IMPV
   If you're going to drink some cane juice, scoop it out with your right hand and drink it!

Negative imperatives carry the suffix -*rã* before the imperative morpheme, whether the subject is singular or plural (see further in §7.15).

(356) Anancio pɨ-a   mũ-ra   tʰabari-**rã**-**tua**
      Anancio 2S-ABL 1S-ABS throw^toward-NEG^IRR-IMPV
      Anancio, don't throw [that rock] at me!

7.9 Polite imperatives. Contrary to ES, which has a specific polite imperative form (Harms 1994:130), NEP adds the irrealis and focus suffixes to form polite commands (see also §6.29). The addition of a stative verb makes the clause more semantically obligative than imperative; see (358).

(357) Patiseko pɨ-ra wã-i-ta   ũtʰɨ
      Patiseko 2S-ABS go-IRR-FOC up
      Patiseko, why don't you climb up? *or* Patiseko, you should climb up.

Clause 97

(358) *paripɨrɨ pɨ-a pio waka-i-ta b-ɨ-a tai traha*
however 2s-ABL much care-IRR-FOC be-PRES-DECL 1p work

pʰan-ɨ-misʰa
be^few-PRES-while
However, you must take very good care [of our children] while we are working.

7.10 Hortatory imperatives. These take the same form as the future plural and are interpreted as hortatory or declarative by context. See §6.25 for hortatory imperatives with other mood markers.

(359) *mãũ hiwa-ta aba-pe bari-di-a*
this bend-ABS^FOC one-LIM fish-FUT^PL-DECL
Let's just fish this bend of the river.

7.11 Imperatives in quotations. Contrary to ES, NE does not have a special marker for quoted commands. This function can be obtained through use of the reportative evidential (§6.30) or by suffixing quoted material with the focus marker *-ta* (§9.12).

When a command is reported in a subordinate clause of purpose, the imperative mood marker *-tua* is not used. However, the negative irrealis suffix *-rã* is preserved.

(360) *mũ-a hara-sʰi-a kʰo mãrẽã*
1S-IO say-PAST-DECL eat PURP
He told me to eat it.

(361) *mũ-a hara-sʰi-a kʰo-rã mãrẽã* (NEP)
1S-IO say-PAST-DECL eat-NEG^IRR PURP
He told me not to eat it.

In EK, however, the negative purpose clause (§9.4) includes a negated verb followed by the imperfective form of the verb 'be', all followed by *mãrẽã*.

(362) *mũ-á hara-sʰi-a kʰo ẽ b-a mãrẽã* (EK)
1S-IO say-PAST-DECL eat NEG be-IMPF PURP
He told me not to eat it. (lit., He told me to be not eating it.)

7.12–7.17 Negation

There are three different negation markers in NE. The standard negative enclitic *ẽ* functions as a verb, since it can take a declarative marker, but it can negate almost any part of speech, as in ES (Harms 1994:131). The habitual negative *-khá* negates only verbs (see §§6.12 and 6.18). The imperative negative *-rã* only occurs in negative imperatives and negative purpose clauses.

Some verbs are irregular in that they do not follow the normal process of negation (§7.16). There are also some constructions which have no specific negative morpheme but rather an understood or inherent negative meaning (§7.17).

7.12 Standard negation. The usual negative construction in a verb phrase consists of the verb stem, the plural suffix *-da/-na* if the subject is plural, the negative enclitic *ẽ,* and the equative verb *pa-* if the tense is not in the present. (363) is of a singular present. (364) is of a singular past.

(363) kʰuriwa mṳ-a pʉ pedea ĩhã   ẽ-a
      guatín   1S-ABL 2S word   believe NEG-DECL
      Guatín, I don't believe you.

(364) ũnṵ ẽ   pa-sʰi-a
      see NEG EQ-PAST-DECL
      He didn't see her.

In EK one example is attested where the equative is not used, and the negative enclitic *ẽ(ã)* is suffixed with tense and mood markers.

(365) ara   mãṵne-ra mṳ-ra   mṳči   trua-edá   wã   b-e
      same then-PIVOT 1S-ABS 1S^COREF land-GOAL go   be-PERF

      ẽã-sʰi-a
      NEG-PAST-DECL
      So then I couldn't go to my land.

In (366) the auxiliary is the equative *pa-* since it is a simple past. Plural cannot be marked in the equative, so it is marked with the addition of *-da/-na* on the verb stem.

(366) mãwã   hara-pʉrʉ-mĩna wapema-pa pʰãnu-**na** ẽ   pa-sʰi-a
      like^this say-PRES-though others-ABL answer-PL NEG EQ-PAST-DECL
      Even though he was saying this, the others did not respond.

To negate a constituent rather than a whole clause, the negative ẽ occurs between the constituent and the stative verb.[37] In (367) ẽ negates 'see-PL', so the clause literally means 'they were those who did not see it'.

(367) ũnũ-na ẽ   pʰan-a-sʰi-a
      see-PL NEG be^few-IMPF-PAST-DECL
      They had not seen it.

In example (368) from EK, ẽã negates the phrase wã b-e, forming a phrase meaning 'unable to walk'.

(368) ara   mãũne tʰepadewa-sʰi-a   mũ wã b-e   ẽã
      same   then   start^walking-PAST-DECL 1S go be-PERF NEG

      tʰa-b-ʉ-tʰa   (EK)
      lie-be-PRES-FOC
      So I started walking, I who had been lying down unable to walk.

The difference between constituent negation and clause negation is shown in (369): the meaning 'poorly' is derived from pia 'good' and ẽ 'NEG'. The second example is simply a negation of the clause '(sg.) is well'.

(369) a. pia ẽ   b-ʉ-a
         good NEG be-PRES-DECL
         (Sg.) is doing poorly.

      b. pia   b-ʉ   ẽ-a
         good be-PRES NEG-DECL
         (Sg.) is not well.

The negative ẽ also combines with the generalizer nẽ to form an encliticized postposition meaning 'without'. In EK, from which (370) comes, this form has become ẽã, developed from ẽ-a and corresponding to the SE wẽã.

---

[37]Thanks to Jamie Enemark, Doug Schermerhorn, and Sharon Tibberts for the appropriate data.

(370) kʰai-pa   trabajo tia-i   **nẽ^ẽã**-maẽ
      who-ABL work   give-IRR without-LOC
      in a place without anyone who would give me work

7.13 Negation of equatives. Just as in ES, equative clauses in NE are negated by addition of the negative *ẽ* and, if in the present tense, suffixation with the appropriate mood marker. In past or future tense, the equative *pa-* with appropriate tense marking is used.

(371) *ačʰe*   imama hãũ-ra   mũ hĩrũ **ẽ**-ma   (NEP)
      friend jaguar that-ABS 1S leg   NEG-VERI
      Hey, jaguar, *that's* not my leg!

7.14 Habitual negation. Habitual clauses are negated by the suffix *-kʰá*. In these cases the negative sense is translated as 'never' or 'never before'.

(372) animarã tau^pʰena ũnũ-na-**kʰá**   akʰu-di   kʰãrẽã
      animal   caged   see-PL-NEG^HAB look-FUT^PL   REASON
      so we could look at animals we had never seen before

7.15 Negative imperatives. As described in §7.8, negative imperatives carry the suffix *-rã* immediately before the imperative morpheme, whether the subject is singular or plural. In EK and Panamanian NEP, however, the negative is placed before the plural marker, as is shown in (375). The plural morpheme becomes nasal in this sentence because it follows another nasal.

(373) *Anancio pu-a   mũ-ra   tʰabari-**rã**-tua*
      Anancio 2S-ABL 1S-ABS   throw^toward-NEG^IRR-IMPV
      Anancio, don't throw [that rock] at me!

(374) *kʰo-da-**rã**-tua*
      eat-PL-NEG^IRR-IMPV
      Don't you all eat it! (Colombian NEP)

(375) *kʰo-rã-**na**-tua*
      eat-NEG^IRR-PL-IMPV
      Don't you all eat it! (EK and Panamanian NEP)

Just as positive commands (§7.8) can add overt aspect through the use of auxiliary verbs, negative commands also do this. However, the typical *-rã* is not used; rather, the standard *ẽ* is employed.

(376) *kʰãĩ-rã-tua*
sleep-NEG-IMPV
Don't sleep [now]!

(377) *kʰãĩ   ẽ   b-a-tua*
sleep NEG be-IMPF-IMPV
Don't sleep at all! (lit., Don't be sleeping!)

7.16 Irregular negative verbs. The negative construction *nẽ ẽ-a* 'be without, there is none' is normally used as the antonym of the verb stem *erob-* 'have' and the existential *para* 'there are'. *ero-b-* can be negated like other verbs but this is not usual.[38]

(378) *iwidi-sʰi-da-a   gasolina-ta   mãũ-ne   kʰãpʰũrĩã-pa*
ask^for-PAST-PL-DECL gasoline-ABS^FOC this-in Latino-ABL

ero-b-ʉ-a   a-sʰi-a
have-be-PRES-DECL say-PAST-DECL
We asked for gasoline. And the Latino said, "I have some."

(379) *mũ-ra   pʰõwã   nẽ   ẽ   baera   batʰa   ẽ   pa-sʰi-a*
1S-ABS rifle GEN NEG because shoot NEG EQ-PAST-DECL
Because I didn't have a rifle, I didn't shoot. (lit., Because I was without a rifle, I didn't shoot.)

7.17 Inherent negatives. Some verbs use an antonym instead of using *ẽ* as the negative. Such is the case with *kʰawa* 'know', which is negated with *atua* 'be ignorant of'.

(380) *mãũ-ne   ũmãkʰĩrã-pa   kʰawa-sʰi-a   mũ   kʰima-ra   animarã-pa*
this-in man-ABL know-PAST-DECL 1S spouse-ABS demon-ABL

ete   wã-pʉrʉ-ta
take go-PRES-ABS^FOC
About that time the man realized, "My wife has been taken by a demon."

---

[38]Phill Harms (pers. comm.) hypothesizes that the phrase *nẽ ẽã* has come from the Spanish *no hay* 'there isn't any'.

(381) či   hohoma   mīā̃   **atua**   bia-sʰi-a
      REF coatí   GEN   be^ignorant   yell-PAST-DECL
      The *coatí* screamed without knowing [what had hit him].

8

Sentence

A sentence may be composed of a sentence introducer or vocative, a main clause, and adverbial clauses. This chapter deals with the order of constituents in the sentence (§8.1) and with sentence introducers (§§8.2–8.6). Adverbial and embedded clauses are further discussed in §§9.1–9.8.

8.1 Sentence formation. Sentence introducers relate the sentences in which they occur to those that precede them. At least one sentence introducer, *mãũne,* may also follow an adverbial clause. Adverbial clauses may precede or follow the main clause and are subordinate to it.[39] They are signaled by certain verb suffixes which are discussed in chapter 9.

NE sentences can be very short. A minimal sentence is a single clause which, in turn, may have only a single constituent.

(382) ũnũ ẽ pa-si-a
 see NEG EQ-PAST-DECL
 He didn't see her.

At the other extreme, NE sentences can be quite complex. In natural text, it is not uncommon for three or four adverbial clauses to precede the main clause as in (383) or for sentence introducers to both introduce the sentence and follow an adverbial clause. This is the case in (383).

---
[39]When a purpose clause occurs with the marker *-de* and its main clause employs a motion verb, the motion verb acts as an auxiliary when it is not in case agreement with the subject noun. See §6.9.

(383) mẽã   wã-na   oča   ẽ   nū-m-ʉ-ta   oča   ẽ
      jungle go-PPRT come^out   NEG   stand-be-PRES-SUBD   come^out   NEG

      nū-m-ʉ-ta   kʰewara   pa-pʉrʉ-de   sʼe-sʰi-a   tida
      stand-be-PRES-SUBD   afternoon   EQ-PRES-in   come-PAST-DECL   home

Having gone into the jungle and not coming out for a long time, when it was afternoon he came home.

(384) ūmãkʰīrã-pa   pakʰuru   bʉa   tʰu-da-pa   hūma   u
      man-ABL   stick   break   chop-PPRT-ABL   all   swat

      kʰẽna-kʰua-pʉrʉ-de   mãū-ne   čora   kʰir-u-ta   bia
      slaughter-REPT-PRES-in   this-in   old^FEM   DESC-PRES-ABS^FOC   yell

      pʰiradrʉ   toko-sʰi-a
      get^up   run-PAST-DECL

As the man was beating them all to death with the stick he had chopped off, an old lady got up screaming and ran after him.

The vocative occurs as the first word in the sentence unless a word of greeting is used before it.

(385) **kʰima**   mū-a   wãtekʰare   pido-ta   batʰa-pue-sʰi-a
      spouse   1S-ABL   upstream   boar-ABS^FOC   shoot-VOL-PAST-DECL

Wife, just upstream I shot a boar.

(386) **ačʰe**   **tʰro**   mū-ra   pʉ-ma   sʼe   b-ʉ-a
      friend   armadillo   1S-ABS   2S-LOC   come   be-PRES-DECL

Hey, armadillo, I (have) come to you.

8.2–8.6 Sentence introducers

As in ES (Harms 1994:142–50), many sentences in NE have introducers which reveal how a given sentence is related to one preceding it. These most often consist, in part, of the demonstrative *mã-* 'this, the' followed by a suffix from the list in (387).[40] Those suffixes in the group listed first require that *-ʉ* be attached to the demonstrative, if such is used. The only correlation between those suffixes requiring *-ʉ* and those which do not is

---

[40]Relationships between clauses are also indicated by verbs combining with the suffixes in the list. These constructions are discussed in §§9.1–9.8.

that those that do require it may do so because they begin with consonants. Those that do not require -ʉ begin with vowels, for the most part.

The indexing stem *ara* 'same, right' (§4.5) may precede the demonstrative in some constructions. The other demonstrative roots *hã* 'that' and *nã* 'this' may also combine with the endings. However, the resulting forms are unusual sentence introducers.[41]

The demonstrative *mã-* refers to something which is currently understood, usually from the previous sentence. The available endings describe the nature of the relationship between the previous information and the current sentence. In natural text the most common sentence introducers are *mãũne* 'then', *mãũpe* or *mãpe* which marks a slight delay between sentences, *mãẽpʉrʉ* which marks the beginning of a scene that leads to an important event, and *ara mãũta* which marks events that are important in a story; these are discussed further in §10.11.

In (387) the suffixes used in sentence introducers are listed with their meanings and with references for further discussion.

(387)
-de/-ne	'in, during'	(§5.7, 9.1)
-de-pa/-ne-pa	'from a specific location'	(§5.10)
kʰãrẽã/kʰarea	'on account of'	(§5.4)
-misʰa	'during, while' (NEP)	(§9.1)
-pe/-ʉpe	'only, time of'	(§10.11)
pẽrã, pera	'because (of)'	(§9.6)
-ta	(subordinate clause suffix)	(§9.2)
-da kʰarea	'sequential, change of subject' (NEP)	(§9.2)
-ẽpʉrʉ	'then'	(§10.11)
-ẽtʰara, ẽtʰeara	'if that's so'	(§8.7)
-i	'sequential, change of subject' (EK)	(§9.2)
-ma	'stationary location'	(§5.7)
-ʉ-pa	'from a specific location'	(§5.10)
-wã	'like (this/that)'	(§2.7, 8.8)
-wã-pʰe(da)	'after (doing this/that)'	(§9.2)

In addition, the nonabsolutive focus suffix *-pʉrʉ* (§§5.1 and 10.8) may follow the suffixes *-ma, -ne, -pe,* and *-wã*.

8.2 Temporal relators. The following temporal relators add unity to an account, especially to a narrative, by joining clauses and sentences in a temporal relationship with one another. Temporal relators include *mãũne* 'then', *mãpe/mãũpe* 'and then, after that, so then' (NEP), and *mãũmisʰa* 'meanwhile'

---

[41]See §10.1 for instances of *hã-* as a sentence introducer.

(NEP). *mãũne* introduces events which occur in the same time frame as that of the previous event, whereas a short lapse of time separates events linked by *mãpe/mãũpe*. There is no logical cause implied with these markers.

In (388), *mãũne (mãũ-ne)* 'this-in' indicates that the events 'they bathed' and 'he picked a flower and gave it to the little boy' occur in the same time frame.

(388) ara mãũ-ta kʰui-sʰi-da-a **mãũ-ne** wárra sʲakʰe-a nẽ
 same this-SUBD bathe-PAST-PL-DECL this-in offspring small-IO GEN

      pʰono-ta bʉa tia-sʰi-a
 blossom-ABS^FOC break give-PAST-DECL
 So they bathed. He picked a flower and gave it to the little boy.

Other events considered to be occurring at the same time are consecutive utterances by different speakers in a reported conversation.

(389) ũmãkʰĩrã-pa iwidi-sʰi-a pʉ-ra sʰãwã sʲe-sʰi
 man-ABL ask-PAST-DECL 2S-ABS how come-PAST
 The man asked, "How did you get here?"

(390) **mãũ-ne** wẽrã-pa hara-sʰi-a mũ-ra tiauru-pa
 this-in woman-ABL say-PAST-DECL 1S-ABS demon-ABL

      ẽne-sʰi-a
 bring-PAST-DECL
 Then the woman said, 'I was brought by a demon.'

mãũne also occurs following adverbial clauses within a sentence. Stephen Levinsohn (personal communication) suggests that this use slows down the story immediately before a significant development or the achievement of a delayed goal, in order to highlight the development. In (391) a man is looking for his wife and son, who have been taken away by a devil.

(391) kʰaidu wã-pʉrʉ-ta kʰaidu wã-pʉrʉ-ta **mãũ-ne** ũnũ-ne
 follow go-PRES-SUBD follow go-PRES-SUBD this-in see-in

      wã-sʰi-a či wárra sʲakʰe hemene
 go-PAST-DECL REF offspring small play

kʰer-a-da-ta
DESC-IMPF-PPRT-ABS^FOC
Following along for a long time, he then saw that his little son had been there playing.

In EK, *māwẽ* is used following an adverbial clause to highlight what follows; see §10.11.

māũne may also introduce an event which occurs at the same time as the previous event, even when there is no logical relationship between the two. The events in (392) transpire in different places but occur at about the same time.

(392) a. hũẽ-na-pʰeda tida   ete   wã-sʰi-a
       arrive-PL-after home take go-PAST-DECL
       After they arrived he [the demon] took her [another man's wife] into his house.

   b. mãũ-ne ũmākʰĩrā-pa kʰawa-sʰi-a   mũ   kʰima-ra
      this-in man-ERG   know-PAST-DECL   1S   spouse-ABS

      animarā-pa ete   wã-pʉrʉ-ta
      take   demon-ABL   GO-PRES-ABS^FOC
      About that time, the man [husband] realized, "My wife has been taken by a demon."

The addition of the nonabsolutive focus marker -*pʉrʉ* (§10.8) to *māũne* (forming *mope-pʉrʉ* in EK) highlights the specific time something happens.

(393) **mãũ-ne-pʉrʉ** mũ-a   kʰawa-sʰi-a   diauru-ta
      this-in-FOC^GI   1S-ABL know-PAST-DECL   demon-ABS^FOC
      That's when I realized he was a demon.

mãpe/mãũpe signals that there is some minor delay between the two events.[42]

(394) warrá to-sʰi-da-a   **mãũpe** ãči-ra to-eda   kʰui-de
      tasty drink-PAST-PL-DECL then   3S-ABS river-into bathe-in

---

[42]In EK, *mope* is cognate with NEP *māpe/mãũpe* but has a different function; see §10.11.

wã-sʰi-da-a
go-PAST-PL-DECL
They drank it heartily. A bit later they went down to the river to bathe.

(395) iči-ra taidu pura wã-sʰi-a   **mãũpe** ũrĩ
3S-ABS down roll go-PAST-DECL then hear

nũ-m-e-sʰi-a
stand-be-PERF-PAST-DECL
It rolled down the hill. Shortly thereafter he began hearing it.

mãũ-misʰa 'this-while' has a stricter use than *mãũne,* in that it can only mark events as happening concurrently with others. The suffix *-misʰa* does not occur in EK and when used in NEP it is almost always found attached to a verb in an overlapping event clause (§9.1).

8.3 Extended time relators. The extended time relators evident in ES (Harms 1994:147) are not attested in NE. Instead, adverbial clauses (§9.2) are used to express such delays.

8.4 Additive relators. Additive relators like *ičaba* 'in addition' and *tewara* 'also' signal that the information they introduce is in an additive relationship to what precedes them. They are interchangeable when beginning clauses but *tewara* also functions as an additive adverb, as is evident in (397), which follows a speech by the same woman.

(396) hara nũpa-sʰ-a   sʼrõã b-a-da-mĩna   **ičaba**   iči-a
  say walk-PAST-DECL old be-IMPF-PPRT-though in^addition 3S-ABL

hara-pa-či-a   iči-ra Ãkʰõrẽ ũmẽ bursʰida b-u-ta
say-HAB-PAST-DECL 3S-ABS God   two happy   be-PRES-ABS^FOC
He went around saying this even though he had become old; in addition he would say that he was happy with God.

(397) *mãũ-ne* **tewara** hara-sʰi-a   werã-pa
  this-in also   say-PAST-DECL woman-ABL
Then the woman also said…

8.5 Logical relators. The sentence introducers *mãũpa, mãũ pẽrã/pera,* and *mãũ kʰãrẽã* all signal logical relationships between the previous and following sentences. While all could be translated as 'because of this', there are differences between the three.

mãũpa signals obvious causal relationships. In (398), for instance, it refers to a constituent which also has the ablative marker, because it describes the means that caused the result.

(398) *paripʉrʉ či hãpa-ra sʲʉkʉa sʲe-pʉrʉ b-a-sʰi-a*
however REF canoe-ABS heavy come-PRES be-IMPF-PAST-DECL

*ñame-pa **mãũ-pa** pʰoa nũ-m-e-sʰi-a*
yam-ABL this-ABL dry stand-be-PERF-PAST-DECL
But the canoe was running heavy because of the yams. Because of this, it got hung up [on a rock].

When the first clause provides the reason for the result, rather than the means for it, the result is introduced with *mãũ pẽrã*.

(399) *pʉ-ta wariˆẽ b-a-sʰi-a **mãũ pẽrã** mũ-ra*
2S-ABSˆFOC alikeˆNEG be-IMPF-PAST-DECL this because 1S-ABS

sʲe-sʰi-a
come-PAST-DECL
He looked just like you. So I came here.

Whereas *mãũ pẽrã/pera* introduces results when the reason is a reality, *mãũ kʰãrẽã* introduces consequences or reasons which are potential. In (400) the reason the monkey fled is that the woman would hit him if he stayed.

(400) *iči-a kʰawa-sʰi-a čipari wẽrã-pa iči-ra u-i-ta*
3S-ABL know-PAST-DECL owner woman-ABL 3S-ABS swat-IRR-ABSˆFOC

***mãũ kʰãrẽã** mĩrũ-sʰi-a či yarre-ra*
this REASON flee-PAST-DECL REF monkey-ABS
[The monkey] knew that the housewife would try to hit him. For this reason [he] fled.

In (401) the reason the speaker came to get the addressee is not because he shot the boar but so that she would help (cut it up for) him.

(401) watekʰare pido-ta   batʰa-pue-sʰi-a   **mãũ kʰãrẽã** mũ-a pɨ
      upstream boar-ABS^FOC   shoot-VOL-PAST-DECL   this REASON 1S-ABL 2S

   eta-de s'e-sʰi-a
   get-in come-PAST-DECL
   Just upstream I shot a boar. That is why I came to get you.

8.6 Comparative relators. The comparative sentence introducer *mãwã* 'like this' is used to compare and contrast the previously mentioned sentence with the following action. In (402) the manner of the action of the final sentence is just as the previous sentence describes it.

(402) iči-ra mãũ-ne taidu pɨra wã-ya-a   tʰɨpɨ uruka
      3S-ABS this-in down roll go-FUT-DECL fire burn

   nũ-m-ɨ-na   **mãwã-pɨrɨ**   pɨ-a pea-ya-a
   stand-be-PRES-GOAL   like^this-FOC^GI   2S-ABL kill-FUT-DECL
   He will go rolling down the hill into the burning fire. It is in this way that you will kill him.

8.7 Conditional relators. Conditional relators like the common *mãẽtʰara* 'if it is this way' indicate that what follows is a conclusion, deduction, or proposition made from information in the preceding sentence. In (403) *mãẽtʰara* introduces the conclusion which the speaker draws from the content of the previous speech.

(403) abaɨ-pa   hara-sʰi-a   pɨ-a   nãũ sʰukʰura   warrá ẽ
      one^of-ABL say-PAST-DECL   2S-ABL this cane^juice tasty NEG

   o-sʰi-a   mãũ-ne iči-a   hara-sʰi-a   **mãẽtʰara**
   make-PAST-DECL this-in 3S-ABL say-PAST-DECL if^so

   pɨ-ta   ya be-tua   tida
   2S-ABS^FOC   now stay-IMPV home
   One of them said, "You didn't make this cane juice very well." And he [who made it] said, "Well, then, *you* stay home [and make it]!"

8.8 *mãwã* as a pro-verb. The sentence introducer *mãwã* 'like this' is used not only as a temporal relator (§8.2) and a comparative relator (§8.6); it is also used as a pro-verb, i.e., it takes the place of a verb. As such, it may take any of the subordinating suffixes described in §§9.1–9.7.

Sentence   111

In (404), for instance, *mãwã* takes the place of the verb 'yell' and is suffixed with the indicators of overlapping events (§9.1).⁴³

(404) a. *Anancio bia-sʰi-a   ay Tío Cabeza mũ-ra čʰiratrʉka-sʰi-a*
Anancio yell-PAST-DECL oh Uncle Head   1S-ABS   slip-PAST-DECL
Anancio yelled, "Oh, Uncle Head, I slipped!"

   b. *mãwã-pʉrʉ-de   poro-de   irʉ-kʰo-b-a-da-ra*
   like^this-PRES-in head-on   have-POS-be-IMPF-PPRT-ABS

   wẽãtʰa-sʰi-a
   throw^off-PAST-DECL
   While he was yelling this he threw off what he had placed on his head.

In (405) *mãwã* obviates the need to repeat 'they searched everyone' and in turn is suffixed with *-mĩna* 'though' to indicate that the sentence following describes an action which is contrary to the expectation of the previous sentence.

(405) *hũma-ẽnã hʉrʉ-sʰi-da-a   **mãwã-mĩna**   tai-ra nẽ   nẽ*
all-into   search-PAST-PL-DECL like^this-though 1p-ABS GEN GEN

   ẽ   pʰan-a-sʰi-da-a
   NEG be^few-IMPF-PAST-PL-DECL
   They searched everyone. Even though [they did] this, we didn't have any [weapons] at all.

---

⁴³*mãwã* is also used to introduce reported speeches, especially in EK; see §9.12.

9

Subordinate Clause

There are are two classes of subordinate clause in NE—adverbial and embedded. Adverbial clauses may precede or follow the main clause. Embedded clauses which act as main clause constituents include relative clauses (§§9.9–9.10) and sentential complements (§§9.11–9.12).

9.1–9.8 Adverbial clause

A sentence may include several adverbial clauses (see §8.1). Whereas the main clause has tense, number, aspect, and mood morphemes (§§6.11–6.30), the adverbial clause has verbal suffixes, postpositions, or subordinating conjunctions which specify temporal, purposive, conditional, or logical relationships between itself and the main clause. In addition, some adverbial clauses contain morphemes that indicate direction, aspect, number, and tense. As stated in §§6.11–6.13, tense in adverbial clauses is not absolute; it is relative to the tense of the main clause. The tense markers usually occur immediately before the indicator of the relationship between the adverbial clause and the main clause.

The following sections describe the relationships of the adverbial clauses to the main clauses and any co-occurrence restrictions. Temporal, conditional, and concessive adverbials usually occur prior to the main clause. Purpose and reason clauses occur principally after the main clause.

9.1 Overlapping event clause. When the event or state described in the adverbial clause overlaps temporally with that of the main clause, the adverbial clause contains either a present progressive suffix -*puru*/-*puta* on the verb or else a stative verb with a present tense vowel. All such constructions end in -*de* (§5.7). The present progressive suffixes are normally used when the adverbial is an action. In (406) the event in the adverbial clause is an act of speaking, so the present progressive suffixes are evident.

(406) ara   mãwã   hara-***puru**-de* Anancio-ra   peu-pa-či-a
       same   like^this   say-PRES-in   Anancio-ABS die-HAB-PAST-DECL
       Just like he said, Anancio died as he had before.

If the adverbial clause refers to a state rather than an action, then the stative verb with a present tense vowel is used. In (407) the adverbial clause indicates that the animal was in the state of needing to urinate.

(407) tʰuetʰuepa-ra   mãũ-ne   čʰiwa   pʰúatʰa   kʰer-a-sʰi-a
       animal^sp.-ABS   this-in urinate   hurt   DESC-IMPF-PAST-DECL

       mãwã   ***b-u-de***   tʰuetʰuepa-pa   wãyã   iwidi-sʰi-a
       like^this   be-PRES-in   animal^sp.-ABL   again   ask-PAST-DECL

       ačʰe   mũ-ra   čʰiwa   pʰúa   nũ-m-u-a
       friend   1S-ABS   urinate   hurt   stand-be-PRES-DECL
       Then the *tuetueba* (bird) had to urinate badly. That being the case, [he] said again, "Hey, I've got to go badly."

In (408) the action of the main clause occurs as the state of the adverbial clause continues. While the echoes of gunshots continue, a man appears.

(408) pʰõwã-ta   hĩkua   nũ-m-e-sʰi-a   mãwã   ***b-u-de***
       rifle-ABS^FOC   sound   stand-be-PERF-PAST-DECL   like^this   be-PRES-in

       sʼe-sʰi-a   ũmãkʰĩrã   sʼa   b-u-ta
       come-PAST-DECL   man   here   be-PRES-ABS^FOC
       A rifle started sounding. While this was happening, there came a man who looked just like him.

Harms (1994:153) states that the suffix -*misʰa* 'while' indicates that the action of the main clause is started and completed during the action of the adverbial clause. This can also be said of NEP, with the stipulation that the adverbial clause action be ongoing and not punctiliar. (In EK, -*misʰa* is not attested, and there is no exact equivalent of it.)

Subordinate Clause 115

(409) paripuru pu-a pio waka-i-ta b-u-a tai traha
but 2S-ABL really care-IRR-FOC be-PRES-DECL 1p work

    pʰan-u-**misʰa** (NEP)
    be^few-PRES-while
but you have to take really good care of them while we're working

(410) māma tau čʰiru b-u-**misʰa** kʰuriwa-ra ẽtru
there-LOC eye sting[44] be-PRES-while guatín-ABS go^out

    wã-sʰi-a (NEP)
    go-PAST-DECL
While [the vulture's] eye was still stinging, the guatín got out [of the hole] and escaped.

Both NE languages, especially EK, attach -*puru-para* 'when, by the time' to the end of the adverbial clause to indicate that as one event is being completed, another event is already being carried out in the main clause.

(411) mu-a mãũ pedea ūrī-***puru-para*** māwã-sʰi-a (EK)
1S-ABL this word hear-PRES-time say-PAST-DECL
When I listened to this voice it said...

(412) māwā čʰũ tʰotʰo-***puru-para*** pʰũãtru sʰida tʰau
like^this quiet go-PRES-time wind also^ABS stop

    tʰotʰo-sʰi-a (EK)
    go-PRES-DECL
When the voice quieted, the wind stopped, too.

(413) tidu hũẽ-***puru-para*** mãũ-ne wẽrã-pa kʰuda-ra hãpa-de
inside arrive-PRES-time this-in woman-ABL baggage-ABS canoe-in

    eda pué eru-b-a-sʰi-a (NEP)
    into load have-be-IMPF-PAST-DECL
By the time he got to the hunting house, the woman had all the baggage loaded into the canoe.

In NEP, -*para* marks contrary-to-fact conditions. See §9.5.

---

[44]It has not been possible to ascertain the exact meaning of this morpheme.

9.2 Sequential event clause. Adverbial clauses describing an action occurring before the main clause event carry the suffixes -*sʰi-de*, -*ta*, -*pʰeda*, or, in NEP, the past participle suffix -*da*/-*na* plus the subordinating conjunction *kʰarea*. The first marker, -*sʰi-de*, provides a temporal setting at the beginning of a story or in a new scene of a story. The next two markers indicate that the same subject has been carrying out the action in the subordinate clause as will carry it out in the main clause. The third marker indicates a change of subject between the two clauses. In EK, -*i* is used instead of -*da*/-*na kʰarea* to mark the change of subject.

The combination of the past tense suffix -*sʰi* with -*de* 'in' provides a temporal setting for a story. If the time of an action by a plural subject provides the temporal setting, then the plural suffix -*da* is inserted between -*sʰi* and -*de*. In (414) from NEP, 'when we were youths' provides the temporal setting at the beginning of the story.

(414) tai   nããna kũtra   pʰan-a-**sʰi-de**   mũ   čapa   na-pema
       1p   before youth   be^few-IMPF-PAST-in   1s   brother ahead-ORIG

       ũmẽ Quía-de-pa   wã-sʰi-da-a   to   Napipí a-pa-ta-da
       two Quía-in-ABL go-PAST-PL-DECL river Napipí say-HAB-PL-GOAL
       Before, when we were youths, my older brother and I went from the Quía [River] to the river called Napipí.

When -*sʰi-de* is used in the middle of a story it provides a new temporal setting, as in (415) from EK.

(415) ya   mãwã   o-de   pʉ-**sʰi-de**   wĩkʰa   ariku   b-a-sʰi-a
       now   like^this trail-in   walk-PAST-in   small   better be-IMPF-PAST-DECL

       pia   ariku   b-a   ẽ   pa-sʰi-a   mãwã-mĩna
       good   better be-IMPF   NEG EQ-PAST-DECL   like^this-though
       After walking on the trail, I felt a little better. I still wasn't feeling that well, though.

The suffix -*ta* signals that a continued action, marked by the present progressive -*pʉrʉ*/-*pʉta* or a stative verb with tense/aspect vowel -*ʉ* (§2.12), ends with the action of the main clause. In (416) the action in the adverbial clause 'going along' ends with the main clause action 'we saw chimpanzees'.

Subordinate Clause

(416) wã-pʉ-ta-**ta**   mãũ-ne tai-pa yerrehe-ta   ũnũ-sʰi-da-a
go-PRES-PL-SUBD this-in 1p-ABL chimpanzee-ABS^FOC see-PAST-PL-DECL

ũme
two

Going along, then we saw chimpanzees, two of them.

In (417) the use of the stative *tuan-* with tense/aspect vowel *-ʉ* portrays the adverbial as lasting for some time before it ends with the action of the main clause.

(417) wẽrã-rã   paira   tuan-e-sʰi-da-a   mãwã   paira
woman-PL dance be^many-PERF-PAST-PL-DECL like^this dance

tuan-ʉ-ta   ãsʰa-podo-de   kʰãĩke-sʰi-da-a
be^many-PRES-SUBD daylight-IMM^FUT-in fall^asleep-PAST-PL-DECL

Women started to dance. Dancing like this until nearly daylight, they fell asleep.

(418) illustrates how *-pʰeda* (*-pʰe* in EK) marks an action as completed before the main clause event is carried out.[45]

(418) Anancio-ra   pʰiratrʉ-**pʰeda** pʰata   o   b-e-sʰi-a
Anancio-ABS get^up-after   plantain make be-PERF-PAST-DECL

After Anancio got up, he began making dinner.

In NEP, the combination of the past participle suffix *-da/-na* with the subordinating conjunction *kʰarea* signals not only that the action of the adverbial clause is completed (see §6.17), but also a change of subject for the main clause which follows.

(419) čipari-rã   kʰewara   tida   hũẽ-**na**   kʰarea   ara   mãũ-ta
parent-PL afternoon home arrive-PPRT DS   same this-SUBD

kʰuriwa-pa nẽ ba-ra   tʰue   tia-sʰi-a
guatín-ABL GEN liquid-ABS scoop give-PAST-DECL

Once the parents came home in the afternoon, the guatín served them the soup.

---

[45]In EK, *-pʰe* is augmented to *kʰãrẽma-pʰe* as a rhetorical slowdown device which builds anticipation before an important event (Mareike Schöttelndreyer, personal communication).

(420) māwã   či   kʰuriwa-pa hara-**da** **kʰarea** imama-ra čʰupʰea
 like^this REF guatín-ABL say-PPRT DS   jaguar-ABS quiet

    pʰan-e-sʰi-da-a
    be^few-PERF-PAST-PL-DECL
    After the guatín said this, the jaguars said no more.

EK does not employ the above construction for completed action and change of subject. Rather, the verb suffix -*i* is used.

(421) māwã   tia-da-***i***   traha nũ-m-e-sʰi-a   mũ-ra
 like^this give-PL-CMPL^DS work stand-be-PERF-PAST-DECL 1S-PIVOT

    ewari ũme-pai traha-sʰi-a   (EK)
    day   two-LIM work-PAST-DECL
    Once they gave me work, I began working; I worked just two days.

In NEP, a special use of the past participle suffix -*da*/-*na* signals that participants in a story are going off stage. In these cases, the thematic demonstrative *mãũ* precedes the verb and the different subject marker *kʰarea* is not used.

(422) **mãũ** wã-**na** b-a-sʰi-a   waa   s'e   ẽ   pa-sʰi-a
 this go-PPRT be-IMPF-PAST-DECL more come NEG EQ-PAST-DECL
    This one was gone. He didn't come again.

(423) mãũpe **mãũ** ũmãkʰĩrã wã-**na** hẽtare   te   wãtekʰare
 then this man   go-PPRT back^DIR house up^river

    pʰõwã-ta   hĩkua nũ-m-e-sʰi-a
    rifle-ABS^FOC sound stand-be-PERF-PAST-DECL
    Then, once this man was gone, just up river from the house a rifle started sounding.

Sequential events in future time are shown by the same markers as above with the difference that future tense marking may appear in the main clause. Alternatively, conditional morphemes may appear in the dependent clause (see §9.5).

(424) ārã-rã   peu   kʰãĩke-**da**   **kʰarea** mũ-a   hũma
 3P^ALT-PL drunk fall^asleep-PPRT DS   1S-ABL all

Subordinate Clause 119

    kʰēnā-ya-a
    slaughter-FUT-DECL
Once they are drunk and have fallen asleep, I will slaughter them all.

In EK, the suffixation of irrealis -i and -eda 'GOAL' on the verb of the adverbial clause expresses 'until'.

(425) pʉ-a   kʰrĩña-pʉrʉ Aurelio sʲe-**i-eda**   mũ ũme tai sʲesʲe
    2S-ABL want-COND Aurelio come-IRR-GOAL 1S two 1p father

    pedea bʉ-da-ya-a   a-sʰi-a
    word put-PL-FUT-DECL say-PAST-DECL
"If you want, you can translate God's Word with me until Aurelio comes," she said.

9.3 Antecedence clause. In NEP, the time adverb *nāẽna* 'before' used as a subordinating conjunction indicates that the event in the main clause occurs before the event in the adverbial clause. The verb in the adverbial clause is marked with the irrealis suffix -i since the event in it is future relative to that of the main clause.

(426) māẽpʉrʉ   či kʰuriwa-ra tida sʲe-sʰi-a   imama
    [new^dev.] REF guatín-ABS home come-PAST-DECL jaguar

    sʲe-i   **nāẽna**
    come-IRR before
Then the guatín came home before the jaguar did.

In EK, quite distinct morphology is employed. The future marker -ya followed by the completive -ma and the limiter -pai together indicate that the verb onto which they are suffixed has not yet taken place when the main clause action transpires.

(427) tiamasʰe kʰãĩ-**ya-ma-pai** sʰopʰua nũ-m-e-sʰi-a   aʉtre
    night sleep-FUT-CMPL-LIM sad stand-be-PERF-PAST-DECL extra

    plata nẽ^ẽã-pa
    money without-ABL
Before I went to sleep that night, I started feeling sad because I had no more money.

9.4 Purpose clause.
As in ES, the different ways of marking purpose clauses in NE depend on whether the purpose is immediate or consequent and, to a lesser extent, on whether the subject of the purpose clause is the same as that of the main clause.

(428) Marker Use
  -de   immediate purpose, same subject (with motion verbs only)
  mãrẽã   immediate purpose, almost always different subject; negative purpose
  -i kʰãrẽã consequent purpose (NEP)
  -i-tʰa   consequent purpose (EK)

If the main verb is one of the motion verbs *wã* 'go' or *sʲe* 'come', its purpose clause is terminated with a verb suffixed with *-de* 'in', as long as the subject of both clauses is the same. Harms says that for ES the purpose must be immediate (1994:158). This seems also to be the case in NE, where the purpose is immediate and obvious.

(429) ara   mãũ   kʰewara   mĩã   huru-de   wã-sʰi-da-a   mũ   čapa
      same   this afternoon GEN   seek-in   go-PAST-PL-DECL 1S   brother

      ũmẽ
      two
      That same afternoon my brother and I went to seduce [a certain young woman].

(430) mãẽpuru   kʰuriwa-ra   wã-sʰi-a   tʰro-ma   pedea-de
      [new dev.]   guatín-ABS   go-PAST-DECL   armadillo-LOC   talk-in
      Then the guatín went to talk to the armadillo.

If the main verb is one of the motion verbs mentioned above but the subject has ergative case marking, then the motion verb is acting as an auxiliary for the verb suffixed with *-de* (§6.9).

In most other purpose clauses, the verb in the purpose clause carries the irrealis suffix *-i* and is followed by the subordinating conjunction *kʰãrẽã*. The purpose in these clauses is not immediate but consequent on other actions being performed first. Since *kʰãrẽã* is the reason marker, the purpose may be viewed as a future reason.

Subordinate Clause

(431) pʰaratʰa eta-i   kʰā̃rēã mū-ra ya   pʰúa b-ʉ-a
      money   get-IRR REASON 1sg-ABS now hurt be-PRES-DECL
      I'm going to have a hard time getting my pay now.

Example (432) has first an immediate purpose by the same subject *(-de)* and then a consequent purpose by a different subject *(-i kʰā̃rēã)*. The nursing of the children depends on the guatín's getting them for the mother.

(432) kʰuriwa ete-de wã-tua mũ wárra-rã   mũ-a   hu
      guatín get-in go-IMPV 1S offspring-PL 1S-ABL breast

      tawa-i   kʰā̃rēã
      give^drink-IRR REASON
      Guatín, go get my children so I may nurse them!

In (433) *-i kʰā̃rēã* is used since the consequent purpose of *wãsʰia* 'went' is to kill the deceitful guatín. The immediate purpose is *pʰe* 'collect' which has been combined with *wãsʰia* in a serial verb meaning 'chase'.

(433) imama-ra kʰuriwa kʰaidu pʰe   wã-sʰi-a   pea-i   kʰā̃rēã
      jaguar-ABS guatín follow collect go-PAST-DECL kill-IRR REASON
      The jaguar chased after the guatín in order to kill her.

Consequent purpose in EK is indicated by the irrealis and focus suffixes *-i-tʰa*.

(434) mãma estudia-i-tʰa   wã-sʰi-mĩna   estudia b-e   ẽ
      there study-IRR-FOC GO-PAST-though study be-PERF NEG

      pa-sʰi-a
      EQ-PAST-DECL
      Even though I was going to study there, I wasn't able to.

When a clause describes the immediate purpose of the main clause but the main verb is not a verb of motion, the marker is *mā̃rēã*. In ES this conjunction indicates that the purpose clause and main clause have different subjects (Harms 1994:159). This is almost always true for NE *mā̃rēã*.

In (432) the mother jaguar told the guatín to get her children so she could nurse them. In that case *-i kʰā̃rēã* was used, since the nursing was consequent on the children being brought. In (435), which also has different subjects in the two clauses, *mā̃rēã* is employed, without *-i* 'irrealis'.

(435) ēnē-pʰeda   či   pʰapʰa-a   tia-sʰi-a   hu   tawa
      bring-after REF mother-IO give-PAST-DECL breast give^drink

   mãrēã
   PURP

   After bringing them, she gave them to their mother so she could nurse them.

Typically, purposes expressed in clauses ending with *mãrēã* are thematic and known or expected. This is consistent with the use of the demonstrative *mã-* to mark thematic information (§10.1). By the time (435) was uttered, the hearers already knew from the context of (432) that the reason for giving the children to their mother was so she could nurse them. The same *mãrēã* marks all negative purpose clauses, regardless of subject, theme or scope.

(436) mũ cinturón pia   hũ-sʰi-a   mũ pantalón wẽã-rã
      1S belt   good   tie-PAST-DECL   1S pants   take^off-NEG^IRR

   mãrēã
   PURP
   I buckled my belt well so my pants wouldn't fall down.

9.5 Conditional clause. Conditional clauses usually occur before their accompanying result clauses. There are two classes of conditionals in NE—contrafactual and factual. Contrafactuals have only one basic marker, so these will be handled first.

Contrafactual conditions are those that are either thought to be currently impossible or are hypothetical conditions from the past and also quite impossible. Both employ the same construction. The verb of the conditional clause in NEP is suffixed with *-para* and the verb of the result clause takes the hypothetical suffix *-kʰá* (Loewen 1958:138, Harms 1994:160–61). This is illustrated in (437), which is from Loewen (1958:171).

(437) mu-ta   kʰakʰua entero pasa-da-**para**   kʰuriwa-ra nẽ ẽ
      1S-ABS^FOC body   entire pass-PPRT-time   guatín-ABS GEN NEG

   pa-**kʰá**-sʰi-a
   EQ-HYP-PAST-DECL
   If I had passed with my whole body, there would be no more rabbits.

Subordinate Clause 123

The EK contrafactual is a true conditional since it uses the conditional suffix -*pɨrɨ*. The hypothetical suffix in EK is -*kʰau*.

(438) *mɨ-ta   kʰakʰua entero pasa-da-pɨrɨ   kʰuriwa-ra nẽ   ẽ*
      1S-ABS^FOC body   entire pass-PPRT-COND guatín-ABS   GEN NEG

   pa-kʰau-sʰi-a
   EQ-HYP-PAST-DECL

   If I had passed with my whole body, there would be no more rabbits.

In NEP, however, the use of the hypothetical suffix -*kʰá* is not attested in any recent text material from Colombian speakers. What is used nowadays by younger speakers is the irrealis suffix -*i* on the main verb and a stative auxiliary verb in number agreement with the subject of the clause and in past tense.

(439) *mū̃-ta   hāũ   ewari-de nãma b-e-da-para   tiauru-pa*
      1S-ABS^FOC that   day-on   here be-PERF-PPRT-time   demon-ABL

   mū̃-ra pea-i   b-a-sʰi-a
   1S-ABS kill-IRR be-IMPF-PAST-DECL

   If I had stayed here that day, the devil would have killed me.

Factual conditionals in the present tense take various forms but all have either -*ra* or -*pɨrɨ*. The quandary of predicting which suffix is used is evident in ES (Harms 1994:159–60). In NE, though, -*pɨrɨ* seems to affirm a condition that, from the context, seems likely anyhow.[46]

(440) *sʰukʰura-ta   to-di-pɨrɨ   pãči huware-pa   hue*
      cane^juice-ABS^FOC drink-FUT^PL-COND 2p   right^hand-ABL scoop

   to-da-tua
   drink-PL-IMPV

   If you're really going to drink some cane juice, scoop it out with your right hand and drink it!

(441) *pɨ-a-pɨrɨ   kʰawa b-ɨ-a   pɨči-ta   mãwã*
      2S-ABL-FOC^GI   know be-PRES-DECL   2S^COREF-ABS^FOC like^that

---

[46] In the SE languages, the cognate suffix combination includes the certainty focus suffix -*pɨ/pɨ̈*.

    wã-i-**pɨrɨ**
    go-IRR-COND
You decide whether you actually want to go like that.

(442) pɨ-a   piyo-pɨrɨ   harra   b-ɨ-**pɨrɨ**   ara   ẽ-a
      2S-ABL very-FOC^GI be^hungry be-PRES-COND reach NEG-DECL
      If you are real hungry, you are not going to fill up.[47]

The suffix *-ra* by itself seems to put the question on whether something will happen. In this sense, it is a true conditional.

(443) ačʰe   hosʰo   pɨ-a   mũ-ta kʰĩrã čupuria-**ra** mũ-a kʰimi
      friend anteater 2S-ABL 1S-ABS face mercy-COND 1S-ABL bee

      hõ-ta   ũnũ iru-b-ɨ-a
      fruit-ABS^FOC see have-be-PRES-DECL
      Anteater, my friend, if you do me a favor, I'll show you where some honey is.

Related to this is the marker *-sʰira*, which apparently is a combination of the past tense marker *-sʰi* and the conditional suffix *-ra*. It marks conditionals that carry the time element 'once X happens/once X is done, after that...'. This marker is also common in procedural discourse, as shown in (445).

(444) mũ kʰo-pue-pɨrɨ-**sʰira**   harra   ẽ-a
      1S   eat-VOL-FOC^GI-COND hunger NEG-DECL
      If he does eat me, after that I won't be hungry any more.

(445) pio   uruka nũ-m-e-**sʰira**   pɨ-ra tida   pʰira s'e-tua
      really burn stand-be-PERF-COND 2S-ABS home run come-IMPV
      Once it really starts burning, come running home!

9.6 Reason clause.
The reason clause ends with the morpheme *-era/-ẽrã* on stative verbs or, in NEP, with the conjunction *pẽrã/pera* after regular verbs.[48] This conjunction is a combination of the equative verb *pa-* and *-era/-ẽrã*. When the conjunction follows the past tense suffix *-sʰi*, the reason is a past action, as in (446). If the conjunction follows *-da/-na*, the reason is a resultant state. In (447) the guatín is in a state of being scared.

---

    [47]This example is from Loewen 1958:165–6.
    [48]This usage is directly related to the use of the sentence introducer *mãũ pẽrã/pera* (§8.5).

Subordinate Clause 125

(446) ara   mãũ-ta   iči-ra   kʰĩrũ-sʰi-a   iči sʰukʰura-ta
same this-SUBD 3S-ABS get^mad-PAST-DECL 3S cane^juice-ABS^FOC

    warrá ẽ   to-sʰi   **pẽrã**
    tasty NEG drink-PAST because
Then he got mad because when he drank his cane juice it didn't taste good.

(447) ačʰe   hãũ kʰuriwa beya   tʰrũ-ni-a   tači pʰera-pue-**da**
friend that guatín   whistle call-FUT^PL-DECL 1p   fear-VOL-PPRT

    pera
    because
Hey, let's call that guatín out by whistling, because he's scared of us.

The EK form *pa-era* reflects more accurately the true morphological structure.

(448) kʰãrẽ o-i   nẽ^ẽ   **paera** trua ãĩ   b-ʉ   paera
what make-IRR without because land outside be-PRES because

    sʼupuria kʰričʰa b-e-sʰi-a
    pity   think   be-PERF-PAST-DECL
Since I had nothing to do and because I was outside my land, I started to pity myself.

9.7 Concessive clause. Concessive adverbial clauses indicate that the information of the following main clause is the opposite of the expectation generated by the previous main clause. In NE concessive clauses are marked by the verb suffix *-mĩna* 'though' or the conjunction *paripʉrʉ* 'but'. The concessive suffix *-mĩna* is most commonly seen acting as a sentence introducer in combination with *mãwã* 'like this' (§8.8).

The concessive suffix *-mĩna* marks an attempt, suggestion, or expectation in the adverbial clause which proves to be unfulfilled or unfruitful by the content of the following main clause. In (449) a character's suggestion has been ignored; *-mĩna* is used to indicate that the expectation was that his suggestion would be followed.

(449) mãwã   hara-pʉrʉ-mĩna wapema-pa pʰãnu-na ẽ   pa-sʰi-a
     like^this say-PRES-though others-ABL answer-PL NEG EQ-PAST-DECL
     Even though he was saying this, the rest of them did not answer.

In (450) mãwã-mĩna introduces an event which was contrary to the expectation created by the previous sentence.

(450) Anancio-pa hẽta akʰʉ-sʰi-a   mãwã-mĩna   Anancio-pa
     Anancio-ABL back look-PAST-DECL   like^this-though Anancio-ABL

     ũnũ ẽ   b-a-sʰi-a
     see NEG be-IMPF-PAST-DECL
     Anancio looked back. Even though [he did] this, he didn't see anything.

On the other hand, *paripʉrʉ* indicates that the clause preceding it contains a factual action which will be tempered by another statement in the clause that follows. Unlike *-mĩna, paripʉrʉ* does not imply that the opposite of this statement would have been expected, only that the statement in some way opposes the previous proposition. In (451) the passengers of a ship can see the hills of Panama City, but this is tempered by the fact that they will not be able to see the city itself for quite some time.

(451) mãwã   nĩ-ne   tãrã-pʉrʉ-de   ũnũ-pa-ri-a   Panama
     like^this walk-in delay-PRES-in   see-HAB-SG-DECL Panama

     eya-ta   paripʉrʉ wadi pida tãrã-pa-ri-a
     hill-ABS^FOC but   still also delay-HAB-SG-DECL

     Panama puru   ũnu-i   kãrẽã
     Panama village see-IRR REASON
     After going like that for a long time, you can see the hills of Panama City, but it is still a long time until you can see the city itself.

9.8 Repeated subordinate clause. NE speakers repeat subordinate verb phrases to indicate that the action concerned took place over an extended period of time and ended with the action of the main clause. The repeated subordinate verb phrase almost always employs the main verb of the previous sentence, and the number of repetitions determines the relative time lapse between the previous and following main clauses. Two

Subordinate Clause

repetitions are normal. Three indicate a longer lapse, and one indicates a comparatively short lapse.

The form of these verb phrases is that of sequential event clauses (§9.2), although not all repeated subordinate clauses are suffixed with -*ta*, as seen in (453).

(452) *ete wã-sʰi-a ete wã-pɨrɨ-ta ete wã-pɨrɨ-ta ara*
take go-PAST-DECL take go-PRES-SUBD take go-PRES-SUBD very

  kʰaitʰa b-a-pɨrɨ-de
  near be-IMPF-PRES-in
  He took them along. Taking them a long way, when they were right near there...

(453) *Anancio-ra pʰata o-sʰi-a pʰata o b-ɨ*
Anancio-ABS plantain make-PAST-DECL plantain make be-PRES

  pʰata o b-ɨ pʰata wi-sʰi-a
  plantain make be-PRES plantain be^ready-PAST-DECL
  Anancio made a meal. He cooked and cooked and then it was ready.

(454) *ete wã-sʰi-a ete wã-ta ete wã-ta či eya ɨra*
take go-PAST-DECL take go-SUBD take go-SUBD REF hill cave^in

  hira b-ɨ-ma hũẽ-sʰi-da-a
  hang be-PRES-LOC arrive-PAST-PL-DECL
  He took them along. He took them on and on and they arrived at the place where the hill was caved in.

9.9–9.10 Relative clause

Like ES (Harms 1994:166), NE has internally headed relative clauses. The noun phrase which acts as the head of the relative clause is most often followed by a restrictive clause, which restricts the reference of the head but, occasionally, the head occurs within the relative clause.

The only NP position which can be relativized is the absolutive. This is also true of ECh but is in stark contrast with ES and ET, where ergatives and obliques can also be relativized. This phenomenon is in general agreement with Keenan and Comrie's noun phrase accessibility hierarchy[49] reformulated as two specific universals, "(a) every language can relativize on subjects; (b) any relative clause strategy must cover a continuous segment of the accessibility hierarchy" (Comrie 1989:158). However, a very important caveat for universal (a) is necessary for NE—that transitive subjects cannot be relativized. Conversely, even though direct objects are putatively less accessible than subjects, they can be relativized in NE. To reiterate, this is because NE only relativizes absolutives. Phenomena of this nature led Fox to challenge Keenan and Comrie "on two counts: (a) it seems to be the category absolutive, rather than subject, which occupies the left-most position on the accessibility hierarchy; and (b) it is the discourse function of S- and P-relatives...which gives them prominence in languages across the world" (Fox 1987:869).

For NE, this hierarchy is indeed one of ease in communication. NE only relativizes absolutives because they do not require a case suffix (see §5.2). Since case suffixes are used obligatorily to demarcate the end of relative clauses (see §9.10), any case marker not used in this way would confuse hearers into thinking that the relative clause had ended in a different place from what a speaker intended. Therefore, it is absolutely necessary, given the morphology of the language, that NE only relativize the absolutive case.

The case marking appropriate to the function of the resulting noun phrase in the main clause is attached to the final word in the relative clause, which is usually the verb, not the head noun. (An exception to this is shown in (456).) The relativized verb is preceded by only one other clause constituent. As in other subordinate clauses, the tense of the verb in a relative clause relates to that of the main clause, not to the time of utterance.

In the examples in §§9.9–9.10, the relative clause is put in brackets, and the case marking it carries is outside the right bracket.

9.9 Noun head. The head of a relative clause is a noun or noun phrase which is most often initial in the relative construction and usually acts as its subject. In the relative clause *pakʰuru bʉa tʰudapa* 'with a stick he had broken off' in (455), *pakʰuru* 'stick' is the direct object in the relative clause; the relative clause as a whole is used as an instrumental phrase and is appropriately marked with the ablative suffix *-pa*.

---

[49]"...the hierarchy subject > direct object > non-direct object > possessor defines ease of accessibility to relative clause formation, i.e., it is, in some intuitive sense, easier to relativize subjects than it is to relativize any of the other positions, easier to relativize direct objects than possessors, etc." (Comrie 1989:156).

Subordinate Clause 129

(455) ūmākʰīrā-pa [pakʰuru bʉa   tʰu-da]-**pa**   hūma u
      man-ABL   stick break chop-PPRT-ABL all   swat

      kʰēnā-kʰua-pʉrʉ-de
      slaughter-REPT-PRES-in
when the man was beating and killing every one of them with a stick he had broken off

In (456) the noun *wárra* 'offspring' is the head of the relative clause but it occurs following the verb rather than first. Since it is the last constituent of the relative clause, the case suffix is attached to it, rather than to the verb.

(456) tiamasʰi mīčʰi-pa [mū ūmẽ sʼe-da   wárra]-**ra**   pia
      night   cat-ABL 1s two come-PPRT offspring-ABS good

      pʰera-pue-sʰi-a
      scare-VOL-PAST-DECL
[That] night, a cat really scared the boy who had come with me.

9.10 Headless relative clause. Many relative clauses in NE do not have syntactic heads. As in ES, the relative clause as a whole refers to a person or object for which its content is true (Harms 1994:168). The English equivalent of this is 'the one that'. The implied head of a headless relative clause must be an understood noun in the absolutive case in the relative clause, since NE only permits absolutives to be relativized. As with headed relative clauses, the case marker denoting the function of the relative clause in the main clause occurs at the end of said relative clause.

Examples (457)–(460) all have headless relative clauses, which are bracketed.

(457) mãũ-ne [tida tuan-u-rā]-**pa**   ūnū-sʰi-da-a
      this-in home be^many-PRES-PL-ABL   see-PAST-PL-DECL
Then those who were at home saw it.

(458) mãũ-ne [poro-de eru-kʰo-b-a-da]-**ra**   wēātʰare-tua
      this-in head-on have-POS-be-IMPF-PPRT-ABS   throw^off-IMPV
Then throw off what you have on your head!

Even in fairly simple noun phrases, the relative clause is preferred over a noun plus an adjective. Harms (1994:166–7) says that in ES, 'dog that was white' is preferable to 'white dog'. This is also true of NE. In (459), rather than saying 'to his friend', the speaker uses a headless relative clause and says 'to the one who had been his friend'. The indirect object suffix -a is attached to the verb *pada* 'had been'.

(459) *hara-sʰi-a*   [*iči či^pia pa-da*]-*a*   *mũ-ra wã-pɨrɨ-a*
      say-PAST-DECL   3S   friend   EQ-PPRT-IO   1S-ABS   go-PRES-DECL

      a-sʰi-a
      say-PAST-DECL
He said to the one who had been his friend, "I'm leaving."

The reason the relative clause 'those who were jaguars' is used in (460) is because 'jaguars' by itself would mean only spotted American jaguars. It is known from the context, however, that this group included black panthers, ocelots, and other species. The verb form *tuanarãra* 'were' carries both the plural and absolutive suffixes.

(460) *mãwã-pɨrɨ-de*   [*imama tuan-a-rã*]-*ra*   *hũma-ẽnã*
      like^this-PRES-in   jaguar   be^many-IMPF-PL-ABS   all-into

      pʰira-kʰua wã-pɨrɨ-sʰi-da-a
      run-REPT   go-PL^MANY-PAST-PL-DECL
When he said this, all of those who were big cats ran away.

9.11–9.12 Complementation

Relative clauses and clauses that involve sentential complement relationships are difficult to distinguish in NE in that both involve the embedding of a clause in the position of an argument. The difference between the two is that in relative clauses the head noun phrase, whether overt or not, is a participant in both the main clause and the relative clause. In complement constructions, however, there is no head, and the entire clause serves as a complement to the verb of the main clause.

9.11 Standard complementation. Cognitive and sensory verbs often have subordinate clauses as their complements, which are marked by the absolutive focus marker *-ta*. Most complement clauses occur after the main verb.

Subordinate Clause

(461) mũ-a mẽã   ũnũ-sʰi-a   itua   to   tuan-u-**ta**
      1S-ABL jungle see-PAST-DECL liquor drink be^many-PRES-ABS^FOC
      In the jungle I saw people drinking liquor!

(462) pʉ-a   pida ũrĩ   b-ʉ-kʰa   tikʰo   hĩkua
      2S-ABL also hear be-PRES-POLAR Victrola sound

    nũ-m-ʉ-**ta**
    stand-be-PRES-ABS^FOC
    Do you also hear the Victrola sounding?

(463) mãũ-ne usʰa-ta   beru b-ʉ-ta   ũrĩ-sʰi-a
      this-in dog-ABS^FOC   bark be-PRES-ABS^FOC   hear-PAST-DECL
      Then he heard a dog bark.

In (464) the complement clause is followed by another in apposition; both are marked with -*ta*.

(464) mãũ-ne ũnũ-sʰi-a   hĩrũ tʰuka wã-pʉrʉ-ta   wãrãka hĩrũ
      this-in see-PAST-DECL   foot step go-PRES-ABS^FOC   up^river foot

    ũme ũmãkʰĩrã   hĩrũ-**ta**   wẽrã   ũmẽ
    two man   foot-ABS^FOC   woman   two
    Then he saw footprints that were going up river. There were two sets: those of man with a woman's.

Complement clauses can be shortened to single words if the complement is an equative clause.

(465) mãũ-ne-pʉrʉ   mũ-a   kʰawa-sʰi-a   tiauru-**ta**
      this-in-FOC^GI   1S-ABL know-PAST-DECL demon-ABS^FOC
      That's when I realized he was a demon.

(466) mũ-a   kʰrĩčʰa-sʰi-a   mĩpu-**ta**
      1S-ABL think-PAST-DECL   fish^sp.-ABS^FOC
      I thought it was a *mĩbu* fish.

9.12 Reported quotations. The transition in NE culture from completely oral storytelling to having some legends written down has put quotation structures in a transition phase. In particular, the orienter which marks the end of a reported speech is no longer obligatory.

Direct quotations employ a main clause orienter stating the action of speaking (usually a verb other than *a-* 'say in a quote') followed by the exact content of the quotation and the closing orienter, which is the verb *a-* provided it is not the first verb. Many quotations still follow this structure and the same structure can be used with sensory verbs as well.

(467) **hara-s^hi-a**   iči či^pia b-a-da-a   mʉ̃-ra wã-pʉrʉ-a
      say-PAST-DECL 3S friend be-IMPF-PPRT-IO 1S-ABS go-PRES-DECL

      a-s^hi-a
      say-PAST-DECL
He told the one who had been his friend, "I'm leaving," he said.

(468) wẽrã-pa   k^hawa-s^hi-a   mʉ̃-ra animarã-pʉrʉ hãwã   ete
      woman-ABL know-PAST-DECL   1S   demon-FOC^GI like^that take

      w̃a-pʉrʉ-k^ha   **a-s^hi-a**
      go-PRES-POLAR say-PAST-DECL
The woman realized, "Am I being taken away by a demon?" were her words.

However, the language change mentioned above is manifest in that the double quotation orienter is not always used. In (469) the form of the verb *a-* is absent.

(469) mãʉ̃-ne iči-a   hara-s^hi-a   mãwã   ẽ-a   Anancio pʉ-a
      this-in 3S-ABL say-PAST-DECL like^this NEG-DECL Anancio 2S-ABL

      hʉ̃k^hara t^hu-de   wã-tua
      vine   chop-in go-IMPV
And he said, "No, Anancio. Go cut a vine!"

Indirect quotations have the same structure as the sensory complement clauses discussed in §9.11, but any reference to the person reporting the speech stays in first person rather than being changed to third person as in English. This is most obvious in (470) from EK.

(470) a. mãwẽ   mʉ̃-a   ariwia   widi-s^hi-a   mãʉ̃   plata   s^hãwã
         [new^dev.] 1S-ABL strong ask-PAST-DECL this money how

Subordinate Clause

  o-i *para-tʰa* *kʰawa-da* *ẽ-a* *a-sʰi-da-a* *ãči-a*
  make-IRR have-FOC know-PL NEG-DECL say-PAST-PL-DECL 3S-ABL
  Then I kept asking [them] how I should spend this money. They said they didn't know.

 b. *mũ-a-pʉrʉ* *kʰawa* *b-ʉ-a* *a-sʰi-da-a* *sʰãwã*
  1S-ABL-FOC^GI know be-PRES-DECL say-PAST-PL-DECL how

  o-i-ra
  make-IRR-ABS
  They said I should decide what to do with it. [lit., "I know, they said how to do it."]

This structure can be used for all speech-like verbs such as *kʰrĩčʰa* 'think'.

(471) *Anancio-pa* ***kʰrĩčʰa-sʰi-a*** *sʰãma* *b-ʉ-ta* *mãwã*
  Anancio-ABL think-PAST-DECL where be-PRES-ABS^FOC like^this

  pedea *b-ʉ-ta*
  talk be-PRES-ABS^FOC
  Anancio wondered where the one talking like this was.

As in ES, the manner adverb *mãwã* is used to introduce reported speeches, especially in EK, from which (472) is taken.

(472) *mope* ***mãwã-sʰi-a*** *tai* *sʹesʹe-tʰa* *mepea* *Renatʰa-á*
  [non-dev.] say-PAST-DECL 1p father-FOC sibling Renata-IO

  pedea-sʰi-pida *pʉ-á* *plata-tʰa* *tia* *mãrẽã* *hara-sʰi-pida*
  speak-PAST-RPRT 2S-IO money-FOC give PURP say-PAST-RPRT

  a *tuke-sʰi-a*
  say come-PAST-DECL
  And she came and reported: "God spoke to sister Renata and told her to give you money," she said.

10
Discourse and Pragmatic Considerations

This chapter discusses the discourse functions of the demonstrative pronouns, tracking of participants, referentials, and highlighting.

10.1 Demonstratives in discourse. The spatial versus social usage of the demonstrative adjectives, adverbs, and pronouns in NE has been discussed in §§2.7–2.8 and §4.4. This section considers the discourse uses of the demonstratives *mã-* and *hã-*, which are similar to those in Waunana (Binder 1978) and ES (Harms 1994:179–83).

Once a noun has been mentioned in a given context, its next mention is preceded by the thematic demonstrative *mã-*, if it is of any importance in the story. Most participants and props are preceded by *mã-* only once in a discourse. In (473) 'the deep place' is where the rest of the story takes place, so it is important enough to be assigned *mã-*.

(473) *hãpa-de-pa   hũẽ-sʰi-da-a   nãpua b-ʉ-mae   **mãʉ̃ nãpua***
      canoe-in-ABL arrive-PAST-PL-DECL deep   be-PRES-LOC this deep

   b-ʉ-mae
   be-PRES-LOC
   We came by canoe to a deep place. At this deep place...

Participants or objects preceded by *mã-* do not necessarily remain on stage for the duration of the discourse. Harms (1994:182) says that this is the way props are introduced in ES when they are crucial to the outworking of the story. In the NE example (474) the crocodile appears only in one scene. Nevertheless, the guatín, the main character, gets back to his home by riding on this crocodile's back. Therefore, the crocodile is introduced and then aptly preceded by *mã-*. (474) is the only occurrence of the word with *mã-*.

(474) sʲe-sʰi-a   kʰore-ta   iči-kʰaitʰa   mã̄ẽpʉrʉ
      come-PAST-DECL crocodile-ABS^FOC 3S-close   [new^dev.]

   kʰuriwa-pa   **mã̄ũ kʰore-ra**   pia   akʰʉ b-e-sʰi-a
   guatín-ABL   this   crocodile-ABS good look be-PERF-PAST-DECL
   A crocodile came close to him. Then the guatín started looking at this crocodile really closely.

Other information related to the use of sentence introducers formed with *mã-* is found in §10.11.

The demonstrative *hã-* (*kʰã-* in EK) 'that' is anaphoric in reference and signals thematic distance, including local theme in some cases. In order for *hã-* to be used, its referent must have been mentioned, seen, or heard previously. In (475) the manner adverb *hãwã* is used after the speaker witnesses the hearer running into the house.

(475) pʉ-ra   kʰãrẽ   kʰãrẽã   **hãwã**   pʰira   uru
      2S-ABS what   REASON   like^that   run   come
      Why have you come running like that?

hã- indicates that the noun it precedes is somewhat distant from the global theme, hence the term THEMATIC DISTANCE. In (476) three hungry animals are arguing over who should get to eat a small piece of bread. One argues that the oldest should get it, appealing to the fact that he was on Noah's ark. Another responds that he, too, was on the ark. Whereas the global theme is the bread, the local theme is the argument about the ark.

(476) mũ-ra   ičaba b-a   ẽ   pa-sʰi-kʰa   **hãũ** Noé   arca-de
      1S-ABS also   be-IMPF NEG EQ-PAST-POLAR that   Noah ark-in
      Wasn't I also on that ark of Noah's?

Whereas *mã-* is used anaphorically in connection with the main theme in past tense accounts, *hã-* is used if the main theme is in the future. In future procedurals, for instance, successive steps are introduced with *hãpe* (the equivalent of *mãpe/mã̄ũpe* 'and then, after that, so then'—§8.2).

Discourse and Pragmatic Considerations

(477) pʉ-a hŭkʰara-ta tʰu-de wã-tua **hãpe** pʉ-a mũ-ra
2S-ABL vine-ABS^FOC chop-in go-IMPV after^that 2S-ABL 1S-ABS

pʰečʰera o-tua
harness make-IMPV
Go cut a vine!...Now make me a harness out of it!

(478) pʉ-a mũ-ra taidu hẽsa-de ete wã-tua **hãpe** pʉ-a
2S-ABL 1S-ABS to^river gut-in take go-IMPV after^that 2S-ABL

mũ-ra bʉa tʰu-pʰeda nẽ ba o-tua
1S-ABS break chop-after GEN liquid make-IMPV
Take me to the river and gut me!...Now break me apart and make soup out of me!

Similarly, in (479), in which a crafty gautín is trying to scare away all the big cats who want to eat him and his friends, the second sentence is introduced with *hãẽpʉrʉ* (the equivalent of *mãẽpʉrʉ*—§10.11), as the action it introduces is future. The guatín feigns that his next step is to kill all the jaguars. This is based on his new liking for jaguar meat, hence the anaphora.

(479) imama čara-ra hãwã warrá b-ʉ-ta mũ-a
jaguar meat-ABS like^that tasty be-PRES-ABS^FOC 1S

atua b-a-sʰi-kʰa **hãẽpʉrʉ** imama-ra hũma
be^unaware be-IMPF-PAST-POLAR [new^dev.] jaguar-ABS all

kʰẽna-ya-a
slaughter-FUT-DECL
I didn't know jaguar meat tasted this good! *Now* I am going to kill off all the jaguars.

10.2 Introduction of participants. The main characters in a discourse are introduced in stative and equative clauses near the beginning of the story. Almost any prop or participant, when first introduced anytime in the story, is marked with the absolutive focus marker *-ta*, whether the clause is active or stative. In (480) the guatín is introduced as the friend of the vulture. In (481) the vulture himself is introduced, postposed after the verb, a common device for highlighting the introduction of a participant (see §7.1).

(480) tači s'rõã-ena kʰuriwa-**ta**   ākosʰo ūmẽ či kʰõpʰa
     1p   old-in guatín-ABS^FOC vulture two REF friend

   pa-sʰi-a
   EQ-PAST-DECL
   A long time ago the guatín was the friend of the vulture.

(481) mãũ-ne pʰʉrrʉa-de   wã-pʉrʉ-de kʰuriwa-pa ūnū-ne wã-sʰi-a
     this-in go^circle-in go-PRES-in guatín-ABL see-in go-PAST-DECL

   či kʰõpʰa ākosʰo-**ta**
   REF friend vulture-ABS^FOC
   Then while walking around he saw his mutual friend the vulture.

New participants can also be introduced to an existing scene with *s'e* 'come' as in (482).

(482) mãwã   b-ʉ-de   s'e-sʰi-a   ūmãkʰīrã s'a b-ʉ-ta
     like^this be-PRES-in come-PAST-DECL man   here be-PRES-ABS^FOC
     While this was happening, there came a man who looked just like him.

The only participants who are introduced in an active role are minor characters. In (483) the *poropʰare* 'tropical kingbird' is a minor participant because he has no part to play in the resolution of the conflict. He goes straight into his role without an introduction, being marked with an ergative.[50]

(483) mãũ-ne ĩpana poropʰare-**pa**   hara-sʰi-a   sí pʉ
     this-in bird tropical^kingbird-ABL say-PAST-DECL yes 2s

   kʰõpʰa-ra   s'okʰai b-ʉ-a
   friend-ABS alive   be-PRES-DECL
   Then a tropical kingbird said, "Yes, your friend is alive."

10.3 Participant tracking. A participant is introduced as described above. Then, as the participant continues having import in the discourse, any overt reference receives normal case marking (§5.1 and §10.8). If the

---

[50]Harms (1994:185-6) says that when a new participant is introduced before the verb, as in this example, it marks a discontinuity in the story. Attention is briefly shifted from the main characters to this minor participant, whose role has little or nothing to do with the resolution of the story.

participant is the subject in consecutive sentences, the subject need not be marked overtly, as the consecutive sentences in (484) demonstrate.

(484) a. *Guayabal-de-pa   tai   ya^barrea   s'e-sʰi-da-a*
   Guayabal-in-ABL 1p   down^river come-PAST-PL-DECL
   From Guayabal we came down river.

   b. *martes   ewari-de   s'e-sʰi-da-a   Peñita-da*
   Tuesday day-in   come-PAST-PL-DECL Peñita-GOAL
   On Tuesday we came to Peñita.

   c. *Peñita-de   kʰãĩ-sʰi-da-a*
   Peñita-in sleep-PAST-PL-DECL
   We slept at Peñita.

   d. *nũrẽma   tiapʰede   pʰata   tʰu-sʰi-da-a*
   next^day morning plantain chop-PAST-PL-DECL
   The next morning we cut plantains.

   e. *abari   ewari-de   s'e-sʰi-da-a   ya^barrea*
   same day-in   come-PAST-PL-DECL down^river
   The same day we came on down river.

If the referent of a direct or indirect object is featured in the previous sentence, no overt reference is necessary unless ambiguity would result. In (485), the answer of the man who has gasoline is just the word 'have', rather than with the overt direct object, as in 'I have gasoline'. In (486) the indirect object 'him' was the subject in the previous sentence and is, therefore, omitted.

(485) *iwidi-sʰi-da-a   gasolina-ta   mãũ-ne   kʰãpʰũrĩã-pa*
   ask-PAST-PL-DECL gasoline-ABS^FOC this-in Latino-ABL

   ero-b-u-a   a-sʰi-a
   have-be-PRES-DECL say-PAST-DECL
   We asked for gasoline. Then a Latin man said, "[I] have [some]."

(486) *ara   mãũ-ta   mũ-a   Ø   becalo-ta   tia-sʰi-a   iči-a*
   same this-SUBD 1S-ABL [IO] becalo-ABS^FOC give-PAST-DECL 3S-ABL

    kʰo   mãrẽã
    eat   PURP
So I gave [him] some becalo to eat.

If zero is the default encoding when the subject is the same in consecutive sentences, then reference by a noun to such a participant is marked in comparison and is significant. In (487) *wẽrã* 'woman' is mentioned overtly in two consecutive sentences, even though she is the subject of both. From this and other clues in the context, we discover that the reason for this apparently needless repetition is that one scene is being summarized in the first sentence while a new scene is being started in the second.

(487) **wẽrã**-pa   hũma   wia-sʰi-a   mãẽpᵻrᵻ   **wẽrã**-ra
      woman-ABL   all   prepare-PAST-DECL   [new^dev.]   woman-ABS

        kʰãĩ   b-e-sʰi-a
        sleep   be-PERF-PAST-DECL
      So the woman prepared all [the meat]. Then the woman fell asleep.

Another reason for referring overtly to a participant who was also the subject of the previous sentence is to highlight what the participant says or does. In (488) the overt reference to the woman (same speaker as before) highlights what she says.

(488) a. maũne-pᵻrᵻ   mũ-a   kʰawa-sʰi-a   diauru-ta
       this-in-FOC^GI   1S-ABL   know-PAST-DECL   demon-ABS^FOC
       That's when I realized he was a demon.

    b. maũne   tewara   hara-sʰi-a   **wẽrã**-pa   kʰima   ãči-ra
       this-in   also   say-PAST-DECL   woman-ABL   spouse   3P-ABS

        nane   kʰewara   itua   to-di-a
        later   afternoon   liquor   drink-FUT^PL-DECL
       Then the woman also said, "Husband, tonight they are going to drink chicha."

When the subject of a sentence is different from that of the previous sentence, normal reference to the new subject is with a noun plus appropriate case marking.

(489) wẽrã   to-eda   sʼe-shi-a   ara   mãũ-ta   ūmãkʰĩrã-pa
      woman   river-into   come-PAST-DECL   same   this-SUBD man-ABL

   iwidi-sʰi-a
   ask-PAST-DECL
   The woman came down to the river [to her husband]. Then the man asked...

10.4 The referential adjective *či* in discourse. The basic uses of *či* were summarized in §4.6. Its discourse use is discussed here. Harms (1994:191) says that in ES *či* always refers to a noun that is relevant but is not itself the main theme. This can also be said of the NE *či*, which relates currently less important participants or props to the 'local VIP' or implies that they are not the local VIP.[51]

The first use, by which *či* denotes objects or participants that are related to the local VIP, is illustrated in (490). The husband from the above story has found his wife's footprints and begins following her. Both *kʰima* 'wife' and *wárra* 'offspring' are preceded by *či*. References to both are thus related to the husband, who is the local VIP and the only participant on stage at the time.

(490) či   kʰima   kʰaidu   wã-sʰi-a   mãũ-ne   ūnũ-ne   wã-sʰi-a   či
      REF   spouse   follow   go-PAST-DECL   this-in   see-in   go-PAST-DECL   REF

   wárra   sʼakʰe   hemene   kʰer-a-da-ta
   offspring   small   play   DESC-IMPF-PPRT-ABS^FOC
   He went after his wife...Then he saw that his little son had been playing.

The second use of *či*, whereby a participant is shown not to be the local VIP, is illustrated in (491), which is an excerpt from a classic Embera Guatín and Jaguar story. The guatín is always the protagonist, but in this story where the guatín kills the jaguar's children, the guatín is usually referred to in the last scene as *či kʰuriwa*. This is probably because in the final scene the jaguar himself becomes the local VIP and ends up getting angry with a vulture who was supposed to help him trap the guatín.

(491) ara   mãũ-ta   ãkosʰo-pa   uria-kʰaitʰa   wã-pʰeda   eda   akʰu
      same   this-SUBD   vulture-ABL   hole-close   go-after   into   look

---

[51] A participant is designated a local VIP (very important person) if s/he is the center of attention for part of a discourse (see Dooley and Levinsohn 1997:52–54).

b-a-sʰi-a   mã̰ü-ne či kʰuriwa-pa ĩpu-ta   tau-ma
be-IMPF-PAST-DECL this-in REF guatín-ABL sand-ABS^FOC eye-LOC

hãma pʰuá-sʰi-a
there blow-PAST-DECL

Then the vulture, after going up close to the hole, looked inside. Then the guatín blew sand in his eye.

10.5 Pronouns in discourse. Only one participant at a time in a third-person narrative can be marked with a personal pronoun.[52] Harms (1994:189) says this participant is prominent until another one is given prominence, presumedly with pronominal marking. While in NE it appears that only one participant can be referred to with a personal pronoun, it does not seem that this participant is prominent. Stephen Levinsohn (pers. comm.) suggests that use of the pronoun implies that the participant is not the local VIP.

A change of subject normally results in an overt reference (with a noun) to the new subject (§10.3). In (492) a woman has been taken away by a demon. In the first sentence, the woman is the subject. The new subject in the second sentence, the demon, should be mentioned overtly but he is assigned a pronoun, *iči*, which signals that, notwithstanding his new initiative, the reader's attention is directed to the woman (and, later, her husband), rather than to the demon.

(492) werã-pa   kʰawa-sʰi-a   mũ-ra animarã-pɨrɨ hãwã   ete
      woman-ABL know-PAST-DECL 1S-ABS demon-FOC^GI like^that take

      wã-pɨrɨ-kʰa   a-sʰi-a   mãẽpɨrɨ   iči-a   hara
      go-PRES-POLAR say-PAST-DECL [new dev.] 3S-ABL say

      nũ-m-e-sʰi-a   pɨ-ra ɨbɨa   s'e-tua
      stand-be-PERF-PAST-DECL 2S-ABS strong come-IMPV

The woman realized, "Am I being taken away by a demon?" she said. Then he (the demon) started saying, "Hurry up!"

This is also illustrated in (493), which is the same story. The husband, who is now the local VIP, tells his wife to run away from the demon's village. The use of *či* with the reference to the wife relates her to the local VIP. The reference to her baby, however, uses the third-person possessive

---

[52]Harms refers to pronouns that end with *-či* as 'marked'.

Discourse and Pragmatic Considerations   143

adjective *iči*. *iči* relates the baby to the wife, which makes him less related to the local VIP and lower again on the scale of local importance.

(493) či kʰima-a   hara-sʰi-a   pu-ra   na   wã-tua   hipʰa   pʰira
      REF spouse-IO   say-PAST-DECL   2S-ABS   ahead go-IMPV straight run

   wã-tua   ara   mãũ-ta   wẽrã   iči wárra   sˡakʰe
   go-IMPV   same   this-SUBD   woman   3S offspring small

   ẽkʰarra-de atʰau   eta-sʰi-a
   back-in   carry   bring-PAST-DECL
   [The husband] said to his wife, "You go ahead! Run straight!" Then the woman took her son along tied on her back.

10.6–10.10 Highlighting

NE uses several devices to highlight words, phrases, and clauses, whether in single sentences or in connected discourse. This section concentrates on the morphological devices used for highlighting. There are two groups of morphological highlighting devices—one for the absolutive case and another for the ergative (ablative) and oblique cases. This is in line with Comrie (1978:337ff.), who says that grammatical categories besides case marking are associated with ergative-absolutive systems. Absolutive focus, which does not have a nonabsolutive counterpart, is discussed in §10.6.[53] The other devices are discussed in §§10.7–10.8.

(494)   Absolutive   Nonabsolutive
     Normal case marking (§§5.1–5.3)   -ra   -pa (ablative),
                                                          -a (indirect obj.)
     Introductory focus (§10.6)   -ta (NEP),   ———
                                         -tʰa (EK)
     Focus on given information   -tru   -puru
     (§10.8)
     Additive (§4.11)   sʰida   pida

10.6 Absolutive focus and pivot. When an object or participant is introduced in a discourse or recalled after being in the background, it is assigned the absolutive focus suffix *-ta*. Complement clauses (§9.11), which are

---

[53]The reason that the absolutive focus marker *-ta/-tʰa* does not have a nonabsolutive counterpart is that nearly all participants are introduced in the absolutive case (§10.2).

absolutives, also are suffixed with -ta. In EK, focus marked with -tʰa is not obligatorily absolutive, as it can be used with the irrealis -i to mark intention or consequent purpose (§9.4). However, it is certainly not ergative.

Once introduced, the participant usually ceases to be marked with this suffix. In (495) the main participants are introduced in the first line of the story.

(495) kʰuriwa-ta ičaba imama-ta ãči-ra či^pia pa-sʰi-a
 guatín-ABS^FOC and jaguar-ABS^FOC 3S-ABS friend EQ-PAST-DECL
 Once there were a guatín and a jaguar; they were friends.

While participants and props remain on stage they are no longer suffixed with -ta but with -ra. In (496) the avocado tree is introduced with -ta, but the next overt reference has the suffix -ra.

(496) mãũ te wãtekʰa beko-ta nũ-m-a-sʰi-a či
 this house up^river avocado-ABS^FOC stand-be-IMPF-PAST-DECL REF

 beko-ra s'au nũ-m-a-sʰi-a
 avocado-ABS produce stand-be-IMPF-PAST-DECL
 Just up river from this house there was an avocado tree. The avocado tree was producing fruit.

In (497) an object is recalled and assigned the absolutive focus suffix -ta rather than the normal absolutive -ra. In this story, the deceitful guatín is killing the jaguar's cubs she is supposed to be caring for. While the cubs' parents are out working, she kills a cub and then serves it to the parents in a soup. When the mother jaguar wants to nurse the cubs, the guatín brings out the three live cubs one at a time; they each nurse well. But in place of the fourth, whom they have unsuspectingly eaten, the guatín brings out the cub who nursed first, so this fact is brought into focus with -ta.

(497) mãwã eta-de wã-sʰi-mĩna abari-ta ẽnẽ-sʰi-a či
 like^this get-in go-PAST-though same-ABS^FOC bring-PAST-DECL the

 nara hu tawa b-a-da-ta
 first breast give^drink be-IMPF-PPRT-ABS^FOC
 Even though she went to get [the fourth cub], she brought out the same one that had been nursed first.

Absolutive focus can also be used to switch focus from one on-stage participant to another. In (498) a man and his wife have been speaking. Then the

Discourse and Pragmatic Considerations   145

woman goes away, and the story is developed through actions involving the man. The use of *-ta* directs the audience to switch its attention to him.

(498) ara   mã̃ü-ta   werã̃   wã-sʰi-a   tida   ũmãkʰĩrã-**ta**
       same   this-SUBD   woman   go-PAST-DECL   home   man-ABS^FOC

      čʰiru-da   wã-sʰi-a
      brush-GOAL   GO-PAST-DECL

So the woman went into the house. And the *man* went into the brush.

The suffix *-ra* (glossed 'PIVOT') is used in EK to direct attention away from the constituent to which it is attached to the next corresponding constituent, so may be considered to be a marker of anticipatory or cataphoric focus. This is especially evident when *-ra* is suffixed to a noun which already has an ergative suffix. If the reference to such an agent does carry a *-ra* suffix, the speaker is signaling that this agent or what he does (the first 'pole') is not what is important; rather, the following agent and what he does (the second pole) is significant. This is the opposite of ES, where *-ra* is used to mark the second pole (Harms 1994:82–83).[54]

In (499), which is from EK, that the boss loaned the money to the speaker is not in focus; rather, what is important follows: the speaker was able to travel with the money he was loaned. In other words, the use of *-ra* directs attention away from the boss to the other participant.

(499) ewari   aba   presta-sʰi-a   patron-pa-**ra**   mã̃ü $450   peso-pa
       day   one   loan-PAST-DECL   boss-ABL-PIVOT   this $450   peso-ABL

      Montería-eda   hũtru   b-e-sʰi-a   mũ-ra
      Montería-GOAL   jump   be-PERF-PAST-DECL   1S-ABS

The boss loaned me a day's pay. With these 450 pesos I took off for Montería.

10.7 Important new information. According to Harms (1994:195) in ES discourse *mata* is used to mark important new developments which lead to the climax of a discourse. In NE, however, the cognate *mãũta* is not used in this way (see §10.11).

10.8 Focus on given information. As mentioned above, the absolutive and nonabsolutive cases (§§5.1–5.2) have different ways of showing focus.

---

[54]Harms calls this *-ra* the marker of comparison, and identifies it with the *-ra* described in §5.13 which is attached to adjectives.

Absolutive constituents which are on stage are brought into focus or emphasized with *-tru*, which replaces the expected *-ra*. Although (500) is from NEP, *-tru* is more common in EK. It appears that NEP is discarding *-tru* in favor of a wider use of *-ta*.

(500) kʰĩrũ-pʉrʉ-pa   hara-sʰi-a   mãũ-**tru**   mũ-a   ũrĩ
       get^mad-PRES-ABL say-PAST-DECL   this-FOC^GI^ABS   1S-ABL   hear

       kʰĩrĩa-kʰá
       want-HAB^NEG
       Out of anger he said, "I didn't want to hear *that!*"

Nonabsolutive constituents employ the suffix *-pʉrʉ*.

(501) pãrã-**pʉrʉ**   kʰawa   pʰan-ʉ-a   wadi   to   bari-di-pʉrʉ
       2p-FOC^GI   know   be^few-PRES-DECL still   river   fish-FUT^PL-COND
       You guys know [should decide] whether we should keep fishing.

10.9 Certainty. The morpheme used to mark certainty in ES is not attested in either NE language. For a presentation of evidentiality, see §6.30.

10.10 Contrastive certainty. A separate morpheme for this notion is not attested in NE. See §10.8.

10.11 Event line and background information. Combinations involving the demonstrative *mãũ* have other important uses in discourse besides what is discussed in §§10.1–10.2. Every sentence that begins with a form of the demonstrative *mã-* is thematic and so, in some sense, presents a new development along the theme line (which, in narrative, will be the main event line). Failure to use *mã-* means that the sentence concerned does not represent a new development along the main theme line. The different *mã-* forms signal different relationships between distinct developmental units. These are discussed below. Differences between NEP and EK are pointed out as they arise.

In NEP, once the main character or characters have been introduced, the beginning of the action is often marked with the sentence introducer *mãũta*.[55] The suffix *-ta* is the same as the subordinate verb suffix 'SUBD' described in §9.2. The function of *-ta* is to signal that what has been transpiring, whether an action in progress, a description of the setting, or the introduction of characters, is now completed with the action that will be presented in

---

[55]For discussion of other sentence introducers, see §§8.2–8.8.

Discourse and Pragmatic Considerations

the following main clause. When *maũta* is used, the characters have been introduced and often the setting has been described as well.

Another common beginning to narrative action is *ewari aba* 'one day'. In (502) and (503) both this and *maũta* occur.

(502) a. tači s'rõã-ena kʰuriwa-ta   ãkosʰo ũmẽ či kʰõpʰa
      1p   old-into guatín-ABS^FOC vulture two REF friend

   pa-sʰi-a
   EQ-PAST-DECL
   A long time ago the guatín was the friend of the vulture.

   b. **maũ-ta**   ewari aba kʰuriwa to   hiwa-da
      [action^begins] day   one guatín river bend-GOAL

   pʰurrua-de   wã-sʰi-a
   go^around-in go-PAST-DECL
   One day the guatín went down to a bend in the river to walk around.

(503) a. tači s'rõã-ena ẽpẽrã-ta   sʰida   kʰĩmãrẽ maũ-kʉ
      1p   old-into person-ABS^FOC also^ABS four   this-very

   ẽpẽrã-rã nũrẽma-s'a   traha-pa-či-da-a
   person-PL next^day-every work-HAB-PAST-PL-DECL
   A long time ago there were four men. These same men worked every day.

   b. **maũ-ta**   nũrẽma   aba tida b-e-sʰi-a
      [action^begins] next^day one home be-PERF-PAST-DECL
   One morning one of them stayed home.

Another common sentence introducer which includes the thematic *mã-* is *maũne*, which indicates that the sentence that follows it takes place within the same time frame as the previous sentence (see §8.2).

The use of *mawã* plus a stative verb in the present progressive tense provides a setting for a new development.

(504) te   wãtekʰare pʰõwã-ta   hĩkua nũ-m-e-sʰi-a
      house up^river rifle-ABS^FOC sound stand-be-PERF-PAST-DECL

> mãwã   b-ʉ-de   sʲe-sʰi-a   ūmãkʰĩrã sʲa
> like^this be-PRES-in come-PAST-DECL man   here
>
> b-ʉ-ta
> be-PRES-ABS^FOC

Just up river from the house a rifle started sounding. While this was happening, there came a man who looked just like him.

Finally, *mãpe* or *mãü̃pe* signals some discontinuity of time between the previous event and the one that follows (see §8.2).

A summary in (505) gives some sequential markers that are used where there is continuity of scene and participants.

(505) | | Developmental | Nondevelopmental |
|---|---|---|
| Main clause presents new event | | *mãẽpʉrʉ* (NEP), *mãwẽ* (EK) | tail-head linkage |
| Logical result (predictable) | | *ara mãü̃ta* (NEP), *ara mãü̃ne* (EK) | asyndeton (α) |

mãẽpʉrʉ signals sequential events that present new developments within the same scene and with the same participants. The significance of the development depends on the dynamism of the scene. *mãẽpʉrʉ* occurs whether or not there is conflict between the participants.[56]

The EK sentence introducer which most closely matches the function of NEP *mãẽpʉrʉ* is *mãwẽ*. The main difference between the two is that *mãwẽ* introduces each new development which leads up to the climax of the thematic unit. This is evident in (506).

(506) a. **mãwẽ**   mãmaʉ-ba wakʰusʰa   mũči   traha
     [new dev.] there-ABL   again   1s^COREF work

   b-a-da-eda   sʲe-i   para   sʲe-sʰi-a
   be-IMPF-PPRT-GOAL come-IRR have come-PAST-DECL
   Then from there I had to go back to where I had been working.

   b. **mãwẽ**   mãü̃   pʰʉwʉrʉ sʲakʰe Cristalina-ne-pa
      [new dev.] this   village   small   Cristalina-in-ABL

---

[56]The reader is referred to the texts in the appendix. In sentences 7–14 of the NEP text (appendix A) there is no conflict while in sentences 15–32 there is conflict. In both, *mãẽpʉrʉ* is used to mark thematic development.

Discourse and Pragmatic Considerations 149

    hɨ̃tɨ-pɨɾɨ-de o-de   oi-tʰa   perabari-i-tʰa   para
    jump-PRES-in trail-in woods-FOC navigate-IRR-FOC have

    pa-sʰi-a
    EQ-PAST-DECL
Then, leaving the small village of Cristalina, I had to make my way back on a trail through the woods.

c. **mãwẽ**   mãũ oi   perabari tʰai-de   mũ kʰaidu
   [new dev.] this woods navigate mouth-in 1s follow

    pʰũãtɨ tuke-sʰi-a
    wind   come-PAST-DECL
As I came up to a fork in the trail a wind came up behind me.

d. **mãwã**   mũ kʰaidu pʰũãtɨ tuke-pɨɾɨ tauĉʰa taĉi-ma mũ-tʰa
   like^this 1s follow wind   come-PRES exact 1p-LOC 1S-FOC

    ũtʰɨ hira eta-pɨɾɨ-kʰa-sʰi-a   pʰũãtɨ-pa
    up hang get-PRES-NEG^HAB-PAST-DECL wind-ABL
As the wind came up behind me, to us it would be like it was supernaturally picking me up in the air.

e. **mãwã**   hira eta-pɨɾɨ-kʰa-pɨɾɨ-de pedea-tʰa
   like^this hang get-PRES-NEG^HAB-PRES-in word-FOC

    ũɾĩ-sʰi-a   mũ-a mũ-á pedea-pɨɾɨ-tʰa
    hear-PAST-DECL 1S-ABL 1S-IO speak-PRES-FOC
As I was being supernaturally picked up I heard a voice, a voice that was speaking to me.

f. **mãwẽ**   mũ-a mãũ pedea ũɾĩ-pɨɾɨ-para mãwã-sʰi-a
   [new dev.] 1S-ABL this word hear-PRES-time say-PAST-DECL
Then when I listened to this voice it said,

g. pɨ-ra kʰãwãweda Montería-eda wã-i para pɨ-ra
   2S-ABS right^away Montería-GOAL go-IRR have 2S-ABS

    kʰãwãweda Montería-eda wã-i para a mãwã čʰũ
    right^away Montería-GOAL go-IRR have say like^this quiet

tʰotʰo-sʰi-a
go-PAST-DECL

"You must go to Montería right away, you must go to Montería right away," it said and was silent.

The NEP sentence introducer *ara mã̰ṵta* signals the logical result of the previous event, which is the very next action in the sequence of events. It signals that the direction of development has not changed. As already noted, the suffix *-ta* signals that what has been happening previously ends with the event which follows, i.e., the logical result. In EK *ara mã̰ṵtʰa* signals not only the very next event but that the event occurred suddenly.

NEP *ara mã̰ṵta* is illustrated in (507). A man has tracked down his wife, who has been taken to another village by a demon. Once the man and his wife make eye contact, the logical result is that they meet together. Therefore, the sentence introducer preceding their meeting is *ara mã̰ṵta*.

(507) a. wẽrã-pa   eda   akʰɨ-pɨrɨ-de mã̰ṵ-ne ṵnṵ̃ b-e-sʰi-a
       woman-ABL into look-PRES-in this-in see be-PERF-PAST-DECL

   ṵmã̰kʰĩrã-pa
   man-ABL
   While the woman was looking down [from the house], the man saw her. *or* she was seen by the man.

b. **ara mã̰ṵ-ta** wẽrã   to-eda   sʼe-sʰi-a
   same this-SUBD woman river-into come-PAST-DECL
   So the woman came down to the river [to her husband].

The EK equivalent to NEP *ara mã̰ṵta* is *ara mã̰ṵne*.

(508) a. mã̰wẽ   plata hita-i-ra   traha b-e   ẽ
      [new dev.] money grab-IRR-PIVOT work be-PERF NEG

   pa-sʰi-a
   EQ-PAST-DECL
   To get money I couldn't work.

b. **ara mã̰ṵne**-ra mṵ-ra mṵči trua-edá wã b-e
   same then-PIVOT 1S-ABS 1S^COREF land-GOAL go be-PERF

ẽã-sʰi-a
NEG-PAST-DECL
So I couldn't go to my land.

Tail-head linkage involves the repetition at the beginning of a sentence (head) of the main verb and, sometimes, other constituents from the end (tail) of an earlier sentence (usually the previous one). In (509), the main verb phrase *te osʰidaa* 'made a house' is repeated at the beginning of the next sentence as *te odapʰeda* 'after making a house'.

(509) hũẽ-na-pʰeda   te   o-sʰi-da-a   te   **o-da-pʰeda**
      arrive-PL-after house make-PAST-PL-DECL   house   make-PL-after

   kʰãĩ   pʰan-e-sʰi-da-a
   sleep   be^few-PERF-PAST-PL-DECL
   After arriving they made a house. After making a house, they went to sleep.

Tail-head linkage is used to link events when the second event does not represent a new development along the theme line. In (509), for instance, that the people go to sleep does not represent a new development but, rather, is one of a series of events that set the scene for the developments that are introduced with a form of *mã-* (see appendix A, sentences 2–6).

In (510) what is important is that the people have arrived at the house. That they go into it does not represent a new development in the theme line but a continuation of the previous development; it belongs in the same developmental unit.

(510) hũẽ-sʰi-da-a   iči   te   to-eda   hũẽ-na-pʰeda   tida   ete
      arrive-PAST-DECL   3s   house   river-into   arrive-PL-after   home   take

   wã-sʰi-da-a
   go-PAST-PL-DECL
   They arrived at the river's edge below his house. After arriving he took her into the house.

When tail-head linkage follows a sentence introducer formed from *mã-*, the event of the main clause represents a new development, and the tail-head linkage is used to slow down the story with the rhetorical effect of highlighting it. For example, (511) begins with *mãwã*, which communicates that what follows is a new development. This is followed by extensive tail-head linkage, which is followed in turn by the introducer *mãwẽ*. All of this has the effect of highlighting the event described in the main clause.

(511) *mãwã   hira   eta-pʉrʉ-kʰa-pʉrʉ-de   pedea-tʰa   ũrĩ-sʰi-a*
like^this   hang   get-PRES-HYPO-PRES-in   word-FOC   hear-PAST-DECL

      *mũ-a   mũ-á   pedea-pʉrʉ-tʰa   **mãwẽ**   mũ-a   mãũ   pedea*
      1S-ABL   1S-IO   speak-PRES-FOC   [new dev.]   1S-ABL   this   word

      ũrĩ-pʉrʉ-para   mãwã-sʰi-a
      hear-PRES-time   say-PAST-DECL

As I was being supernaturally picked up I heard a voice that was speaking to me. Then, when I listened to the voice it said...

Four uses of asyndeton (i.e., the absence of a sentence introducer or tail-head linkage) have been found: to introduce a comment on a previous event, to introduce specific information about a prior generic event, to introduce parallel nonevents, and to introduce the second part of an event cluster.

The lack of sentence introducer or tail-head linkage before the second sentence in (512) introduces a comment on or summary of what the woman has been doing. (The absence of a sentence introducer is marked by *α*.)

(512) *mãẽpʉrʉ   parawa-de   ũtʰʉ   pué   hira-bʉ-sʰi-a*   *α*
[new dev.]   rack-in   up   load   hang-put-PAST-DECL

      wẽrã-pa   hũma   wia-sʰi-a
      woman-ABL   all   prepare-PAST-DECL

Then she put [the meat] up on the smoking rack. The woman prepared all [the meat].

In (513) the absence of a sentence introducer indicates that the second sentence is a parallel non-event with the previous sentence.

(513) *mãũ-ne   ẽpẽrã-pa   pakʰuru-ta   bʉa   tʰu*
this-in   person-ABL   stick-ABS^FOC   break   chop

      eru-b-a-sʰi-a   *α nekʰo-ta*
      have-be-IMPF-PAST-DECL   machete-ABS^FOC

eruɨ-b-a-sʰi-a
have-be-IMPF-PAST-DECL
Now the man had a stick he had broken off. He had a machete, too.

(514) shows how the absence of sentence introducers is used to introduce specific information which amplifies a generic event.

(514) tidu   hũẽ-pʰeda   hɨrɨ-sʰi-a   a na   barrea
      inside   arrive-after   search-PAST-DECL   ahead   downˆriver

      hɨrɨ-sʰi-a   a⁵⁷   ũnũ ẽ   pa-sʰi-a   a wãrãka
      search-PAST-DECL   see NEG   EQ-PAST-DECL   upˆriver

      hɨrɨ-sʰi-a
      search-PAST-DECL

After arriving inside the house he looked for her. He looked for her further down river. He didn't see her. He searched up river.

Finally, asyndeton is used when the second sentence forms an event cluster with the first.

(515) maũne   wárra   sʲakʰe-a   nẽ   pʰono-ta   bɨa
      this-in   offspring   small-IO   GEN   blossom-ABSˆFOC   break

      tia-sʰi-a   a wárra   sʲakʰe-ra   ĩpɨ-de   hemene
      give-PAST-DECL   offspring   small-ABS   sand-in   play

      akʰɨ-b-e-sʰi-a
      sit-be-PERF-PAST-DECL

He picked a flower and gave it to the little boy. The little boy sat there on the sand playing with it.

Related to the NEP use of asyndeton is the EK use of *mope,* which is the cognate of NEP *mãpe/mãũpe.* EK *mope* is nondevelopmental in that it is used to link two parts of an event cluster. In (516) *mope* groups together the actions 'she came up' and 'she said'.

(516) mãũ-pa   ipʰida   nũ-m-ɨ-ne   mepea   Kʰerapataɨ
      this-ABL   laugh   stand-be-PRES-in   sibling   Kerabadau

---

⁵⁷Asyndeton is used here because the second sentence is part of the same event complex as the first; see (515).

  tuke-sʰi-a *mũ-má* **mope** *mãwã-sʰi-a*
  come-PAST-DECL 1S-LOC [non dev.] say-PAST-DECL
  As I was laughing about this, sister Kerabadau came up to me. And she said

mope is also used to introduce a speaker comment, i.e., a sentence that is off the event line, as in (517).

(517) a. *nãma nãũ Montería-de ẽpẽrã werã-tʰa čʰu-b-ʉ-a*
   here this Montería-in person woman-FOC sit-be-PRES-DECL

   a-sʰi-a
   say-PAST-DECL
  "Here in Montería there is an Embera woman," he said.

 b. **mope** *mũ-a nãũ pʰʉwʉrʉ sʼroma-ne mãũ ẽpẽrã*
   [non dev.] 1S-ABL this village big-in this Embera

   werã kʰãrẽ o b-ʉ-tʰa kʰrĩčʰa b-e-sʰi-a
   woman what make be-PRES-FOC think be-PERF-PAST-DECL
  And I started wondering what an Embera woman was doing in this big city.

Appendix A

Northern Embera Proper text

(1) ẽpẽrã werã diauru-pa ete-da
Embera woman demon-ABL take-PPRT
How an Embera woman was taken by a demon

(2) tači s'rõã-ẽnã to kʰẽpɨ-da wã-sʰi-da-a ũmãkʰĩrã-ta
1p old-into river nose-GOAL go-PAST-PL-DECL man-ABS^FOC

werã-ta
woman-ABS^FOC
A long time ago a man and a woman went to the headwaters.

(3) wárra s'akʰe-ta aba ete wã-sʰi-da-a
offspring small-ABS^FOC one take go-PAST-PL-DECL
They took along one little son.

(4) wã-pɨ-ta-ta wã-pɨ-ta-ta hũẽ-sʰi-da-a
go-PRES-PL-SUBD go-PRES-PL-SUBD arrive-PAST-PL-DECL
Going along for a long time, they arrived.

(5) hũẽ-na-pʰeda te o-sʰi-da-a
arrive-PL-after house make-PAST-PL-DECL
After arriving they made a house.

(6) te o-da-pʰeda kʰãĩ pʰan-e-sʰi-da-a
house make-PL-after sleep be^few-PERF-PAST-PL-DECL
After making a house they went to sleep.

(7) *nũrẽma ũmakʰīrã mẽã wã-sʰi-a*
next^day man jungle go-PAST-DECL
The next morning the man went into the jungle (= went hunting).

(8) *mẽã wã-na oča ẽ nũ-m-ʉ-ta oča ẽ*
jungle go-PPRT come^out NEG stand-be-PRES-SUBD come^out NEG

   nũ-m-ʉ-ta kʰewara pa-pʉrʉ-de sʲe-sʰi-a
   stand-be-PRES-SUBD afternoon EQ-PRES-in come-PAST-DECL

   tida
   home
   Having gone into the jungle and not coming out for a long time, when it was afternoon he came home.

(9) *pio nẽ pea-sʰi-a*
very GEN kill-PAST-DECL
He killed a lot [of animals].

(10) *maẽpʉrʉ wẽrã-pa nẽ kʰarama-sʰi-a*
[new dev.] woman-ABL GEN burn^hair-PAST-DECL
Then the woman burned the hair off the animals.

(11) *tʰʉpʉ-de wẽ-pʰeda to-eda ete-pʰeda hẽsʰa-kʰua-pʰeda*
fire-in shave^off-after river-into take-after gut-REPT-after

   tida ẽne-sʰi-a
   home bring-PAST-DECL
   Then after scraping the burnt hair off, she took them down to the river and gutted them all and then brought them back to the house.

(12) *maẽpʉrʉ parawa-de ũtʰʉ pué hira-bʉ-sʰi-a*
[new dev.] rack-on up load hang-put-PAST-DECL
Then she put [the meat] up on the smoking rack.

(13) *wẽrã-pa hũma wia-sʰi-a*
woman-ABL all prepare-PAST-DECL
The woman prepared all [the meat].

(14) *maẽpʉrʉ wẽrã-rã kʰāī b-e-sʰi-a*
[new dev.] woman-ABS sleep be-PERF-PAST-DECL
Then the woman fell asleep.

Appendix A

(15) nūrēma ūmākʰīrā mēā wã-sʰi-a
next^day man-ABS jungle go-PAST-DECL
The next morning the man went into the jungle [to hunt].

(16) mãüpe mãü̃ ūmākʰīrā wã-na hētare te wãtekʰare
then this man go-PPRT back house up^river

    pʰõwã-ta hīkua nũ-m-e-sʰi-a
    rifle-ABS^FOC sound stand-be-PERF-PAST-DECL
Then, once the man was gone, just up river from the house a rifle started sounding.

(17) mãwã b-ʉ-de sʲe-sʰi-a ūmākʰīrā sʲa
like^this be-PRES-in come-PAST-DECL man here

    b-ʉ-ta
    be-PRES-ABS^FOC
While this was happening, there came a man who looked just like him.

(18) maẽpʉrʉ wẽrã-a a-sʰi-a kʰima mũ-a wãtekʰare
[new dev.] woman-IO say-PAST-DECL spouse 1S-ABL upstream

    pido-ta batʰa-pue-sʰi-a
    boar-ABS^FOC shoot-VOL-PAST-DECL
Then he said to the woman, "Wife, just upstream I shot a boar.

(19) mãũ kʰãrẽã mũ-a pʉ eta-de sʲe-sʰi-a
this REASON 1S-ABL 2S get-in come-PAST-DECL
That is why I came to get you."

(20) ara mãũ-ta wẽrã ete wã-sʰi-a
same this-SUBD woman take go-PAST-DECL
So he took the woman along.

(21) wã-pʉ-ta-ta wã-pʉ-ta-ta mãũ-ne ẽkʰarra-de tau urua
go-PRES-PL-SUBD go-PRES-PL-SUBD this-in back-on eye burn

    hira-b-e-sʰi-a
    hang-be-PERF-PAST-DECL
They went along for a long time and the baby on her back stayed awake.

(22) mãũ-ne-pɨrɨ werã-pa kʰawa-sʰi-a
    this-in-FOC^GI woman-ABL know-PAST-DECL
    That's when the woman realized.

(23) mũ-rã animarã-pɨrɨ hãwã ete wã-pɨrɨ-kʰa a-sʰi-a
    1S-ABS demon-FOC^GI like^that take go-PRES-POLAR say-PAST-DECL
    "Am I being taken away by a demon?"

(24) maẽpɨrɨ iči-a hara nũ-m-e-sʰi-a pɨ-ra ubɨa
    [new dev.] 3S-ABL say stand-be-PERF-PAST-DECL 2S-ABS strong

    sʲe-tua
    come-IMPV
    Then he started to say, "Hurry up!"

(25) maẽpɨrɨ iči-a hara-sʰi-a nãũ kʰewara nẽ
    [new dev.] 3S-ABL say-PAST-DECL this afternoon GEN

    asʰea-ta to-di-a mũ tida
    bitter-ABS^FOC drink-FUT^PL-DECL 1S home
    Then he said,"This afternoon we will drink chicha at my house.

(26) tači-ra kʰui-di-a nãma
    1P-ABS bathe-FUT^PL-DECL here
    We will bathe here/now." or Let's bathe here/now."

(27) ara mãũ-ta kʰui-sʰi-da-a
    same this-SUBD bathe-PAST-PL-DECL
    So they bathed.

(28) mãũ-ne wárra sʲakʰe-a nẽ pʰono-ta bɨa
    this-in offspring small-IO GEN blossom-ABS^FOC break

    tia-sʰi-a
    give-PAST-DECL
    He picked a flower and gave it to the little boy.

(29) wárra sʲakʰe-ra ĩpɨ-de hemene akʰu-b-e-sʰi-a
    offspring small-ABS sand-in play sit-be-PERF-PAST-DECL
    The little boy sat there on the sand playing with it.

Appendix A

(30) māwã   kʰui   pʰan-a-pʰeda   wã-sʰi-da-a
like^this bathe be^few-IMPF-after go-PAST-PL-DECL
After bathing like this for a while they went on.

(31) wã-pʉ-ta-ta   wã-pʉ-ta-ta   hũẽ-sʰi-da-a   iči te
go-PRES-SUBD go-PRES-PL-SUBD arrive-PAST-PL-DECL 3s house

    to-eda
    river-into
They went along for a long time and then arrived at the river's edge below his house.

(32) hũẽ-na-pʰeda   tida   ete   wã-sʰi-a
arrive-PL-after home take go-PAST-DECL
After arriving he took her into his house.

(33) mãũ-ne   ũmakʰĩrã-pa   kʰawa-sʰi-a   mũ   kʰĩma-ra   animarã-pa
this-in man-ABL know-PAST-DECL 1s spouse-ABS demon-ABL

    ete   wã-pʉrʉ-ta
    take go-PRES-ABS^FOC
Then the man (her husband) realized: "My wife has been taken by a demon."

(34) ara   mãũ-ta   tida   sʲe-sʰi-a
same this-SUBD home come-PAST-DECL
So he came home.

(35) tidu   hũẽ-pʰeda   hʉrʉ-sʰi-a
inside arrive-after search-PAST-DECL
After arriving inside the house he looked for her.

(36) na   barrea   hʉrʉ-sʰi-a
ahead down^river search-PAST-DECL
He looked for her further down river.

(37) ũnũ   ẽ   pa-sʰi-a
see NEG EQ-PAST-DECL
He didn't see her.

(38) wārāka hᵻrᵻ-sʰi-a
 up^river search-PAST-DECL
 He searched up river.

(39) mãũ-ne ũnũ-sʰi-a hīrū tʰᵻka wã-pᵻrᵻ-ta wārāka
 this-in see-PAST-DECL foot step go-PRES-ABS^FOC up^river
 Then he saw footprints that were going up river.

(40) hīrū ũmẽ ũmākʰīrā hīrū-ta werã ũmẽ
 foot two man foot-ABS^FOC woman two
 There were two sets: those of a man with a woman's.

(41) ara mãũ-ta či kʰīma kʰaidu wã-sʰi-a
 same this-SUBD his spouse follow go-PAST-DECL
 So he went after his wife.

(42) kʰaidu wã-pᵻrᵻ-ta kʰaidu wã-pᵻrᵻ-ta mãũ-ne ũnũ-ne
 follow go-PRES-SUBD follow go-PRES-SUBD this-in see-in

   wã-sʰi-a či wárra s'akʰe hemene
   go-PAST-DECL REF offspring small play

   kʰer-a-da-ta
   DESC-IMPF-PPRT-ABS^FOC
 Following along for a long time, he then saw that his little son had been there playing.

(43) īpᵻ-de nẽ phōno hĩs'uatʰa kʰer-a-sʰi-a
 sand-in GEN blossom scatter DESC-IMPF-PAST-DECL
 He had been scattering all the petals on the sand.

(44) ara mãũ-ta ũmākʰīrā wã-sʰi-a waa wārā
 same this-SUBD man go-PAST-DECL more up^river
 So the man kept going up river.

(45) wã-pᵻrᵻ-ta hũẽ-ne wã-sʰi-a diauru te-da
 go-PRES-SUBD arrive-in go-PAST-DECL demon house-GOAL
 He went along and arrived at the house of the demon.

(46) maẽpᵻrᵻ ũmākʰīrā čʰirua-de-pa akʰᵻ b-e-sʰi-a
 [new dev.] man brush-in-ABL look be-PERF-PAST-DECL
 Then the man started looking out from the underbrush.

Appendix A

(47) *werã-pa   eda   akʰʉ-pʉrʉ-de mãũ-ne ũnũ b-e-sʰi-a*
woman-ABL into look-PRES-in this-in see be-PERF-PAST-DECL

   ũmākʰīrã-pa
   man-ABL
While the woman was looking down [from the house] the man saw her. *or* she was seen by the man.

(48) *ara   mãũ-ta   werã   to-eda   sʲe-sʰi-a*
same this-SUBD woman river-into come-PAST-DECL
So the woman came down to the river [to her husband].

(49) *ara   mãũ-ta   ũmakʰīrã-pa iwidi-sʰi-a   pʉ-ra sʰãwã sʲe-sʰi*
same this-SUBD man-ABL   ask-PAST-DECL 2S-ABS how   come-PAST
Then the man asked, "How did you get here?"

(50) *mãũ-ne werã-pa   hara-sʰi-a   mũ-ra diauru-pa ẽne-sʰi-a*
this-in woman-AB say-PAST-DECL 1S-ABS demon-ABL bring-PAST-DECL
Then the woman said, "I was brought by a demon.

(51) *pʉ-ta   wariˆẽ   b-a-sʰi-a   mãũ pẽrã   mũ-ra*
2S-ABSˆFOC alikeˆNEG be-IMPF-PAST-DECL this because 1S-ABS

   sʲe-sʰi-a
   come-PAST-DECL
He looked just like you. So I came here.

(52) *ya   warã   b-a-pʉrʉ-de   mãũ-ne ẽkʰarra-de taupara*
already upˆriver be-IMPF-PRES-in this-in back-on   magic

   hira-b-e-sʰi-a
   hang-be-PERF-PAST-DECL
When I was already a ways up river, he cast a spell on the baby.

(53) *mãũ-ne-pʉrʉ   mũ-a   kʰawa-sʰi-a   tiauru-ta*
this-in-FOCˆGI 1S-ABL know-PAST-DECL demon-ABSˆFOC
That's when I knew he was a demon."

(54) *mãũ-ne tewara hara-sʰi-a   werã-pa   kʰīma ači-ra nane*
this-in also   say-PAST-DECL woman-ABL spouse 3p-ABS later

      kʰewara   itua   to-di-a
      afternoon liquor drink-FUT-PL-DECL
      Then the woman also said, "Husband, tonight they are going to drink chicha."

(55) mãũ-ne ũmakʰĩrã-pa hara-sʰi-a   mãẽtʰara pia b-ʉ-a
      this-in   man-ABL   say-PAST-DECL if^so   good be-PRES-DECL
      Then the man said, "If that's so, then that's fine."

(56) ãrã-rã peu   kʰãĩke-da   kʰarea mũ-a   hũma
      3p-PL   drunk fall^asleep-PPRT DS   1S-ABL all

      kʰẽna-ya-a
      slaughter-FUT-DECL
      Once they are drunk and have fallen asleep I will slaughter them all."

(57) ara   mãũ-ta   ũmakʰĩrã-pa hara-sʰi-a   wẽrã-a   pʉ-ra kʰãĩ
      same   this-SUBD man-ABL   say-PAST-DECL woman-IO 2S-ABS sleep

      ẽ   b-a-tua
      NEG be-IMPF-IMPV
      So then the man said to the woman, "Don't sleep at all!"

(58) mãũ-ne wẽrã-pa   pʰãnu-sʰi-a   pia   b-ʉ-a
      this-in woman-ABL answer-PAST-DECL good be-PRES-DECL

      a-sʰi-a
      say-PAST-DECL
      Then the woman answered, "O.K.," she said.

(59) ara   mãũ-ta   wẽrã   wã-sʰi-a   tida
      same   this-SUBD woman go-PAST-DECL home
      So the woman went into the house.

(60) ũmakʰĩrã-ta   mãũ-ne čʰiru-da   wã-sʰi-a
      man-ABS^FOC this-in brush-GOAL go-PAST-DECL
      The *man* went into the brush.

(61) čʰirua-de-pa akʰʉ b-a-pa-či-a
      brush-in-ABL look be-IMPF-HAB-PAST-DECL
      He was looking out from the brush as he had been before.

Appendix A

(62) *māwã   b-u-de   ēpẽrã-rã   s'e-s'e-sʰi-da-a*
like^this be-PRES-in person-PL come-come-PAST-PL-DECL
While he was doing that, people started arriving little by little.

(63) *ara   mãũ-ta   ãči-ra   itua-ta   to*
same this-SUBD 3p-ABS liquor-ABS^FOC drink

   tuan-e-sʰi-da-a
   be^many-PERF-PAST-PL-DECL
Then they started drinking liquor.

(64) *mãũ-ne či   ūmakʰīrã-pa čʰiru-ta   s'a   nũ-m-e-sʰi-a*
this-in REF man-ABL reed-ABS^FOC play stand-be-PERF-PAST-DECL
Then the man [demon] started playing the flute.

(65) *mãũ-ne hĩrũ-pa tambora-ta   s'a   nũ-m-e-sʰi-a*
this-in foot-ABL drum-ABS^FOC play stand-be-PERF-PAST-DECL
Then he started to play a drum with his feet.

(66) *wẽrã-rã   baira tuan-e-sʰi-da-a*
woman-PL dance be^many-PERF-PAST-PL-DECL
Women started to dance.

(67) *māwã   paira   tuan-u-ta   āsʰa-podo-de*
like^this dance be^many-PRES-SUBD daylight-PRES^IMM-in

   kʰāīke-sʰi-da-a
   fall^asleep-PAST-PL-DECL
Dancing like this until nearly daylight, they fell asleep.

(68) *mãũ-ne ēpẽrã-pa   pakʰuru-ta   bʉa   tʰu   eru-b-a-sʰi-a.*
this-in person-ABL stick-ABS^FOC break chop have-be-IMPF-PAST-DECL
Now the man had a stick he had broken off.

(69) *nekʰo-ta   eru-b-a-sʰi-a*
machete-ABS^FOC have-be-IMPF-PAST-DECL
He had a machete, too.

(70) *ara   mãũ-ta   ēpẽrã   tidu   wã-sʰi-a*
same this-SUBD person inside go-PAST-DECL
So the man went into the house.

(71) či kʰĩma-a   hara-sʰi-a   pʉ-ra   na   wã-tua   hipʰa   pʰira
     REF spouse-IO   say-PAST-DECL   2S-ABS ahead go-IMPV straight run

     wã-tua
     go-IMPV

He said to his wife, "You go ahead! Run straight!"

(72) ara   mãũ-ta   werã   iči wárra   sʲakʰe ēkʰarra-de atʰau
     same this-SUBD   woman 3S   offspring small   back-in   carry

     eta-sʰi-a
     bring-PAST-DECL

Then the woman took her son along tied on her back.

(73) mãẽpʉrʉ   wã-sʰi-a   tiamasʰi
     [new dev.] go-PAST-DECL   night

Then she left while it was still dark.

(74) ara   mãũ-ta   ũmakʰĩrã-pa pakʰʉrʉ bʉa   tʰu-da-pa   hũma
     same this-SUBD   man-ABL   stick   break chop-PPRT-ABL   all

     u   kʰẽna-kʰua-pʉrʉ-de   mãũ-ne   čora   kʰir-u-ta
     swat slaughter-REPT-PRES-in   this-in   old^fem   DESC-PRES-ABS^FOC

     bia   pʰiratrʉ toko-sʰi-a
     scream get^up   run-PAST-DECL

Then, as the man was beating them all to death with the stick he had chopped off, an old lady got up screaming and ran after him.

(75) ara   mãũ-ta   orra^eta-sʰi-a
     same this-SUBD   attack-PAST-DECL

So he attacked her.

(76) udu   hĩtrʉ toko-de mãũ-ne ēpẽrã-pa   hĩrũ-ma
     down jump run-in this-in person-ABL leg-LOC

     tʰu-pue-sʰi-a
     chop-VOL-PAST-DECL

Jumping out of her way, the man chopped her on the leg.

Appendix A

(77)   *iči-ra hɨ̃rũ moč^{h}a p^{h}ira wã-s^{h}i-a*
      3S-ABS leg limping run   go-PAST-DECL
      She ran away limping.

(78)   *ara mãũ-ta ẽpẽrã-ra či tõme k^{h}õã^manorã udu*
      same this-SUBD person-ABS REF stairpole rope^ladder down

      k^{h}iap^{h}e hĩtrɨ wã-s^{h}i-a
      quietly jump go-PAST-DECL
      Then the man went down the rope ladder and quietly jumped to the ground.

(79)   *ara mãũ-ta ẽpẽrã p^{h}ira wã-s^{h}i-a*
      same this-SUBD person run go-PAST-DECL
      Then the man ran away.

(80)   *p^{h}ira wã-ta p^{h}ira wã-ta ot^{h}a ũnatrɨ-s^{h}i-a*
      run go-SUBD run go-SUBD on^trail dawn-PAST-DECL
      He ran and ran and while he was still on the trail dawn came.

(81)   *tidu hũẽ-pɨrɨ-para mãũ-ne wẽrã-pa k^{h}ɨda-ra hãpa-de*
      inside arrive-PRES-time this-in woman-ABL baggage-ABS canoe-in

      eda pué eru-b-a-s^{h}i-a
      into load have-be-IMPF-PAST-DECL
      By the time he got to the hunting house, the woman had all the baggage loaded into the canoe.

(82)   *ara mãũ-ta wã-s^{h}i-da-a barrea*
      same this-SUBD go-PAST-PL-DECL down^river
      Then they went down river.

(83)   *wã-pɨ-ta-ta wã-pɨ-ta-ta tidu hũẽ-s^{h}i-da-a*
      go-PRES-PL-SUBD go-PRES-PL-SUBD inside arrive-PAST-PL-DECL
      They went a long ways and then arrived at their house.

(84)   *hũẽ-na-p^{h}eda p^{h}ãn-ɨ-ta tomia aba pa-pɨrɨ-de ak^{h}ɨ-de*
      arrive-PL-after be^few-PRES-SUBD week one EQ-PRES-in look-in

s'e-sʰi-da-a
come-PAST-PL-DECL

After arriving and being there a week, they came to look [at the hunting house].

(85) akʰɨ   s'e-pɨ-ta-para   te-ra   tʰeka kʰo-b-a-sʰi-a
look come-PRES-PL-time house-ABS fall   POS-be-IMPF-PAST-DECL
By the time they came to look, the house was already knocked down.

(86) ẽpẽrã-pa   kʰrĩčʰa-sʰi-a   mɨ-ta   hãɨ̃ ewari-de nãma
person-ABL think-PAST-DECL 1S-ABS^FOC that day-on   here

b-e-da-para   tiauru-pa   mũ-ra   pea-i   b-a-sʰi-a
be-PERF-PPRT-time demon-ABL 1S-ABS kill-IRR be-IMPF-PAST-DECL
The man thought, "If I had stayed here that day, the demon would have killed me."

(87) ara   mãma-pe   tači   s'rõã-ẽnã-pema   nẽpɨrɨ
same here-LIMIT 1p   old-in-ORIG   story
And the story from our old times ends right here.

Appendix B

Embera-Katío text

(1) mũ tai s'es'e pedea ĩhã-sʰi-de mũ sʰãwã kʰrĩčʰa
    1s 1p father word believe-PAST-in 1s how   think

   b-e-da-tʰa   mũ-a   nepиrи-ya-a
   be-PERF-PPRT-FOC   1S-ABL tell-FUT-DECL
   I will tell you about how I began thinking when I believed God's Word.

(2) mũ kʰrĩčʰa-ra   nãũ pa-sʰi-a   ũrĩ   kʰo-pʰan-a-tua
    1s thought-ABS   this EQ-PAST-DECL   hear POS-be^few-IMPF-IMPV
    This was my thinking; sit and listen!

(3) ẽpẽrã-rã   ũrãka wã-i-tʰa   kʰrĩčʰa b-e-sʰi-a
    person-PL   teach go-IRR-FOC   think   be-PERF-PAST-DECL
    I began thinking that I would go teach people.

(4) kʰapana   tai s'es'e pedea ĩhã   tuan-и   ũrãka
    big^group 1p   father word believe be^many-PRES teach

   b-a-i-tʰa   mãwã   kʰrĩčʰa b-a-sʰi-a
   be-IMPF-IRR-FOC   like^this   think   be-IMPF-PAST-DECL
   To teach big groups of believers was my thinking.

167

(5) māwã kʰrĩčʰa b-ʉ-de wẽrã tai sʼesʼe pedea ĩhã
    like^this think be-PRES-in woman 1p father word believe

    b-ʉ-á pedea-sʰi-a tai sʼesʼe-tʰa kʰaĩmokʰara-de
    be-PRES-IO speak-PAST-DECL 1p father-FOC dream-in

As I was thinking like this, God spoke in a dream to a woman who believed his word.

(6) mãʉ̃ māwã pedea-pʉrʉ-de-ra hara-sʰi-a mʉ̃ Córdoba-eda
    this like^this speak-PRES-in-PIVOT say-PAST-DECL 1S Córdoba-GOAL

    wã-i para-tʰa ãči kʰaidu
    go-IRR have-FOC 3p follow

In this speaking He (via the woman) said that I should go with them (her group) to Córdoba.

(7) mʉ̃-tʰa ãči kʰaidu wã ẽ-pʉrʉ mʉ̃-a kʰrĩčʰa b-ʉ-tʰa
    1S-FOC 3p follow go NEG-COND 1S-ABL thought be-PRES-FOC

    ari b-a-era mope iči-a mʉ̃ kʰẽnabari-i-tʰa
    follow be-IMPF-because [non dev.] 3S-ABL 1S punish-IRR-FOC

    hara-sʰi-a
    say-PAST-DECL

If I did not go, because I would be following my own desire I would be punished, He said (via the woman).

(8) mãʉ̃ pedea-tʰa mãʉ̃ wẽrã tai sʼesʼe pedea ĩhã
    this word-FOC this woman 1p father word believe

    b-ʉ-pa hara-i mʉ̃ ãči kʰaidu wã-i para
    be-PRES-ABL say-CMPL^DS 1S 3p follow go-IRR have

    sʼe-sʰi-a Cordoba-eda
    come-PAST-DECL Córdoba-GOAL

Because of this word the believing woman said I had to go with them and came to Córdoba.

(9) māwẽ wã-sʰi-a kʰaidu
    [new dev.] go-PAST-DECL follow

Then I went with them.

Appendix B

(10)   *māma estudia-i-tʰa wã-sʰi-mĩna estudia b-e ẽ*
      there study-IRR-FOC go-PAST-though study be-PERF NEG

      pa-sʰi-a
      EQ-PAST-DECL
      Even though I was going to study there, I wasn't able to.

(11)   *māmĩ mũ kʰrĩčʰa-de-ra ariwia b-a-sʰi-a ẽpẽrã-rã*
      however 1s thought-in-PIVOT strong be-IMPF-PAST-DECL person-PL

      ũrãka-i-tʰa
      teach-IRR-FOC
      But I still felt strongly I should teach people.

(12)   *mãũ-tʰa mũ sʰo-de nũ-m-a-sʰi-a*
      this-FOC 1s heart-in stand-be-IMPF-PAST-DECL
      This was in my heart.

(13)   *māwã b-ʉ-de māwã kʰrĩčʰa b-ʉ-de-ra nẽ kʰo*
      like^this be-PRES-in like^this think be-PRES-in-PIVOT GEN eat

      ẽã čiwidi-bi-da-pa-či-a tai sʼesʼe-a sʼarea widi
      NEG pray-CAUS-PPRT-HAB-PAST-DECL 1p father-IO strength ask

      b-ʉ-tʰa kʰrĩčʰa widi b-ʉ-tʰa
      be-PRES-FOC thought ask be-PRES-FOC
      Thinking like this, I prayed to God and fasted, asking for strength and asking for wisdom.

(14)   *ara mãũ-ne widi b-e-sʰi-a mũ-á kʰrĩčʰa hi mãrẽã*
      same this-in ask be-PERF-PAST-DECL 1S-IO thought give PURP

      ẽpẽrã-rã ũrãka wã-i-tʰa ẽpẽrã-rã be-sʼa
      person-PL teach go-IRR-FOC person-PL be^individual-every
      So I asked him to give me wisdom so I could go teach people wherever they were.

(15)   *māwã kʰrĩčʰa b-ʉ-de tai sʼesʼe-pa mũ-á sʼarea*
      like^this think be-PRES-in 1p father-ABL 1S-IO strength

        tia-sʰi-a   *wãrĩnu*
        give-PAST-DECL truly
As I was thinking like this, God truly gave me strength.

(16) *kʰaya-ũrũ čiwidi-pɨrɨ-de b-e   b-a-sʰi-a*
      sick-upon pray-PRES-in be-PERF be-IMPF-PAST-DECL
      When I laid hands on the sick I could heal them.

(17) *mãwã b-ɨ-de   Cordoba-de-pa wakʰusʰa mũči   trua-eda*
      like^this be-PRES-in Córdoba-in-ABL again   1S^COREF land-GOAL

      Chocó-eda wã-i-tʰa kʰrĩčʰa-sʰi-a
      Chocó-GOAL go-IRR-FOC think-PAST-DECL
      As this was going on, I thought again about going from Córdoba back to my land in the Chocó.

(18) *kʰãrẽ o-i   nẽ ẽ   paera   trua ãĩ   b-ɨ   paera*
      what make-IRR GEN NEG because land outside be-PRES because

      sʼupuria kʰrĩčʰa b-e-sʰi-a
      pity   think   be-PERF-PAST-DECL
      Since I had nothing to do and because I was outside my land, I started to pity myself.

(19) *mãwã   kʰrĩčʰa b-a-pʰe   kʰapʰũrĩã-maẽ traha*
      like^this think be-IMPF-after Latin-LOC   work

      b-e-sʰi-a   mũči   trua-eda wã-i-tʰa Chocó-eda
      be-PERF-PAST-DECL 1S^COREF land-GOAL go-IRR-FOC Chocó-GOAL
      After thinking like this for a while, I began working for a Latin in order to go to my land in the Chocó.

(20) *mãwã   traha nɨ-m-e-pɨrɨ-de   kʰaya-sʰi-a pio*
      like^this work stand-be-PERF-PRES-in sick-PAST-DECL very

      kʰɨwa-sʰi-a
      fever-PAST-DECL
      When I started to work I got sick; I had a high fever.

(21) *mãũ-pa pʰiratrɨ b-e   ẽ   pa-sʰi-a*
      this-ABL get^up be-PERF NEG EQ-PAST-DECL
      Because of this I couldn't get up.

Appendix B

(22) mãwã pʰiratɨ b-e ẽã nɨ̃-m-ɨ-ne wá-pɨrɨ kʰaya
like^this get^up be-PERF NEG stand-be-PRES-in more-EMPH sick

    wã-sʰi-a
    go-PAST-DECL
Being unable to get up, I got even sicker.

(23) peu-i kʰĩrã-kʰa nɨ̃-m-e-sʰi-a ara mãɨ̃-ne
die-IRR face-SIM stand-be-PERF-PAST-DECL same this-in
I started feeling like I was going to die right then.

(24) mãwẽ plata hita-i-ra traha b-e ẽ pa-sʰi-a
[new dev.] money get-IRR-PIVOT work be-PERF NEG EQ-PAST-DECL
To get money I couldn't work.

(25) ara mãɨ̃-ne-ra mɨ̃-ra mɨ̃či trua-edá wã b-e
same this-in-PIVOT 1S-ABS 1S^COREF land-GOAL go be-PERF

    ẽã-sʰi-a
    NEG-PAST-DECL
So I couldn't go to my land.

(26) mope mɨ̃ mãwã kʰaya tʰa-b-e-pɨrɨ-de mɨ̃-a tai
[nondev.] 1S like^this sick lie-be-PERF-PRES-in 1S-ABL 1p

    s'es'e-a widi b-e-sʰi-a kʰãrẽ-ne-pa mɨ̃ kʰaya
    father-IO ask be-PERF-PAST-DECL what-in-ABL 1S sick

    nɨ̃mina-tʰa
    DUR-FOC
Lying there sick like that, I began asking God what had been making me sick for so long.

(27) kʰačirua o-pɨrɨ-de-pa kʰaya nɨ̃mina-tʰa o tači nẽ
sin make-PRES-in-ABL sick DUR-FOC or 1p GEN

    hura-pa o ãtʰomia-pa mãwã s'upuria eru-nɨ̃mina-tʰa
    enemy-ABL or devil-ABL like^this suffering have-DUR-FOC

171

kʰawa ẽã b-e-sʰi-a
know NEG be-PERF-PAST-DECL
Whether I had done evil or whether an enemy or the devil had a curse on me I didn't know.

(28) mãũ-pa tiamasʰe ewari-de čiwidi b-e-sʰi-a mãwã
this-ABL night day-in pray be-PERF-PAST-DECL like^this

kʰaya tʰa-b-e-pʉrʉ-pa
sick lie-be-PERF-PRES-ABL
Because of this, I began praying day and night about being sick in bed like that.

(29) pʰiratrʉ ẽ pa-i kʰĩrã-kʰa nũ-m-ʉ-ne peu-i kʰĩrã-kʰa
get^up NEG EQ-IRR face-SIM stand-be-PRES-in die-IRR face-SIM

nũ-m-ʉ-ne tai s'es'e-pa mũ-á kʰrĩčʰa tia-sʰi-a
stand-be-PRES-in 1p father-ABL 1S-IO thought give-PAST-DECL
When I was unable to get up, feeling like I was going to die, God gave me a thought.

(30) mũ-ra mãma tʰa-b-a b-e ẽã-tʰa o mãma traha-pʰe
1S-ABS there lie-be-IMPF be-PERF NEG-FOC or there work-after

mũči trua-eda wã b-e ẽã-tʰa awara iči-a kʰrĩña
1S^COREF land-GOAL go be-PERF NEG-FOC rather 3S-ABL want

b-ʉ-tʰa aribae-i para-tʰa
be-PRES-FOC line^up-IRR have-FOC
It wasn't about my lying there sick or going to my land but about my lining my life up with what He wanted.

(31) mãwẽ mãũ kʰrĩčʰa-tʰa tia-sʰi paera mũ-tʰa iči
[new dev.] this thought-FOC give-PAST because 1S-FOC 3S

pedea hara wã ẽã-ne-pa mãwã kʰaya nũmina-pʉrʉ
word say go NEG-in-ABL like^this sick DUR-COND

mãwã itrua tha-b-ʉ-tʰa pʰiratrʉ-pi mãrẽã
like^this worse lie-be-PRES-FOC get^up-CAUS PURP

Appendix B

        hara-s^{h}i-a   mũ-a
        say-PAST-DECL 1S-ABL
Then, because he gave me this thought, if my being sick was so I wouldn't go preach, I asked him to raise me up from my sickbed.

(32) b-e-pi   mãrẽã hara-s^{h}i-a   hip^{h}a
      be-PERF-CAUS PURP say-PAST-DECL straight
I told him directly to heal me.

(33) ara   mãũ-ne mũ-a k^{h}awa-i-t^{h}a mũ iči pedea hara wã-i
      right this-in 1S-ABL know-IRR-FOC 1S 3S word say go-IRR

      para-t^{h}a k^{h}rĩña b-u-t^{h}a   iči-a
      have-FOC want   be-PRES-FOC 3S-ABL
So that way I would know if He wanted me to go preach.

(34) ara   mãũ-ne mũ mãwã itrua hip^{h}a-de k^{h}ak^{h}ua
      same this-in 1S like^this worse straight-in body

      nomantru   t^{h}a-b-u-t^{h}a   ara   mãwã   p^{h}iratru-i
      weak^nauseous lie-be-PRES-FOC same like^this get^up-IRR

      para-s^{h}i-a
      have-PAST-DECL
So, being in bad shape and weak and dizzy, I had to get up.

(35) ũt^{h}re k^{h}ãi b-a-s^{h}i-a   k^{h}ãp^{h}ũrĩã teda   mũči   traha
      above sleep be-IMPF-PAST-DECL Latin   home 1S^COREF work

      b-u-mãẽ
      be-PRES-LOC
I was sleeping upstairs in the Latin's house where I worked.

(36) mãmĩ   p^{h}úa-pa k^{h}ãi b-e   ẽ   pa-s^{h}i-a   ewari-de mĩã
      however pain-ABL sleep be-PERF NEG EQ-PAST-DECL day-in   GEN

      tiamas^{h}e pida
      night   also
However, because of the pain I couldn't sleep day or night.

(37) ara   mãũ-ne mãmau-pa p^{h}iratru-p^{h}e mũ-a   mãwã-s^{h}i-a   tai
      same this-in there-ABL get^up-after 1S-ABL say-PAST-DECL 1p

  s'es'e-a mʉ̃ nãmaʉ-pa pʰinantrʉ tʰotʰo-pʉrʉ-de
  father-IO 1s here-ABL jump go-PRES-in

So, having gotten up from there, I said to God as I was jumping down from there,

(38) pʉ-a mʉ̃ kʰakʰua hõma s'area-pi-kʰua-tʰa-tua
   2S-ABL 1s body all strong-CAUS-REPT-SUM-IMPV

  mʉ̃-a ara mãʉ̃-ne kʰawa-ya-a pʉ-a pʉči pedea
  1S-ABL same this-in know-FUT-DECL 2S-ABL 2S^COREF word

  hara wã-i-tha kʰrĩ̃a b-ʉ-tʰa
  say go-IRR-FOC want be-PRES-FOC

"Make every part of my body strong and then I will know that you want me to go and preach your word."

(39) mãwã pedea-pʰe o mãwã čiwidi b-a-pʰe
   like^this speak-after or like^this pray be-IMPF-after

  mãmaʉ-pa pʰiratrʉ-pʰe wa b-e-da-pʰe
  there-ABL get^up-after clothes be-PERF-PPRT-after

  mãma-ʉ-pa-ra ʉ̃tʰʉ paera tume nẽ ẽ paera
  there-in-ABL-PIVOT up because stairpole GEN NEG because

  pʰinantrʉ-i para pa-sʰi-a
  jump-IRR have EQ-PAST-DECL

Having spoken or prayed like that, after I got up from there and got dressed, because I had to get down from there and there was no ladder, I had to jump down.

(40) mãwẽ mãwã pʰiratrʉ-pʰe pʰinantrʉ-sʰi-a mãmaʉ-pa
   [new dev.] like^this get^up-after jump-PAST-DECL there-ABL

Then after I got up I jumped down from there.

(41) mãwã-pʉrʉ-de wãrĩnu mʉ̃ kʰakʰua s'area etaʉ
   like^this-PRES-in truly 1s body strength get

  nʉ̃-m-a-ne wã-sʰi-a
  stand-be-IMPF-in go-PAST-DECL

Doing that, my body actually had a little bit of strength.

Appendix B

(42) ara   mãũ-ne   tʰepadewa-sʰi-a   mũ wã b-e   ẽã
      same   this-in start^walking-PAST-DECL   1s go be-PERF NEG

   tʰa-b-ʉ-tʰa
   lie-be-PRES-FOC
   So I started walking, I who had been lying down unable to walk.

(43) mãwẽ   mũ pia   tʰepadewa-sʰi-a   mãmi   hipʰa
      [new dev.] 1s good start^walking-PAST-DECL however straight

   b-e   tʰotʰo ẽ   pa-sʰi-a
   be-PERF go   NEG EQ-PAST-DECL
   I started walking OK; however, I couldn't walk that well.

(44) wadi   pʰupʰukʰa kʰo-b-a-sʰi-a   kʰakʰua-ra o   wadi   pʰúa
      still shaky   POS-be-IMPF-PAST-DECL body-ABS   or still pain

   nũ-m-a-sʰi-a
   stand-be-IMPF-PAST-DECL
   I was still rather shaky; in other words, my body still hurt.

(45) ara   mãũ-ne   mãmi   wã-sʰi-a   tʰotʰo-sʰi-a
      same   this-in however go-PAST-DECL go-PAST-DECL
      Right then I went anyway; I took off.

(46) ara   mãũ-ne   mũ-ra   pʰʉwʉrʉ s'akʰe-tʰa   Cristalina
      same   this-in 1s-PIVOT   village small-FOC   Cristalina

   a-pa-ta-eda   wã-i-tʰa   kʰrĩčʰa-sʰi-a
   say-HAB-PL-GOAL   go-IRR-FOC   think-PAST-DECL
   Then I thought about going to a small village called Cristalina.

(47) mãwã   wã-i-tʰa   kʰrĩčʰa-pʰe   edá   tʰepadewa-sʰi-a
      like^this   go-IRR-FOC   think-after   into start^walking-PAST-DECL

   mũ-ra   ũtʰʉ-pa   kʰatʰuma-ne-pa
   1s-PIVOT   up-ABL   hill-in-ABL
   After thinking like this, I started walking down from up on a hill.

(48) mãwã   ara   mãũ-ne   hũẽ-sʰi-a   mũ-ra   Cristalina
      like^this   same   this-in arrive-PAST-DECL 1s-PIVOT Cristalina

       pʰɨwɨrɨ-idu
       village-inside
       Going like this, I then arrived in the village of Cristalina.

(49) *mã-ĩnu   hũẽ-pɨrɨ-para   mũ-a   kʰrĩčʰa-sʰi-a   mãma*
      there-into arrive-PRES-time 1S-ABL think-PAST-DECL there

       mã-ĩnu-pa   ẽpẽrã-rã   ũrãka wã-i-tʰa   ẽpẽrã-rã
       there-into-ABL person-PL teach go-IRR-FOC person-PL

       be-sʼa   wã-i-tʰa
       be^individual-every go-IRR-FOC
       When I arrived there, I thought I would go out from there to teach the people wherever they were.

(50) *mãwã-mĩna   mãwã   ẽ   pa-sʰi-a   tai sʼesʼe*
      like^this-though like^this NEG EQ-PAST-DECL 1p father

       kʰrĩčʰa-ra   mã-ĩnu   hũẽ-pi-pɨrɨ-ra   ici-a kʰãrẽ
       thought-PIVOT there-inside arrive-CAUS-PRES-PIVOT 3S-ABL what

       o-i-tʰa   kʰrĩna b-ɨ   pia   kʰawa-pi-i   kʰarea
       make-IRR-FOC want be-PRES good know-CAUS-IRR REASON

       mã-ĩnu   hũẽ-pi-sʰi-a   awara
       there-into arrive-CAUS-PAST-DECL rather
       But that wasn't what God wanted; he had made me come there so I would know his will was different.

(51) *mãwẽ   mãmaɨ-pa wakʰusʰa mũči   traha*
      [new dev.] there-ABL again   1S^COREF work

       b-a-da-eda   sʼe-i   para sʼe-sʰi-a
       be-IMPF-PPRT-GOAL come-IRR have come-PAST-DECL
       Then from there I had to go back to where I had been working.

(52) *mãwẽ   mãũ pʰɨwɨrɨ sʼakʰe Cristalina-ne-pa   hũtrɨ-pɨrɨ-de*
      [new dev.] this village small Cristalina-in-ABL jump-PRES-in

Appendix B

       o-de   oi-tʰa   perabari-i-tʰa   para pa-sʰi-a
       trail-in woods-FOC navigate-IRR-FOC have EQ-PAST-DECL
       Then, leaving the small village of Cristalina, I had to make my way back on a trail through the woods.

(53) mãwẽ   mãũ oi   perabari tʰai-de   mũ kʰaidu pʰũãtrʉ
      [new dev.] this woods navigate mouth-in 1S follow wind

      tuke-sʰi-a
      come-PAST-DECL
      As I came up to a fork in the trail a wind came up behind me.

(54) mãwã   mũ kʰaidu pʰũãtrʉ tuke-pʉrʉ taučʰa tači-ma mũ-tʰa
      like^this 1S follow wind   come-PRES exact 1p-LOC 1S-FOC

      ũtʰʉ hira eta-pʉrʉ-kʰa-sʰi-a   pʰũãtrʉ-pa
      up hang get-PRES-NEG^HAB-PAST-DECL wind-ABL
      As the wind came up behind me, to us it would be like it was supernaturally picking me up in the air.

(55) mãwã   hira eta-pʉrʉ-kʰa-pʉrʉ-de   pedea-tʰa ũrĩ-sʰi-a
      like^this hang get-PRES-NEG^HAB-PRES-in word-FOC hear-PAST-DECL

      mũ-a   mũ-á   pedea-pʉrʉ-tʰa
      1S-ABL 1S-IO speak-PRES-FOC
      As I was being supernaturally picked up I heard a voice, a voice that was speaking to me.

(56) mãwẽ   mũ-a mãũ pedea ũrĩ-pʉrʉ-para   mãwã-sʰi-a pʉ-ra
      [new dev.] 1S-ABL this word hear-PRES-time say-PAST-DECL 2S-ABS

      kʰãwãweda Montería-eda wã-i para pʉ-ra kʰãwãweda
      right^away Montería-GOAL go-IRR have 2S-ABS right^away

      Montería-eda wã-i para a   mãwã   čʰũ   tʰotʰo-sʰi-a
      Montería-GOAL go-IRR have say like^this quiet go-PAST-DECL
      Then, when I listened to this voice it said, "You must go to Montería right away, you must go to Montería right away," it said and was silent.

(57) mãwã   čʰũ   tʰotʰo-pʉrʉ-para pʰũãtrʉ sʰida   tʰau
      like^this quiet go-PRES-time   wind also^ABS stop

    tʰotʰo-sʰi-a
    go-PRES-DECL
  When the voice quieted, the wind stopped, too.

(58) māwã-pʉrʉ-pa mũ ũtʰʉ ewara-de pʰũãbari tʰai kʰĩrã-kʰa
   like^this-PRES-ABL 1S up outside-in air normal face-SIM

    tʰai-de wakʰusʰa kʰenetʰa-pʉrʉ-para mũ-ra tači
    mouth-in again leap-PRES-time 1S-PIVOT 1p

    tʰai-de tʰotʰo-sʰi-a wakʰusʰa
    normal-in go-PAST-DECL again
  While I continued out in the open at the fork in the trail feeling light-footed, when I leaped once more I found I was walking normally again.

(59) ara mãũ-ne mũ-ra pari ĩapa-sʰi-a wãẽpa-sʰi-a
   same this-in 1S-ABS free breathe-PAST-DECL go^fast-PAST-DECL

    mũči traha nũ-m-a-na-ẽnã
    1S^COREF work stand-be-IMPF-PPRT-GOAL
  So I took a deep breath and started walking quickly back to where I had been working.

(60) mãma sʼe-pʰe trabajo widi-sʰi-a wakʰusʰa
   there come-after work ask-PAST-DECL again
  Once I got there I asked for work again.

(61) ya māwã o-de pʉ-sʰi-de wĩkʰa ariku
   now like^this trail-in walk-PAST-in small better

    b-a-sʰi-a
    be-IMPF-PAST-DECL
  Now, walking on the trail, I felt a little better.

(62) pia ariku b-a ẽ pa-sʰi-a māwã-mĩna
   good better be-IMPF NEG EQ-PAST-DECL like^this-though
  I still wasn't feeling that well, though.

(63) ara mãũ-ne sʼe-kʰãrĩ-ma-pʰe trabajo widi-pʉrʉ-para
   same this-in come-REASON-CMPL-after work work

      trabajo   *tia-s^hi-da-a*
      ask-PRES-time give-PAST-PL-DECL
      Then, after I had gotten there, when I asked for work they gave me a job.

(64) *māwā*   *tia-da-i*   *traha* *nũ-m-e-s^hi-a*   *mũ-ra*
     like^this give-PL-CMPL^DS work stand-be-PERF-PAST-DECL 1S-PIVOT
     Once they gave me work, I began working.

(65) *ewari ũme-pai traha-s^hi-a*
     day two-LIM work-PAST-DECL
     I worked just two days.

(66) *či waa-pema presta widi-s^hi-a*
     REF more-ORIG loan ask-PAST-DECL
     The rest I asked them to loan me.

(67) *māwẽ*   *presta tia-s^hi-a*   *patron-pa-ra*
     [new dev.] loan give-PAST-DECL boss-ABL-PIVOT
     Then the boss loaned it to me.

(68) *ara mãũ-ne ewari-ra* *$150 pa-da paera dos día*
     same this-in day-PIVOT $150 EQ-PPRT because two day

          traha-pʉrʉ-pa $300 tia-s^hi-da-a   *mũ-á*
          work-PRES-ABL $300 give-PAST-PL-DECL 1S-IO
     Because it was 150 pesos a day, for two days' work they paid me 300 pesos.

(69) *y audu eru-b-a-s^hi-a*   *ewari aba*
     and extra have-be-IMPF-PAST-DECL day one
     And I had one more day's pay.

(70) *ewari aba presta-s^hi-a*   *patron-pa-ra*
     day one loan-PAST-DECL boss-ABL-PIVOT
     The boss loaned me a day's pay.

(71) *mãũ $450 peso-pa Montería-eda hũtrʉ b-e-s^hi-a*
     this $450 peso-ABL Montería-GOAL jump be-PERF-PAST-DECL

    mũ-ra
    1S-ABS
With these 450 pesos I took off for Montería.

(72) ara   mãũ-ne mũ-ra pʰuwuru Uré a-pa-ta-eda   wã-sʰi-a
      same this-in 1S-ABS village Uré say-HAB-PL-GOAL go-PAST-DECL
So I went to a village called Uré.

(73) māma hũẽ-pʰe   či kʰārẽ-ma wã-puru kʰawa ẽã-tʰa   miã
      there arrive-after REF what-LOC go-PRES know NEG-FOC GEN

      kʰai-ma wã-puru kʰawa ẽã-tʰa   wã-sʰi-a   Montería-eda
      who-LOC go-PRES know NEG-FOC go-PAST-DECL Montería-GOAL
After I got there, I went on to Montería not knowing for what or for whom I was going.

(74) mũ-a-ra   kʰrĩčʰa b-a-sʰi-a   Montería-de kʰarepa
      1S-ABL-PIVOT think be-IMPF-PAST-DECL Montería-in help

      b-u-tʰa   mũ-itʰa o mũ-á plata   tia-da-i-tʰa   mũ
      be-PRES-FOC 1S-BEN or 1S-IO money give-PL-IRR-FOC 1S

      mũči   trua-eda   wã-i-tʰa o tai s'es'e pedea hara
      1S^COREF land-GOAL go-IRR-FOC or 1p father word say

      wã-i-tʰa
      go-IRR-FOC
I was thinking that in Montería there would be help for me or someone would give me money so I could go to my land or go preach.

(75) māmĩ   mãwã   ẽ   pa-sʰi-a
      however like^this NEG EQ-PAST-DECL
However, that wasn't it.

(76) tai s'es'e-pa-ra   awara iči-a kʰrĩña-tʰa o   mãrẽã
      1p father-ABL-PIVOT rather 3S-ABL wish-FOC make PURP

      s'okʰa-sʰi paera   mãwã   mĩõ-pa   mũ-á plata
      send-PAST because like^this nobody-ABL 1S-IO money

Appendix B

        tia-da   ẽ   pa-sʰi-a
        give-PL NEG EQ-PAST-DECL
        Because God had do *His* will, no one gave me any money at all.

(77) *māwẽ   Montería-eda   hũẽ-pʰe   pastor Juan Gonzales*
[new dev.] Montería-GOAL arrive-after pastor Juan Gonzales

        a-pa-ta   teda   hũẽ-sʰi-a
        say-HAB-PL home arrive-PAST-DECL
        Then, after arriving in Montería, I went to the home of the one called Pastor Juan Gonzales.

(78) *mope   mũ-a   neрʉrʉ-sʰi-a mũ kʰaya nũ-m-ʉ-tʰa   y*
[nondev.] 1S-ABL tell-PAST-DECL 1S sick stand-be-PRES-FOC and

        mũ wā kʰrĩña b-ʉ-tʰa   Antioquia-eda tai sʼesʼe pedea
        1S go want be-PRES-FOC Antioquia-GOAL 1p father word

        hara-de
        say-in
        I told how I had been sick and how I wanted to go to Antioquia to preach.

(79) *māwā-mĩna   plata   tia-da   ẽ   pa-sʰi-a*
like^this-though money give-PL NEG EQ-PAST-DECL
However, they didn't give me any money.

(80) *plata nẽ ẽ-a   a-sʰi-da-a*
money GEN NEG-DECL say-PAST-PL-DECL
"We don't have any money," they said.

(81) a. *ara   māũ-ne mũ kʰāĩ-ña-ma-pai   pastor-pa māwā-sʰi-a*
      same this-in 1S sleep-FUT-CMPL-LIM pastor-ABL say-PAST-DECL

        mũ-á
        1S-IO
        Right then, before I went to sleep, the pastor said to me,

    b. *nāma nāũ Montería-de ēpẽrã   wẽrā-tʰa   čʰu-b-ʉ-a*
      here this Montería-in Embera woman-FOC sit-be-PRES-DECL

a-sʰi-a
say-PAST-DECL
"Here in Montería there is an Embera woman," he said.

(82) mope   mũ-a   nãũ   pʰɨwɨrɨ sʲroma-ne mãũ ẽpẽrã wẽrã
     [nondev.] 1S-ABL this village big-in   this person woman

     kʰãrẽ o   b-ɨ-tʰa   kʰrĩčʰa b-e-sʰi-a
     what   make be-PRES-FOC   think   be-PERF-PAST-DECL
     And I started wondering what an Embera woman was doing in this big city.

(83) mãwã   kʰãĩ-sʰi-a   ara   mãũ-ne
     like^this   sleep-PAST-DECL   same this-in
     And I fell asleep wondering about that.

(84) a. iči-a   mũ-á   mãũ   hara-pɨrɨ-de-ra
        3S-ABL 1S-IO this say-PRES-in-PIVOT
        He said to me,

     b. tiapʰeda a   la   5   čiwidi-de sʲe   čʰu-b-ɨ-a   mãũ
        morning at   the 5   pray-in   come   sit-be-PRES-DECL this

        ẽpẽrã   wẽrã-ra   a-sʰi-a
        person woman-PIVOT   say-PAST-DECL
        "Tomorrow morning at 5 this Embera woman is coming," he said.

(85) mãwã-i   mãũ-ũrũ   kʰrĩčʰa kʰãĩ-sʰi-a   mũ-ra
     like^this-CMPL^DS this-upon   think   sleep-PAST-DECL   1S-PIVOT

     mãũ ẽpẽrã wẽrã   pʰɨwɨrɨ sʲroma-ne kʰãrẽ o
     this person woman village big-in   what   make

     b-ɨ-tʰa
     be-PRES-FOC
     When he had said this, I fell asleep thinking, "What is an Embera woman doing in the big city?"

(86) ara   mãũ-ne   ũnatrɨ-i   iči pastor mũ-ma   sʲe-pʰe
     same this-in   awake-CMPL^DS   3S   pastor 1S-LOC come-after

Appendix B

ãpa wã-sʰi-da-a tai iglesia-de eda čiwidi-de
together go-PAST-PL-DECL 1p church-in into pray-in
When I had awakened, after the pastor came to me we went together to the church to pray.

(87) ara mãũ-ne tʰepadewa-sʰi-a warĩnu
same this-in start^walking-PAST-DECL truly
Then we actually walked in.

(88) a. ara mãũ iči pastor-pa mũ-á hara-sʰi-a
right this 3S pastor-ABL 1S-IO say-PAST-DECL
Right then the pastor said to me:

b. hari uru-a ẽpẽrã wẽrã-ra a-sʰi-a
there come-DECL person woman-PIVOT say-PAST-DECL
"That lady coming over here is the Embera woman," he said.

(89) mãwẽ mũ-a akʰu-pʉrʉ-para ãĩpema Alemania-ne-pema
[new dev.] 1S-ABL look-PRES-time foreigner Germany-in-ORIG

mũ-a Salaquí-de ũtu-da-tʰrʉ tʰepa-sʰi-a awara
1S-ABL Salaquí-in see-PPRT-FOC^GI walk^up-PAST-DECL rather
Then, when I looked, to my surprise, up walked a foreigner from Germany whom I had met on the Salaquí River.

(90) tači ẽpẽrã wẽrã ẽ pa-sʰi-a
1p person woman NEG EQ-PAST-DECL
She wasn't an Embera woman.

(91) mãmĩ tači pedea-tʰa kʰawa čʰu-b-a-era ẽpẽrã
however 1p word-FOC know sit-be-IMPF-because person

wẽrã a-sʰi-a
woman say-PAST-DECL
However, since she knew our language he called her "Embera woman."

(92) ara mãũ-ne-ra warĩnu iči pastor pedea-pi
same this-in-PIVOT truly 3S pastor speak-CAUS
So it was true what the pastor had said.

(93) ara māū̃-ne mū-a ya   ūtu kʰawa baera   saluda-pʰe
     same this-in 1S-ABL already see know because greet-after

     ya   čiwidi perabari-i   iči tedá ete-sʰi-a
     already pray   navigate-CMPL^DS 3S home take-PAST-DECL

     Kʰerapaɟau-pa
     Kerabadau-ABL
     So since I already knew her I greeted her, and then after the prayer meeting she took me to her house, Kerabadau did.

(94) iči tʰrū-ra   Kʰerapaɟau-a
     3S   name-ABS   Kerabadau-DECL
     Her name was Kerabadau.

(95) māwā   iči tedá ete-pʰe   nẽ hi-sʰi-a   mū-ra nẽ
     like^this 3S home take-after GEN give-PAST-DECL 1S-ABS GEN

     kʰo-sʰi-a
     eat-PAST-DECL
     So after taking me to her house she fed me; I ate.

(96) mope   kʰrīčʰa b-e-sʰi-a   mū māū̃ tiapʰeda-ra
     [nondev.] think be-PERF-PAST-DECL 1S this morning-PIVOT

     mū kʰārẽ o-de   ibaritʰa   kʰāpāẽã kʰaya
     1S what trail-in pass^time badly   sick

     nū-m-ɟ-tʰa   y   pʰúa nū-m-ɟ-tʰa
     stand-be-PRES-FOC and pain stand-be-PRES-FOC
     I started thinking that morning about what I should do about my sickness and pain.

(97) māwā   kʰrīčʰa b-e-sʰi-a
     like^this think be-PERF-PAST-DECL
     I kept thinking about this.

(98) tiamasʰe khāī-ya-ma-pai   sʰopʰua nū-m-e-sʰi-a   aɟtre
     night   sleep-FUT-CMPL-LIM   sad   stand-be-PERF-PAST-DECL extra

> plata nẽ^ẽã-pa
> money without-ABL
>
> Before I went to sleep that night I started feeling sad because I had no more money.

(99) ya hō-sʰi-a   plata
     now end-PAST-DECL money
     It had run out.

(100) miã či sʰāmá wã-i   nẽ^ẽã-ne   kʰārē-pa mŭči   trua-eda
      GEN REF where go-IRR without-in what-ABL IS^COREF land-GOAL

> wã-i   nẽ^ẽã-ne   pʰuwuru s'roma-ne eda   b-e-sʰi-a
> go-IRR without-in village big-in   into be-PERF-PAST-DECL
>
> eda   māū-ne kʰai-pa trabajo tia-i   nẽ^ẽã-maẽ
> into then   who-ABL work   give-IRR without-LOC
>
> Without money to go anywhere and no way to travel to my home, I was stuck in a big city where no one would give me work.

(101) a. māwã   ara   māū-ne   kʰāī-ya-ma-pai   sʰopʰua
         like^this same this-in sleep-FUT-CMPL-LIM   sad

> nũ-m-u-ne   mũ kʰrīčʰa-de tuke-sʰi-a
> stand-be-PRES-in   1S thought-in come-PAST-DECL
>
> So these kinds of thoughts came into my head when I was trying to go to sleep,

  b. ah mũ kʰārēã sʰopʰua b-a-i   nesʰida nẽ   ē-a
     oh 1S why   sad   be-IMPF-IRR need   GEN   NEG-DECL
     "Oh, why am I sad? I'm not in any need."

(102) ara^maũtʰa mũ čiwidi nũ-m-e-sʰi-a
      suddenly   1S pray   stand-be-PERF-PAST-DECL
      Suddenly I started praying.

(103) māmī   māwã   i-pia-de   čiwidi ẽ   pa-sʰi-a
      however like^this lip-good-in pray   NEG   EQ-PAST-DECL
      However, I didn't pray in a good way.

(104) a. tai s'es'e-a kʰĩrũ čiwidi-sʰi-a
       1p father angry pray-PAST-DECL
       I prayed angrily to God,

   b. mũ kʰãrẽã s'okʰa-sʰi-tʰa kʰãmá plata nẽ^ẽã-ra
       1S REASON send-PAST-FOC there money without-PIVOT

      kʰãrẽ-ma s'e-sʰi-tʰa
      what-LOC come-PAST-FOC
      "Why did you send me to this place with no money?! What have I come for?!

   c. mãwẽ puči-a s'okʰa-sʰi paera mũ-ra atua
      [new dev.] 2S-ABL send-PAST because 1S-ABS unaware

      kʰãĩ-pi-rua a-sʰi-a mũ-a
      sleep-CAUS-IMPV say-PAST-DECL 1S-ABL
      If you really have sent me here, make me sleep peacefully!" I said.

(105) mãwã čiwidi nũ-m-a-pʰe kʰãĩ-sʰi-a
      like^this pray stand-be-IMPF-after sleep-PAST-DECL
      After praying like this for a while I went to sleep.

(106) aurre ẽã-ne mũ hipʰa kʰãĩ tʰotʰo-sʰi-a
      extra NEG-in 1S straight sleep go-PAST-DECL
      Before long I went right to sleep.

(107) mãwẽ mũ nrũẽma ũrũma-puru-para sʰopia
      [new dev.] 1S next^day awaken-PRES-time happy

      ũrũma-sʰi-a
      awaken-PAST-DECL
      Then when I awoke the next morning, I woke up happy.

(108) mũ-a kʰawa ẽ pa-sʰi-a kʰãrẽã sʰopia ũnatru-puru-ra
      1S-ABL know NEG EQ-PAST-DECL why happy awaken-PRES-PIVOT
      I didn't know why I woke up so happy.

(109) mãũ-ne tiapʰeda nẽ kʰo-i-tʰa tʰrũ-sʰi-da-a ãči-a
      this-in morning GEN eat-IRR-FOC call-PAST-PL-DECL 3S-ABL
      Then they called me to breakfast.

Appendix B

(110) māwẽ   tiapʰeda   nẽ   kʰo-i-tʰa   tʰrū-na-i
[new dev.] morning GEN eat-IRR-FOC call-PL-CMPL^DS

    heweda-sʰi-a nẽ kʰo-i-tʰa
    sit-PAST-DECL GEN eat-IRR-FOC
    After they called me to eat, I sat down to eat.

(111) a. nẽ kʰo perabari-pʰe   mepea Kʰerapatau-pa mū-á
      GEN eat navigate-after sibling Kerabadau-ABL 1S-IO

    māwã-sʰi-a
    say-PAST-DECL
    After we finished eating, sister Kerabadau said to me,

  b. pu-a   ewara-tʰa   akʰu kʰrĩña-puru balcón-ūrū
     2S-ABL outside-FOC look want-COND balcony-upon

    hewedasʰia⁵⁸ b-u-a   a-sʰi-a
    sit-PAST-DECL be-PRES-DECL say-PAST-DECL
    "If you want to look outside, you can sit up on the balcony," she said.

(112) māwã-i   hewedapari ete-pʰe   māma heweda
like^this-CMPL^DS chair   take-after there sit

    b-e-sʰi-a   mū
    be-PERF-PAST-DECL 1S
    After she said this, after I took a chair up I remained seated there.

(113) māwẽ   carro wã pʰan-a-pa-ri-tʰa   akʰu
[new dev.] car go be^few-IMPF-HAB-SG-FOC look

    b-e-sʰi-a
    be-PERF-PAST-DECL
    I started looking at the cars going by.

(114) māwẽ   carro akʰu nū-m-u-ne   carro tači ipʰida kʰrĩña
[new dev.] car look stand-be-PRES-in car 1p laugh want

---

⁵⁸Frozen form. The word is derived from *heweda-sʰi-a* 'sat'.

    čʰu-b-e-tʰa   ũtu nũ-m-ʉ-pa   ipʰida
    sit-be-PERF-FOC see stand-be-PRES-ABL laugh

    nũ-m-a-sʰi-a   mũ
    stand-be-IMPF-PAST-DECL 1S

Then, as I was looking, because I saw some cars that we want to laugh at, I was laughing.

(115) ũkʰʉrʉ ũrũ-pema nẽ^ẽã čʰu-bea-sʰi-a   carro-ra
     some upon-ORIG without sit-be^indiv-PAST-DECL car-PIVOT
     Some of the cars were without tops.

(116) mũ-má-ra   neida čʰu-bea-sʰi-a
     1S-LOC-PIVOT funny sit-be^indiv-PAST-DECL
     To me they looked funny.

(117) mãũ-pa ipʰida nũ-m-ʉ-ne   mepea Kʰerapataʉ
     this-ABL laugh stand-be-PRES-in sibling Kerabadau

    tuke-sʰi-a   mũ-má
    come-PAST-DECL 1S-LOC
    As I was laughing about this, sister Kerabadau came up to me.

(118) mope   mãwã-sʰi-a tai sʼesʼe-tʰa mepea Renatʰa-á
     [nondev.] say-PAST-DECL 1p father-FOC sibling Renata-IO

    pedea-sʰi-pida pʉ-á plata-tʰa tia mãrẽã hara-sʰi-pida
    speak-PAST-RPRT 2S-IO money-FOC give PURP say-PAST-RPRT

    a   tuke-sʰi-a
    say come-PAST-DECL
    And she reported, "God spoke to sister Renata and told her to give you money," she said.

(119) makʰua tai sʼesʼe-pa mũ-á plata-tʰa tia mãrẽã
     wonderful 1p father-ABL 1S-IO money-FOC give PURP

    hara-sʰi-pʉrʉ pika a-sʰi-a   mũ-a
    say-PAST-EMPH fine say-PAST-DECL 1S-ABL
    "How wonderful of God to tell her to give me money!" I said.

Appendix B

(120) ara   maũ mepea wã-sʰi-a
same this sibling go-PAST-DECL
Right then the sister left.

(121) aɯrre ẽã-ne   tuke-pɯrɯ-tʰa dos mil   peso kʰãrĩ
extra NEG-in come-PRES-FOC two thousand peso REASON

tuke-sʰi-a
come-PAST-DECL
And she came right back to give me two thousand pesos.

(122) mãwẽ   mũ mãũ plata ũtu-pɯrɯ-pa sʰopia
[new dev.] 1S this money see-PRES-ABL happy

nɯ-m-ũ-ne   eda   wetʰá-pɯrɯ sʰopia-sʰi-a
stand-be-PRES-in into more-EMPH   happy-PAST-DECL
Then, being happy because I saw this money, I became even happier.

(123) mãwẽ   mãũ plata či   sʰãwã o-i   kʰawa ẽ
[new dev.] this money REF how   make-IRR know   NEG

pa-sʰi-a   mũ-a
EQ-PAST-DECL 1S-ABL
But I didn't know what to do with this money.

(124) ewari tres   cientocincuenta-de-ra mũ-má-ra   mãũ   pari
day   three 150-in-PIVOT   1S-LOC-PIVOT this free

tiaʰ-pɯ-ta   paera   hipʰa   plata sʰroma pa-sʰi-a
give-PRES-PL because straight money big   EQ-PAST-DECL
For me, who had had only three days' pay at 150 pesos a day, this gift was a lot of money.

(125) ara   mãũ-ne   kʰawa-sʰi-a   wãrĩnu iči   tai sʰesʰe-pa
same this-in   know-PAST-DECL truly   3S   1P   father-ABL

sʰokʰa-da-tʰa
send-PPRT-FOC
So I knew for sure that God had sent it.

(126) mãwẽ   mũ-a   ariwia widi-sʰi-a   mãũ   plata   sʰãwã
      [new dev.] 1S-ABL strong ask-PAST-DECL   this money   how

      o-i   para-tʰa
      make-IRR   have-FOC
      Then I kept asking [them] how I should spend this money.

(127) kʰawa-da   ẽ-a   a-sʰi-da-a   ãči-a mũ-a-pɨrɨ   kʰawa
      know-PL   NEG-DECL   say-PAST-PL-DECL   3S-ABL 1S-ABL-FOC^GI   know

      b-ɨ-a   a-sʰi-da-a   sʰãwã o-i-ra
      be-PRES-DECL   say-PAST-PL-DECL   how   make-IRR-ABS
      They said they didn't know and that I should decide what to do with it.

(128) ara   mãũ-ne   mũ-ra   wakʰusʰa mũči   traha b-a-da-eda
      same   this-in 1S-ABS again   1S^COREF   work   be-IMPF-PPRT-GOAL

      sʲe-sʰi-a   Uré-eda   sʲõrã-rã   pʰan-ɨ-ĩnu
      come-PAST-DECL   Uré-GOAL   elderly-PL   be^few-PRES-inside

      mũči   b-a-da-idu   mũči   traha b-a-da-idu
      1S^COREF   be-IMPF-PPRT-inside   1S^COREF   work   be-IMPF-PPRT-inside

      mũči   kʰaya   nɨ-m-a-na-ĩnu
      1S^COREF   sick   stand-be-IMPF-PPRT-inside
      So I came back to where I had been working, to Uré, back to the old people, to where I had been, to where I had been working, to where I had been sick.

(129) mãwã   ara   mãũ-ne   wãrĩnu mũ-ra   ari^wawá   mãmaɨ-pa
      like^this   same   this-in truly   1S-ABS   further^on   there-ABL

      ẽpẽrã   ara   kʰaitʰa nɨ-m-ɨ   paera   ari^wawá
      person   right close   stand-be-PRES   because   further^on

      ẽpẽrã-rã   ũrãka-de   wã-sʰi-a
      person-PL   teach-in   go-PAST-DECL
      Because I was now so close to lots of Emberas, I went further on from there to teach them.

(130) wãrĩ mũ-ra ara mãũ-ne ẽpẽrã-rã ũrãka a tʰotʰo
 truly 1S-ABS same this-in person-PL teach say go

    bákʰade wã-sʰi-a
    place^to^place go-PAST-DECL
So I really took off and went from place to place teaching the people.

(131) mãwã ẽpẽrã-rã ũrãka b-a-pʰe wã-sʰi-a
 like^this person-PL teach be-IMPF-after go-PAST-DECL

    Montería-eda wakʰusʰa
    Montería-GOAL again
After teaching the people like this for a while, I went back to Montería again.

(132) ara mãũ-ne mepea-pa mũ-á mãwã-sʰi-a Kʰerapatau-pa
 same this-in sibling-ABL 1S-IO say-PAST-DECL Kerabadau-ABL

    pʉ-a kʰrĩ̃a-pʉrʉ Aurelio s'e-i-eda mũ ũme tai
    2S-ABL WANT-COND Aurelio come-IRR-GOAL 1S two 1p

    s'es'e pedea bʉ-da-ya-a a-sʰi-a
    father word put-PL-FUT-DECL say-PAST-DECL
Then sister Kerabadau said to me, "If you want, you can translate God's Word with me until Aurelio comes," she said.

(133) pika a-sʰi-a mũ-a mope-ra
 fine say-PAST-DECL 1S-ABL [nondev.]-PIVOT
And at this I said, "O.K."

(134) mãwã ara mãũ-ne tai s'es'e pedea bʉ hũtrʉ-sʰi-a
 like^this same this-in 1p father word put jump-PAST-DECL
So just like that I took off at translating God's Word.

(135) ara mãũ-ne idi pasʰi-idu tai s'es'e pedea bʉ
 same this-in today pass-inside 1p father word put

    b-ʉ-a mũ-ra
    be-PRES-DECL 1S-PIVOT
Even today I am translating God's Word.

(136) mãũ-tʰa kʰrĩña b-a-sʰi-a   iči tai sʹesʹe-pa
      this-FOC want be-IMPF-PAST-DECL 3S 1p father-ABL
      This is what God wanted all along.

(137) mãũ kʰarea Montería-eda sʹokʰa-sʰi-a   mũ
      this REASON Montería-GOAL send-PAST-DECL 1S
      This is why he sent me to Montería.

(138) mãwã ara mãũ-ne iči tai sʹesʹe či sʹokʰa-de b-ʉ-a
      like^this same this-in 3S 1p father REF send-in be-PRES-DECL

      idipaira   Bogota-de
      here^today Bogotá-in
      Today this sending by God involves my living in Bogotá.

(139) nãma-pai-a   mũ перʉ-ra
      here-LIM-DECL 1S story-ABS
      My story is up until here.

(140) mũ-ra Abel
      1S-ABS Abel
      By Abel. (lit., "I am Abel.")

References

Aguirre-Licht, Daniel. 1995. Fonología del ēbēra-chamí de Cristianía (departamento de Antioquia). In Descripciones 8: Estudios fonologícos del grupo chocó, 9–86. Santa fé de Bogotá: Universidad de los Andes.
Binder, Ronald. 1978. Los enlaces temáticos en el discurso Waunana. Lenguas de Panamá 4:29–68. Panamá: Instituto Lingüístico de Verano.
Comrie, Bernard. 1978. Ergativity. In Winfred Lehmann (ed.), Syntactic typology, 329–94. Austin: University of Texas Press.
———. 1989. Language universals and linguistic typology. (2nd ed.). Chicago: University of Chicago Press.
Constenla-Umaña, Adolfo and Enrique Margery-Peña. 1991. Elementos de fonología comparada chocó. Filología y Lingüística XVII (1–2):137–91.
Dooley, Robert A. and Stephen H. Levinsohn. 1997. Analyzing discourse: Basic concepts. Grand Forks: Summer Institute of Linguistics and University of North Dakota.
Enemark, James Lee, and Douglas Schermerhorn. n.d. Embera language learning lessons. ms.
Fox, Barbara A. 1987. The noun phrase accessibility hierarchy revisited. Language 63:856–70.
Greenberg, Joseph H. 1966. Some universals of grammar with particular reference to the order of elements. In Joseph H. Greenberg (ed.), Universals of language, 73–113. Cambridge, Mass.: MIT Press.
———. 1987. Language in the Americas. Stanford, Calif.: Stanford University Press.

Harms, Phillip Lee. 1994. Epena Pedee syntax. Summer Institute of Linguistics and University of Texas at Arlington Publications in Linguistics 118. Dallas.

Hopper, Paul J. and Sandra A. Thompson. 1980. Transitivity in grammar and discourse. Language 56:251–99.

Loewen, Jacob Abram. 1958. An introduction to Ẽpẽra speech: Sambú dialect. Ph.D. dissertation. University of Washington.

———. 1963. Choco 1: introduction and biography. International Journal of American Linguistics 29:239–63.

Mortensen, Charles A. 1994. Nasalization in a revision of Embera-Katío phonology. M.A. thesis. University of Michigan. Ann Arbor: University Microfilms.

Pardo-Rojas, Mauricio and Daniel Aguirre-Licht. 1993. Dialectología chocó. Estado actual de la clasificación de las lenguas indígenas de Colombia, 270–312. Santafé de Bogotá: Instituto Caro y Cuervo.

Rasmussen, Edel M. and Gregorio Mesúa. 1985. Nociones gramaticales de ẽberã. (no publisher).

Rex, Eileen. 1975. On Catío grammar. M.A. thesis. University of Texas at Arlington.

Schöttelndreyer, Mareike. 1977. La narración folclórica catía como un drama en actos y escenas. In Estudios en camsá y catío, 96–206. Lomalinda, Colombia: Editorial Townsend.

ERRATA
for
A Reference Grammar of the Northern Embera Languages

Charles A Mortensen

Page	For	Read
72, line 8	Immediate past and future	Immediate future and past
72, fn. 30 lines 2-3	...auxiliary which means	...auxiliary which can mean 'to do while going away' or represent punctiliar aspect. The example below illustrates punctiliar aspect.
72, fn. 30 line 6	The very same thing broke him as he was running away.	The very same thing broke him apart instantly.

www.ingramcontent.com/pod-product-compliance
Lightning Source LLC
Chambersburg PA
CBHW051523230426
43668CB00012B/1719